CRIME AND
GOD'S JUDGMENT
IN SHAKESPEARE

CRIME AND GOD'S JUDGMENT IN SHAKESPEARE

ROBERT RENTOUL REED, JR.

THE UNIVERSITY PRESS OF KENTUCKY

Copyright © 1984 by The University Press of Kentucky

Scholarly publisher for the Commonwealth,
serving Bellarmine College, Berea College, Centre
College of Kentucky, Eastern Kentucky University,
The Filson Club, Georgetown College, Kentucky
Historical Society, Kentucky State University,
Morehead State University, Murray State University,
Northern Kentucky University, Transylvania University,
University of Kentucky, University of Louisville,
and Western Kentucky University.

Editorial and Sales Offices: Lexington, Kentucky 40506-0024

Library of Congress Cataloging in Publication Data

Reed, Robert Rentoul, 1911-
   Crime and God's judgment in Shakespeare.

   Includes bibliographical references and index.
   1. Shakespeare, William, 1564-1616—Political and
social views. 2. Shakespeare, William, 1564-1616—
Religion and ethics. 3. Justice in literature.
I. Title.
PR3017.R43 1983   833.3'3   83-19701
ISBN 0-8131-1502-7

CONTENTS

INTRODUCTION

The present book treats divine retribution both in Shakespeare's English history plays and in several of his major tragedies, each of which has satisfied the precondition that the retribution is a principal force—and sometimes the main force—behind the play's tragic inevitability. In the histories, God's judgments are motivated principally (but not entirely) by the biblical doctrine of inherited guilt; in the tragedies, by the immediate guilt of a living man. The purpose of my introduction is to respond to those critics, most of them recent, who have repudiated the presence of divine punishment in the histories—in particular, the two tetralogies—and to whom, in my analyses of the plays, I have found no appropriate place to respond. As for the tragedies, I find no urgent compulsion to respond, collectively, to readers who have dissented from affirmations of divine retribution in them, for such affirmations, until now, have not been recognized as a motif prominent enough to encourage much adverse commentary.

My response is necessarily confined to the English history plays, and even here the imperative behind it is not overriding: the most energetic repudiations of the existence of divine retribution in these plays have been, at best, periodic and in substance not unduly impressive. On the other hand, even though E.M.W. Tillyard introduced the Tudor myth theme as far back as 1944, little that can be termed both perceptive and comprehensive has since been published in support of the providential shaping of destiny within the history plays, in particular as determined by God's judgment upon violations of the divine law. In short, the principal studies rejecting divine retribution in the English history plays are approximately as numerous as those that affirm it and are, in general, more concentrated in their focus. The Naysayers—and this is the crucial point—have exhibited a persuasive talent, more evident in their arresting phrases than in the substance of their arguments, not even approximated in the scholarly and hence less evocative syntax of the Affirmers.

When Shakespeare wrote the *Henry VI* plays in the early 1590s, his interest in retribution was focused primarily on the "blood will have blood" stimulus, or the vendetta, and only rarely (and then with a somewhat misted clarity) on God's judgment upon the transgressor. *Richard III*, by contrast, indicates an awakened awareness of God's power of retribution, which had been a preoccupation more of the Elizabethan pulpit than of the theater. Two or three critics of the past twenty years—responding basically to Tillyard's insistence upon the "Tudor myth"—have marked the relative absence of divine justice in the *Henry VI* plays and have exploited this absence in rejecting Tillyard's arguments. Others, a bit bolder, have focused their disagreements only on *Richard III*. Of the former, David Frey, in a recent book (1976), cites the "innocent human suffering" of Henry VI as proof of the absence of God's justice of any kind. He finds "God's historical justice" both in the Tudor chroniclers' accounts of Henry VI and in Shakespeare's *Henry VI* plays "to be shockingly negligent in protecting [an] anointed king, the innocent Henry VI." Frey then proceeds: "If Providence," as recorded by the chroniclers, "did not protect Henry VI, was it likely [Shakespeare seems to have asked] that it defeated Richard III and planted Richmond on England's throne? Thus, at the same time that he [Shakespeare] revivifies Henry VI to question the 'Tudor myth,' he enlarges on Richard III to nullify it, and he diminishes Richmond to demolish it."[1]

This statement of thesis, in suggesting Shakespeare's total disavowal of Providence, contains two flaws which Frey makes no later attempt to correct. First, it does not take appropriate account of two notable affirmations of God's supremacy over men on the occasion of Duke Humphrey's death in *2 Henry VI*, namely, that Humphrey may be a victim of "God's secret judgment" and Henry VI's statement: "If my suspect [about Humphrey's murderers] be false, forgive me God, / For judgment only doth belong to Thee" (*2 Hen 6*, III.ii.139-40)—for the death of Humphrey, the King's uncle and Lord Protector, is an event that no critic can lightly bypass: it is to expose the weak-minded King to certain destruction by the house of York, itself a claimant to the throne, and more important in the present context, it brings God's judgment upon Humphrey's murderers. Second, Frey's statement totally ignores the divinely imposed Lancastrian affliction of inherited guilt (of which Humphrey is one of the victims) as carefully established—indeed, planted with artful "foresight"—by Shakespeare in the historically earlier play *Richard II* only a year or two after he had completed (in *Richard III*) his first and historically later tetralogy. It is in this web of inherited guilt (the deferred legacy of the usurper and murderer Henry IV) that both Humphrey and Henry VI, however innocent themselves, are caught up. Of these and other workings of Providence, Frey takes no account.

In Humphrey's death there is only the indication of "God's secret judgment" upon him. By contrast, if we are willing to give credence to a single word—"ordain'd"—customarily used by Shakespeare with God as the understood agent, Henry VI's untimely death, as shown late in *3 Henry VI*, can be justified, almost irrefutably, in terms of the inherited guilt imposed by God upon Henry IV's heirs. Richard of Gloucester, having heard himself painted by Henry, whose son he has recently murdered, as a cutthroat incurably addicted to the shedding of English blood, recoils in unbridled anger: "I'll hear no more. Die, prophet, in thy speech. [*Stabs him.*] / For this, amongst the rest, was I ordain'd" (*3 Hen 6*, V.vi.57-58).[2] In view of the fact that the spoken word of a character was the Tudor playwright's principal medium of instructing his audience, Shakespeare, almost certainly, would not have put the phrase "For this [the stabbing of Henry] was I ordain'd" in Richard's mouth if he did not intend his audience to understand Richard as a divinely appointed scourge; if we consider Richard's prideful independence of worldly officialdom, by what high authority other than God can he have been "ordain'd" to kill not only Henry VI but other men as well? At the very least, Richard thinks himself ordained as a scourge by a higher power, and if we hold in mind God's curse upon Henry IV's heirs (a theme, as chapter 1 will show, enunciated in the historically earlier plays), what Richard thinks about himself in terms of a divine sanction to kill a Lancastrian heir—in this instance, Henry VI—happens to fit in precisely with the judgment of "God omnipotent" upon the house of Lancaster as twice foretold in *Richard II*. The task at hand authenticates Richard's boast.

Ignorant of providential matters or not, Frey seems to have been intent on exploding the "Tudor myth," first spelled out, although in a somewhat patchwork format, by Tillyard in 1944. Tillyard, for example, in his chapter on the play *Richard II*, overlooks (as Frey has done) the theme of inherited guilt which, first implanted in that play, does much to illuminate the historically later chronicle plays, including (of course) Richard of Gloucester's murder of Henry VI. Tillyard, in short, did not make the best use of the materials available to him, an oversight which Frey has not hesitated to exploit. Of those critical writings that question Tillyard's "Tudor myth," Michael Quinn's article "Providence in Shakespeare's Yorkist Plays" (*Shakespeare Quarterly*, 1959), which treats *2-3 Henry VI* and *Richard III*, is refreshingly evenhanded, for it recognizes both a "particular providence," in which the motives of men are the "efficient secondary causes," and a "general providence" inseparable from "the Primary Cause," which is God and which is "indicated by [the] curses and prophecies" of the actors.[3] Quinn, however, like Tillyard earlier and Frey later, seems to have been unaware of the curse that, twice foretold in *Richard II* and conditioned on Henry Bolingbroke's usurpation, imperils the house of Lancaster; nor does he take specific note of the later curse imposed upon the house of York because of its own ancestral crimes. He does not, in discussing *2 Henry VI*, see the untimely death of the Lancastrian Duke Humphrey as an effect of the inherited guilt arising from Bolingbroke's violation of divine right and specifically forecast, at that early time, by both Richard II (*R2*, III.iii.85-90) and the Bishop of Carlisle (IV.i.133-49). He is prompt, however, to recognize God's immediate judgment upon Humphrey's murderers: "The deaths of Winchester and Suffolk in *The Second Part* (of *Henry VI*) are sufficient warning for the ungodly that God can, when He wills, strike suddenly and without warning."[4] Quinn is aware enough of God's power of retribution, but not in terms of inherited guilt. His perspective, like Frey's, is restricted by an exclusive focus on the first tetralogy. For this reason his view of divine judgment does not extend beyond its isolated manifestations.

Among others who have called to account Tillyard's argument that the Tudor myth structures *1-3 Henry VI* and *Richard III* are Wilbur Sanders and, less vigorously, Moody E. Prior. Sanders attacks the myth only at its strongest point, *Richard III*, for this is the play upon which Tillyard, having overlooked the curse on the house of Lancaster, has focused his principal argument in support of the myth. In speaking of Margaret's major curse upon the Yorkists (*R3*, I.iii.195-214), Sanders acknowledges its "invocation of divine sanctions" but adds that, like the less elaborate curses in the play, it "is so deeply intertwined with personal malice . . . that it is dangerous to take any of it at its face value."⁵ Prior argues that "its hatred . . . and lust for vengeance" cancels out its claim to prophetic veracity.⁶ The fact remains, however, that God is invoked and that every one of the Yorkists marked for death in the curse is, as Margaret has foretold, "cut off" (with short shrift in the double sense) "by some unlook'd for accident" (l. 214), behind which lie the machinations of Richard of Gloucester. It is appropriate, I believe, to evaluate her curse upon the Yorkists in the context of Henry VI's prophecy—a much neglected one—which, coming late in *3 Henry VI*, categorizes Richard of Gloucester as a scourge of English blood (now and in time to come) only moments before Richard, in slaying Henry, retorts with the boast that he is, indeed, such a scourge (in fact, an "ordain'd" one). The identity of those who are to be slain by Richard is not specified in Henry's prophecy which (unlike Margaret's in *Richard III*) is apocalyptic in the biblical sense and not (as hers will be) incisive and denotative; Henry addresses Richard of Gloucester:

> And thus I prophesy, that many a thousand
> Which now mistrust no parcel of my fear,
> And many an old man's sigh and many a widow's,
> And many an orphan's water-standing eye—
> Men for their sons, wives for their husbands,
> Orphans for their parents' timeless [untimely] death—
> Shall rue the hour that ever thou wast born.
> [*3 Hen 6*, V.vi.37-43]

Only moments later comes Richard's affirmation that he is not merely a scourge but one ordained by God to kill King Henry and other men, whom he does not name. Not only has Richard claimed for himself a divine ordination, but in terming Henry a "prophet" he has acknowledged, by the associations of that term, the much more hallowed ordination of his antagonist; for the latter, as Richard knows, has spoken the truth, and such self-assured foresight—as in Hellenic and biblical precedents—was thought to come only from God. The confrontation of the outraged visionary and the impudent scourge, with its pronouncements which are later to be authenticated, is at the very least indicative of divine promptings. By means of Henry's prophecy, moreover, the audience is allowed to see the future, as it were, through a veil only;

Margaret's curse, coming only four scenes later in terms of the tetralogy itself, has the effect of tearing apart the veil and revealing, in hard detail, the precise victims—all of them Yorkists—upon whom the scourge Richard is yet to work his machinations. Even if we put aside Richard's inherent wickedness, he too, because he is a scourge and not a minister, must be destroyed by Providence, as Margaret is prompt to project (*R3*, I.iii.217-21).

In light of the total context—Henry's apocalyptic prophecy, Richard's self-identification as a divinely ordained scourge, Margaret's curse (which is, in reality, a prophecy), and the ultimate validation of the authentic character of each of these three components—I find no compulsion to doubt, especially in view of the repeated invocations to God throughout *Richard III*, that Shakespeare intended to show his audience (in contrast to our skeptical selves) anything other than what it was attuned to comprehend: namely, the control of Providence, even though the acts are ostensibly those of men, over the world of the play. The prophecies, the invocations, the repeated curses, and Henry of Richmond's unflagging image of himself as "[God's] captain" are not (to use Sanders's term) mere "proclamations": they are the guideposts designed to illuminate for the audience the otherwise incomprehensible workings of the divine law.

Most Elizabethans had either read in the Geneva Bible (in one of the forty-odd editions[7] printed in their Queen's reign) or heard from the pulpit the perquisite "Vengeance is mine: I wil repaye, saith the Lord" (Rom. 12.19); it had become a staple of their time, and hence (as I shall show in detail) they had no compulsion to doubt God's function of Supreme Arbiter, for this function had also been established—and established firmly—in the medieval trial by combat and remained a basic of their legal institutions. The public magistrate, for example, looked upon himself, above any other consideration, as a minister of God.[8] Hence Richard of Gloucester as a scourge and Henry of Richmond as a minister become in *Richard III*, in which ordinary processes of law have been replaced by anarchic privilege, instruments of God's judgment, which is yet to be fulfilled on the house of York. Quinn is correct in identifying a "particular providence," as well as a "general" one, and in observing in the malign craft of Richard the principal "efficient secondary cause" of events, while Sanders reflects more of Freud than of Shakespeare in his emphasis on Richard's "intransigent naturalism."

The fact is that, if we are to believe what Richard, at the end of *3 Henry VI*, has said of himself—namely that he has been "ordain'd" to put other men to death—then the particular, or naturalistic, providence becomes, in terms of Shakespeare's world view, a secondary phenomenon controlled, at certain critical points, by God's ordinance. In Shakespeare's time and in the centuries preceding it, the particular providence (if I may again use Quinn's dichotomy) appears to have borne much the same relationship to the general providence as did the geocentric universe, in terms of the Ptolemaic principle of cosmography, to the Primum Mobile. The rejection of the Ptolemaic theory, which not only postulated a finite physical cosmos but, for centuries, had supported conceptions of an intelligent cosmic hierarchy correspondent to the physical, is undoubtedly a factor behind the flurries of modern skepticism directed at Shakespeare's conception (in his time, quite logical) of a Providential government over important human events, especially those centered upon kings; for high magistrates, as deputies of God, were thought, in the conduct of their duties, to be specifically answerable to Him,[9] Who alone (like the Primum Mobile) was absolute.

Those critics, finally, who have treated Richard's vision of Ghosts and his subsequent throes of conscience as though the whole business were nothing more than an attack of acid indigestion are, I believe, either ignorant of the Elizabethan concepts of conscience (which include its divine origin) or, equally likely, indifferent to them. A. L. French has contended that Richard, by means of sophisticated word play (V.iii.182-92), quibbles the seizure of conscience into a virtual nonentity; to French, the seizure is little more than "a feeling of uneasiness,"[10] which is promptly dispelled. Sander's argument on Richard's seizure of conscience is somewhat more substantive than is that of French: "Shakespeare . . . , after permitting Richard to dance about on the brink of moral awareness, restores him to the certainties of the Machiavellian world where 'Conscience is but a word that cowards use.' "[11] Richard, as French has stressed, is uncommonly adroit at playing a "multiplicity of parts."[12] The passage in which Richard plays the word-splitting logician, and which begins three lines after his outcry "O coward conscience, how dost thou afflict me!" (l. 179) and ends with "Fool, do not flatter," is conspicuous testimony of this adroitness and is clearly a reflex, though postured, attempt to shake himself free of the double grip of conscience and fear. The attempt (as French has failed to note) is not successful. At line 193, Richard is again pommeled by the lash of conscience: "My conscience hath a thousand several tongues, / And every tongue . . . condemns me for a villain"; fourteen lines later, he concludes, with a shuddering recall of the vision itself: "And every [Ghost] did threat / Tomorrow's vengeance on the head of Richard" (ll. 205-206).

Richard's ensuing depression of mind, which is sustained, is broken only by Norfolk's urgent reminder "Arm, arm, my lord; the foe vaunts in the field" (l. 288). Prompted thus to state the order of battle, he puts on his accustomed public front (the readiest of his postures); but even this front cannot rub from his mind the recollection of the Ghosts for, indicative of his preoccupation with them, his concluding instructions to Ratcliffe and Norfolk are addressed as much to the preoccupation that has unnerved him as to the order of battle:

> Let not our babbling dreams affright our souls;
> Conscience is but a word that cowards use,
> Devis'd at first to keep the strong in awe.
> Our strong arms be our conscience, swords our law.
>
> [V.iii.308-11]

What has suddenly gripped Richard is, I believe, a reactivation of conscience which, in the shape of "babbling dreams" [the vision of accusing Ghosts] and the "conscience/coward" syndrome, has broken through his self-control and has injected itself into his speech patterns. He instinctively accommodates this tension by integrating his responses so that, in exhorting himself to withstand the reproaches of conscience ("Let not our babbling dreams affright our souls"), he maintains the appearance of exhorting his officers. But this containment of the encroachments of conscience is to prove tenuous only; for, in the closing couplet of the exhortation, it is displaced unexpectedly by the blatant illogic of a mind shorn totally of its self-discipline: "March on, join bravely, let us to it pell-mell; / If not to heaven, then hand in hand to hell" (ll. 312-13). This outcry is sheer bravado untempered by an iota of reason. Richard has said, in effect: "Let us 'join bravely' with our adversaries and be heroically slaughtered," for how otherwise can the ensuing reward of battle be "heaven" or, more likely, a comradely descent into "hell"?

In contrast to the conclusions of French and Sanders that Richard suffers only a brief qualm of conscience and then is restored to stability of mind, the "March on, join bravely" couplet, placed critically on the threshold of battle, vibrates with the unfocused bravado indicative of a mind possessed by deep-set and as yet irresolvable disconcertions.

Throughout Richard's earthy speech addressed to his army at large and placed (allowing for a pause) immediately after the doomsday couplet, his public front is again in control—that is, until he hears the report of Lord Stanley's desertion. At this critical moment Richard's tentative self-control explodes into a series of bombastic platitudes (ll. 347-51) indicative of impatience and parroted (almost verbatim) from *Lieutenant Pistol's Lexicon.*[13] Beyond this point—as his remaining six lines, all hyperbolic, are to attest—he is sustained by the intoxication of a strange excitement. When he cries out in his final speech, "Slave, I have set my life upon a cast, / And I will stand the hazard of the die" (V.vi.9-10), he provides a hint of the cause behind this excitement. Although I agree with Sanders that Richard has pitted success or failure upon "chance," I do not agree that the basic motive springs from "Epicurean convictions."[14] Why, for example, is Richard so anxious to find and, if he can, to kill Richmond? "Five [Richmonds] have I slain to-day," he cries, "instead of him." Is the hunt for Richmond a metabolic response that, in energizing and refocusing his mind, has alleviated the torments of conscience? It has, I believe, a larger substance than that. Mindful of the Ghosts' threat of "tomorrow's vengeance on the head of Richard," he has seen in the desertion of Lord Stanley and his men the high probability of the success of that threatened vengeance. Richard, always impatient and aware that Stanley's desertion has placed his cause at an unexpected disadvantage, is seeking (I believe) to put the threat of the Ghosts, without further delay, to its ultimate test: if he can kill Richmond, he will have proved his vision of Ghosts nothing but "a babbling dream." If he himself is killed—and, in the light of his most recent experiences, he is hard put to hope otherwise—there is, even in that, a satisfaction: he will not again, on lonely midnights to come, be compelled to grapple with the spine-chilling phantasms of conscience. Whether this analysis is correct or not is apart from my central point. Are we to accept in its place—and here is the point—the proposition made by Sanders that Richard's motive in risking probable death derives

solely from "a kind of moral duty" that compels him to "demon-
strate . . . the courage of his Epicurean convictions"? An observation
such as this, in my judgment, takes little thoughtful account of Shakespeare's text and none at all of Tudor concepts.

Problems of conscience, painstakingly studied and preserved, for later
times, in the Tudor theories of Timothy Bright and William Perkins,
and supported shortly by those of Robert Burton, were not regarded
lightly by the Elizabethans; for it was widely thought, as Perkins spells
out with particular care, that the conscience, to which was ascribed the
function of "accusing and condemning," was structured on God's laws
as contained "in the booke of the old & new Testament."[15] Bright
states the problem of conscience, as viewed by the Elizabethans, in terms
of offense and punishment: it is not, he says, "the breach of humane
laws . . . but of the Law divine" that prompts, upon the offender,
God's "fierce wrath"[16] in the shape of intolerable anxieties. Unlike
Sanders and French, among many other moderns, the Elizabethans did
not think of a seizure of conscience (depending, of course, on the inten-
sity of the seizure) as a mental disturbance that could be lightly dismissed, and certainly Shakespeare did not think so, as will be evident
from my analyses (in later chapters) of Richard III and Macbeth, including some comments on Lady Macbeth, each of whom is punished
through conscience by God. It seems to me, in conclusion, that critics
who often write most engagingly on Shakespearean topics find an advantage, however precarious it may be, in substituting modern and
sometimes personal criteria (whether in terms of theology, agnosticism,
or psychology) for established Tudor concepts. The use of modern
criteria is not in itself wrong; Shakespeare, in writing for the Elizabethan stage, also wrote unknowingly for our time. They become
misleading, however, when they are used to reach conclusions that, in
terms of Tudor criteria, are illogical or invalid.

Critics who object to Tillyard's Tudor myth and the many facets of
experience that relate to it may not, in all details, be mistaken. They
have, nevertheless, habitually ignored the Tudor concepts upon which,
in its *broadest* sense, the myth is based. These concepts include the
biblical principle of inherited guilt; the doctrine that God is the fountainhead of retribution and that man (whether the magistrate, the
scourge, or the next of kin) is merely His worldly instrument; and third,
and not necessarily least, the fundamentally divine function of the con-

science, in particular when its Old Testament dictates are violated. These three principles—familiar to all knowledgeable Elizabethans, including Shakespeare—are central to my comprehension of both the English history plays and certain providentially oriented tragedies which, collectively, are the subject of this book.

ONE

The Structure
of Shakespeare's
Eight-Part Epic

Of Shakespeare's themes in the history plays and the tragedies, none is so commonly enunciated as is the theme of political homicide, prompted by self-interest, and God's ultimate judgment upon the perpetrator or his heirs. This theme is fundamental to the structure of the two historical tetralogies, binding the two into an intelligible whole, while it informs, independently, each of the two Richard plays; it is, moreover, a central theme of at least three important tragedies. The homicide, because it is committed against a man of high status, inevitably shapes much of the subsequent action, customarily in the form of political confrontations, and invites, ultimately, retribution upon the criminal. To the unpracticed eye, the ultimate judgment may seem to be the work of one or more men; but a careful perusal of the text (as in *Richard II* and *Macbeth*, for example) makes it clear that the agent of punishment has acted in behalf of God, to Whom alone belonged, in the biblically oriented Tudor mind, the right of vengeance. The cornerstone of this belief was the New Testament statement "Vengeance is mine: I wil repaye, saith the Lord" (Rom. 12.19). The principle of God as the highest avenger serves, with special effectiveness, the theme of inherited guilt, for the crimes of Henry Bolingbroke are, two generations later, to be paid for in the *Henry VI* plays, and those of the Yorkists (as opposed to the Lancastrians) are brought to judgment in *Richard III*. In short, crimes which most men in time forget, God ultimately brings to account, thus visiting "the iniquitie of the fathers" upon the descendants. The working of divine judgment is equally apparent in the tragedies that I shall discuss, but in these plays, since the guilt arising from homicide is intrinsic and not inherited, the reality of divine intervention does not depend largely upon ancient prophecies and reminders of unpaid-for crimes but rather takes shape (sometimes subtly) from the immediate context. The homicide and the judgment, finally, are two parts of a causality, and in my analyses, neither of the two will, or can, be organically isolated from the other. Without a crime against the divine law, there can be no judgment by God.

In several plays, especially the histories and *Hamlet*, more attention will be given to the political repercussions of the crime than to the crime itself. Even so, without the crime (on occasion merely reported), we would have no play, for the crime is the mainspring of the action, a fact especially evident in *Richard II* and *Hamlet*. Meanwhile, from the political repercussions, an instrument of vengeance, such as Bolingbroke, Richmond, or Macduff, emerges. Although in popular conception an avenger, he is, in actuality, only an agent of God, or of God's Laws, for he cannot rightly usurp (as Shakespeare is careful to imply) the high Authority upon which the laws of the Western world are founded: "God's is the quarrel," states John of Gaunt; "Let heaven revenge." Ironically, in acting as God's magistrate in the punishment of King Richard II, Bolingbroke knowingly violates the divine law; in consequence, the crimes for which he and his heirs will be punished take shape even while he is fulfilling God's judgment upon Richard. Elsewhere, especially in *Macbeth*, it will be necessary to focus at some length on the genesis of the crime, for in it are extenuating circumstances which provide, properly enough, a degree of empathy favorable to the principal perpetrator. In consequence, we share with him some of the pain that attends the providential judgment upon him.

My purpose, in the treatment of God's judgment in certain of Shakespeare's plays and, in particular, of His retribution in behalf of persons unjustly murdered, departs considerably from that of former evaluations of the theme, which customarily take the form of a chapter; examples are M.E. Prior's commentary on *Richard III* (chap. 3) and *Henry V* (chap. 4) in his book *The Drama of Power* (1973) and E. I. Berry's useful chapter "Richard III: The Self-Alone," in *Patterns of Decay* (1975). Elsewhere, from E.M.W. Tillyard (1944) through R.B. Pierce (1971) and Robert Ornstein (1972), commentary on God's judgment in the English history plays is an occasional corollary of a more central concern. The work closest in purpose to my own is H.A. Kelly's *Divine Providence in the England of Shakespeare's Histories* (1970); Kelly focuses chiefly, however, on the English chroniclers, not on Shakespeare. More the scholar than the critic, Kelly in his commentary on the history plays recognizes divine intervention but, preferring to state alternative conclusions, very rarely takes a positive stance. His interest lies in Shakespeare's borrowings from the chroniclers and not in how, and to what purpose, he shaped these borrowings. A central purpose of mine, by contrast, is to show how a study of God's judgments, as it interrelates with the internal problems of the play, such as the crime of homicide, the obligations of kin right, and the murderer's violated conscience, has a capacity to open up new interpretations of what Shakespeare meant. To his conception of God, the prototype of which is the Old Testament image, I pay careful attention. The workings of divine retribution, however, are best observed in the instruments of God's wrath, such as Bolingbroke and Hamlet, and, equally well, in its objects, such as Richard III and Macbeth, for in them God's wrath is manifested primarily through the tormented conscience. Hence, for the purposes of precision and comprehensiveness, this study of God's judgments in Shakespeare's plays has an uncommonly strong internal focus.

Let us first consider two concepts of unity, one of biblical origin, as a means to understanding the structure of Shakespeare's two historical tetralogies which, as illustrated in *An Age of Kings* (a popular TV series of the 1960s), are after all a single prolonged stage play of interdependent parts and have the advantage of continuity when so produced. Shakespeare almost certainly had a unified plan in mind, as my evidence will show, when he began the writing of his second tetralogy, which covers the historically earlier period. The structure that binds the eight plays, and derives only in part from the recurrent stress on divine intervention, makes of them a kind of epic better unified than the *Iliad* but, unlike the *Odyssey* and the *Aeneid*, having no flesh-and-blood central character. There is, however, an idealistic and unifying concept which, when personified, embodies the English spirit (as well as that of England's late medieval kings) and which, flagging almost to extinction throughout much of the eighty-seven-year period (1398-1485) covered by the two tetralogies, is ultimately, with the manifest help of God, restored to vigor.

Both E.M.W. Tillyard and, among Shakespeare's contemporaries, Samuel Daniel in *The Civil Wars* have sensed a unity in this span of history, whether noted in Shakespeare's plays or, when Daniel wrote his poem, in the recent Tudor chronicles. Tillyard's personification of the unifying element, which he calls *Res Publica*, is somewhat less fitting, I think, than is Daniel's term "Genius of England," for the latter denotes the spirit of the people and not basically the physical kingdom and its documents of law. The French term *noblesse oblige* is pertinent but is not adequately comprehensive. A related word, however, defines the spiritual qualities of valor and selflessness, as typified by the ideal medieval warrior-statesman, better than does Daniel's less specific phrase "Genius of England" and is more comprehensive (and grammatically more appropriate) than is *noblesse oblige*. It contains those qualities that Gaunt and York in *Richard II* recall to mind in speaking of the reign of their father, Edward III—qualities almost extinct in England during the last years of Richard II's sovereignty. The term is *Nobilitas*. Hotspur has a share of Nobilitas: he has the valor but nothing of the selflessness, for his chief objective is personal honor. Prince Hal, before he becomes king, is Shakespeare's best example of Nobilitas, although by no means perfect, within the frame of the eight-part historical epic. Henry V, Duke Humphrey and, somewhat more so, Lord Talbot exemplify the high qualities expected of England's leaders. Nobilitas distinguishes a leader from the average man, and when its qualities do not appear within the ruling house of a nation, they are unlikely to occur in that land at all. Talbot, not a member of the ruling house, is an exception. His story, as told in *1 Henry VI*, reminds the reader of that lordly self-denial—namely, Nobilitas—which the decadent house of Lancaster must re-acquire, at least in large part, or it will soon be destroyed.

The main value of Kelly's book on providential justice lies in his analysis of those chroniclers—medieval and Renaissance—who wrote on British affairs from the downfall of Richard II to the coronation of Henry Tudor. The closing third of his book treats Shakespeare's two historical tetralogies. In analyzing the pre-Tudor, or mid-fifteenth-century, chroniclers, he reaffirms several points of interest, of which one, in my opinion, basically shapes and unifies the structure of Shakespeare's eight-part historical epic, perhaps more so than does the principle of Nobilitas. It has to do with the problem of the "third heir" and, in consequence, with Henry VI, grandson of Henry IV. John Hardyng, in the Yorkist (or later) version of his *Chronicle*, discerns in the troubles of Henry VI (as paraphrased by Kelly) "the providential punishment of the house of Lancaster" for Henry IV's and his descendants' "unjust possession of the realm."[1] In this context Hardyng quotes an old adage: "Of evil gotten good the third [heir] should not enjoice."[2] The Burgundian John de Waurin, who, like the French chroniclers Froissart and Créton, was sympathetic to Richard II, not only brands Henry Bolingbroke "the usurper of the crown of the glorious King Richard" but adds: "De male acquisitis non gaudebit tertius heres" ("Of goods wickedly obtained the third heir shall not have joy").[3] A third late medieval chronicler, who writes from hindsight, is quoted by Kelly to the same effect: "Heritage holden wrongfully / shall never chieve ne with the third heir remain."[4] The loss of the kingship by Henry VI was thus anticipated, and confirmed, in terms of an unavoidable destiny arising from the crimes of his grandfather. The "third heir" principle had its roots not only in the observations made by men but, much more deeply, in God's Old Testament warning that He would visit "the iniquitie of the fathers upon the children, upon the third *generacion* and upon the fourth" (Exod. 20.5).[5] The breaking of a commandment—a trespass which God had termed an "iniquitie"—becomes in consequence a peril not only for oneself but equally much for one's descendants.

Polydore Vergil, as historian to the Tudor kings, was not completely free to observe in the overthrow and murder of a Lancastrian king the handiwork of God. He ascribes to other writers, however, the belief that Henry VI was the victim of "divine justice, because the realm," as Vergil sums up these writers, "had been acquired through force by Henry IV . . . , so the sin of the grandfather redounded upon the grandchildren."[6]

Of the sixteenth-century chroniclers, Edward Hall, as interpreted by Kelly, is more reluctant than is Raphael Holinshed to identify divine retribution as the principal cause of the overthrow of Henry VI. Kelly notes in Hall "a basic tendency . . . to cast doubt on the facile explication of God's motivations and to stress the mysterious and the unknown factors in the movements of divine providence."[7] Of those who wrote of miracles, Hall (a devout Protestant) asks: "What shall a man say of such writers who took upon themselves to know the secrets of God's judgment?"[8] He was also unwilling to affirm, because of mundane considerations, the theory of Henry VI's inherited guilt: "Hall," Kelly contends, "has toned down the theme of [Henry Bolingbroke's] usurpation, perhaps to avoid showing Henry V in a bad light."[9] Hall was, nevertheless, aware of the large segment of opinion with regard to which he hesitated to commit himself. On the topic of Henry VI's overthrow and death, "Hall . . . reports, as the opinion of certain men. . . . , the theory of the inherited guilt and [providential] punishment of the house of Lancaster."[10] He is, moreover, quite ready to place the opinion that the Lancasters had inherited guilt, which is also England's, into the mouth of a speaker: Richard, Duke of York, as treated by Hall, is allowed to harangue at length on the wrongness of Henry IV's seizure of the crown and to attribute all the "tormentes" that God has imposed upon "this miserable Isle," including the untimely death of Henry V, to "the fyrste ungodly usurpacion," the act of a man "untruely called kyng Henry the iiij."[11] In consequence, when Shakespeare came to write his two tetralogies, he found available in Hall's chronicle, as well as elsewhere, ample support for the principle of inherited guilt and its providential punishment. He would also be aware that Hall, while holding that God had absolute power over man, felt that the method behind such power was inscrutable and, finally, that Hall himself, partially because of his extensive debt to the *Historia Anglica* by Polydore Vergil and partially because of his own particular sentiments, had some reservations about the wrongness of the Lancastrian occupation of the throne.

Kelly's interpretation of Holinshed's account of the late years of Henry VI's reign and the events that affected them is more troublesome than is his interpretation of Hall's. Too many of Holinshed's sources are involved: added to Vergil-Hall are the *Wethamstede Register*, the Yorkist *History of the Arrival of Edward IV*, and ultimately the *Chronicles* of John Stow. In addition, especially since Shakespeare is thought to have used the second edition of *The Chronicles of England, Scotland, and Ireland*, published after Holinshed's death, there are the hands of too many scribes, including the 1587 editor John Hooker and, in particular, the ambitious self-appointed "editor" Abraham Fleming. The result is a potpourri of facts, half facts, and some contradictions, which Kelly inherits from his source materials. Kelly's analysis indicates that Holinshed, unlike Hall, accepts both the wrongness of Henry IV's seizure of England's throne and, with some qualification, the inherited guilt theme as applied to Henry VI. After commenting on two possible, although related, motives behind the untimely death of so innocent a person as Henry VI, Holinshed (as noted by Kelly) reaches the explanation that he finds most plausible: more likely, concludes Holinshed, Henry VI died "for his father's, his grandfather's, and his own unjust usurping and detaining

of the crown."[12] This statement—the best of the three conjectures—
finds support in two much earlier pronouncements by Holinshed (to
whom I now refer directly) on the topic of inherited guilt. The first of
them is found in Holinshed's post-mortem analysis of Richard II's harsh
fate and comments moralistically on Henry Bolingbroke's "revenge"
upon Richard in behalf of their murdered uncle Thomas Duke of Gloucester: "The duke of Hereford [Bolingbroke, later Henry IV] tooke
upon him to revenge his [Gloucester's] death, yet wanted he moderation . . . , for the which both he himselfe and his lineall race were
scourged afterwards, as due punishment unto rebellious subjects."[13]
The second of the two earlier statements that substantiate the theme of
inherited guilt between the first and the third generations of the house
of Lancaster is an observation made by Holinshed early in the account
of Henry IV's reign: because of Henry's "violent" dethronement and
murder of King Richard, "he and his posteritie," Holinshed tells us,
"tasted such troubles as put them still in danger of their states, till their
direct succeeding line was quite rooted out by the contrarie faction."[14]
Kelly's commentary on this passage, which he paraphrases (and does
not quote), is worth repeating: "Once again, it is conceivable that Holinshed here is implying . . . a purely natural cause-and-effect series of
events, but it is perhaps more likely that some kind of providential punishment for sin is implied in the statement."[15]

To this point, with two notable exceptions (Polydore Vergil and
Richard of York, as recorded by Hall), the statements about inherited
guilt that I have from the chroniclers, both pre-Tudor and Tudor, make
no direct mention of God's part in the punishment of that guilt. And
in the words that I have just cited from Holinshed, the "contrarie faction," meaning the house of York, is identified as the ultimate destroyer
of Henry IV's "posteritie." Kelly apparently shares my viewpoint: that
the passage just presented, not unlike Holinshed's previous statements
on inherited guilt that I have quoted, strongly implies "providential
punishment for sin" and that "the contrarie [or Yorkist] faction" is intended only as the necessary agent, and not as the prime mover, in the
fulfillment of God's curse upon the Lancastrian heirs. This conclusion
is affirmed by the testimony of Exodus, as quoted above, namely, that
"the iniquitie of the fathers" can be visited by God at His pleasure
"upon the third *generacion* and upon the fourth." The not infrequent
neglect of a direct mention of God in Tudor (and pre-Tudor) statements

about inherited guilt probably reflects the fact that His function in the punishment of such guilt was widely acknowledged. In a memorable statement, John Donne, speaking from the pulpit, confirms the orthodox Renaissance thinking upon the theme of inherited guilt: "Thy Fathers, thy Grandfathers have sinned against him [God], and thou has been reprieved but for two sessions, two generations, and now maiest come to execution."[16]

In emphasizing the background of the theme of inherited guilt, I have sought to establish a well-known formula upon which Shakespeare has consciously shaped his two tetralogies into a unified whole. The principle of inherited guilt, embracing three or four generations, is thus very important. It does not much matter, however, whether God or "natural cause and effect" is responsible. Either way, the principle is capable of unifying relatively long periods of time. Shakespeare, as will soon be evident, unquestionably felt that it was founded largely—perhaps entirely—upon a judgment made by God. But Shakespeare was not adamant, perhaps for the reason that a traditionalist has less impulse (although sometimes more cause) to mount a soapbox than does a social radical. Because traditional beliefs, both medieval and Renaissance, helped to mold Shakespeare, and probably as much as tradition has molded any other great writer, I shall return briefly to Hall and Holinshed, his principal sources of material for the English history plays, closing out the background on inherited guilt.

Hall, in not endorsing the inherited guilt principle as ascribed by other writers to the Lancaster family, nevertheless, came far short of denying its reality. He and Holinshed share agreement on this principle as it related to the house of York. Moreover, in the catastrophes that exterminated the male issue of the York faction, both Hall and Holinshed, unlike some of their predecessors, make it amply clear that God is the principal avenger. Of the two, Hall's account, which follows, is the more difficult. When Edward IV returned, in 1471, from his short French exile and sought entrance to the city of York, the citizens, who held him to be "onelie duke," insisted that he "swere . . . to be obedient . . . to all kyng Henryes commaundementes and preceptes." Hall then explains that Edward, "in the next mornyng, at the gate where he should enter . . . in the masse tyme, receyvying the body of our blessed Savior, solemply [swore] to kepe and observe" allegiance to King Henry VI, whereas his intention at that very time, when he was in God's presence, "was . . . to persecute kyng Henry, & to spoile him of his kingdome." Such men, Hall continues, who "take an othe by by the immortal God which they know perfitly, shalbe broken and violate hereafter, . . . [are later] worthely scorged for their perjurie, in so much oftentymes that the blot of suche offence of the parentes is punished in the sequele & posteritie," and he adds, "the progeny of Edward escaped not untouched for this open perjurie."[17] In Edward's act of perjury, committed in holy church, God is so manifestly the party against whom the crime is directed that to insist upon Him as the principal avenger upon "the progeny" of Edward IV becomes, I think, tautological. Holinshed, by contrast, is unmistakably explicit in identifying the author of the inherited guilt that wipes out the house of York. Henry Bolingbroke, although clearly sinful because he had no valid claim to England's throne, had made a virtually bloodless coup in attaining it. The Yorkists, by contrast, came to the throne soaked in Lancastrian blood. For their "bloudie" methods, Holinshed tells us, "the Lords vengeance appeared more heavie towards the same [York] than toward the other [Lancaster], not ceasing till the whole issue male of the said Richard duke of Yorke was extinguished."[18] In short, for the crimes of Richard of York and his sons (including Edward), God's vengeance extended to the third generation, beyond which it had no need to reach. Holinshed's God, who visits destruction upon the innocent heirs of both Lancaster and York for crimes committed by their forebears, is a God of severe impartiality and, for this reason, much more closely approaches the Old Testament prototype than does Hall's proLancastrian deity.

To establish the unity that would bind together, in epic form, the two tetralogies—the first of which (although historically the later in time) had already been written—it was incumbent on Shakespeare to introduce the theme of inherited guilt into *Richard II* in a manner that would clearly extend to the existing *Henry VI* plays. One passage from Holinshed's *Chronicles* is tailor-made for Shakespeare's purpose and, being conspicuously placed within the chronicler's account of Richard II, may even have suggested that purpose to him, namely, the statement that delineates the immoderation of Henry Bolingbroke's revenge upon King Richard and its promise that not only Bolingbroke but also "his lineall race [would be] scourged afterwards, as due punishment for rebellious subjects." These words, even if Shakespeare had no knowledge of

Holinshed's other pronouncements on inherited guilt, which are placed in the accounts of later kings, were in themselves a sufficient spur (and for him an adequate guide) to incorporate the theme in *Richard II*.

The notion of inherited guilt naturally presupposes the existence of an instrument, or instruments, through which God will punish that guilt. As the evidence that I have cited suggests, there can be little doubt that the late medieval and Renaissance mind, being biblically oriented, regarded God as the avenger of the deposed and murdered Richard II. In the widely circulated Geneva Bibla, the literate Elizabethan had read, in effect, that God in all things was the avenger: "Vengeance is mine: I wil repaye, saith the Lord" (Rom. 12.19). In the punishment of crime, God was thought to have a choice of infinite instruments; among those available to Him in the Bible were floods, brimstone, pestilence, plague, civil war (or an alien army), palace rebellion, animals, champions such as Samson, and human scourges (e.g., Zimri and Nebuchadnezzar). That the Wars of the Roses were God's ultimate instrument in His long-purposed destruction of the house of Lancaster has been objected to by an occasional critic, principally on the contention that they were not necessarily an effect of Richard II's deposition. Reappraisals made by modern historians of course have no bearing on the materials available to Shakespeare in the 1590s. It is very difficult to find in the chroniclers or in Shakespeare's double tetralogy any important cause behind the Wars of the Roses more compelling than the vacuum created in the right of kingship by Henry IV's usurpation and the palace imprisonment of Richard II's rightful heir, the younger Edmund Mortimer. Robert B. Pierce has correctly contended: "In Shakespeare, as in the chroniclers, one major link . . . that leads to the Wars of the Roses is Bolingbroke's seizure of the throne, displacing Richard II's rightful line."[19] Citing the quarrels between King Richard and his uncles, Robert Ornstein makes the suggestion that the family dissension, predating by many years the usurpation, was the initial cause of the later civil wars: "The dissension [is] climaxed in the Wars of the Roses."[20]

Most Yorkist and Tudor chroniclers shared the argument that Henry VI's ineptitude of mind was a politically important factor in bringing about the Wars of the Roses. Hall, who circumvented the inherited guilt principle as applied to the house of Lancaster, was well aware that other chroniclers, such as John Hardyng, had strongly supported it: "Other there be that ascribe [Henry VI's] infortunitie [mental short-

comings] onely to the stroke & punishment of God" and, in consequence, contend "that the kyngdome" usurped by Henry IV "could not
by very divyne justice, longe contynew in that injurious stocke: And
that therefore God by his divine providence punished the offence of the
grandfather, in his sonnes sonne."[21] Several modern critics have
stressed the irony behind Henry's godlike ideals and his innate administrative inadequacies, both in Shakespeare's triology (the *Henry VI*
plays) and in the chronicles, and two or three of them see in that political
weakness the working of Providence. Ornstein, commenting on the inadequacy of Henry VI's brand of high morality, as shaped by Shakespeare, when it is extended into the field of politics, sums up: "Henry
is not 'too good' to rule; he is unable to translate his goodness into
political action."[22] Pierce, in his remarks on Shakespeare's plays, notes
that Henry V, a strong king, would not be expected, by natural genetic
causes, to beget a weak one, and he hypothesizes: "Henry VI's weakness
is a delayed effect of the curse on his grandfather's usurpation."[23]
Again, while commenting specifically on the *Henry VI* plays, Pierce explains why Henry kept the throne as long as he did: "Even now [end
of part 1] it is only the strong will and benevolence of Gloucester, the
Protector, that prevent the onset of civil war."[24] As Pierce has just
suggested, two factors, in addition to the high ambitions of Richard,
Duke of York, bear importantly upon the Wars of the Roses: the
political ineptitude of Henry VI and, temporarily counterbalancing that
ineptitude, the practical judgment and iron will of Gloucester, better
known as Duke Humphrey.

It is, of course, the murder of Duke Humphrey in *2 Henry VI* by the
Queen's faction, led by Suffolk and Cardinal Beaufort, that removes the
final restraint to the civil wars destined at the time of Richard II's
deposition. As Michael Manheim aptly notes: "Humphrey's downfall,
then, leads directly to York's Machiavellian leap for power."[25] The
deposition and murder of Richard II, capped by Bolingbroke's usurpation, had not, in a cause-and-effect sense, made totally inevitable the
Wars of the Roses and, as a consequence, the long predicted overthrow
of the house of Lancaster. Essential to complete the inevitability of these
Wars were the political ineptitude of Henry VI; the forced resignation
from office and the murder of the just and iron-willed Protector, Duke
Humphrey; and, through an incredible blunder by the conniving Suffolk
and Cardinal Beaufort, the acquisition of an army by the heretofore

powerless Richard, Duke of York. The claim of York to the throne which derives principally from his mother, a Mortimer, owes much of its broad political acceptance, in both the chronicles and Shakespeare's trilogy, to Henry VI's uncommon weakness as an administrator, a weakness "ascribed" by some contemporaries to the "punishment of God."

Pierce, as I have shown, contributes to the view that inherited guilt is a motif that does much to bind together Shakespeare's two tetralogies, but his focus on his chosen topic precludes a full endorsement. Ornstein neither rejects nor supports the theme of inherited guilt as a Shakespearean motif, and Kelly, although far from rejecting it, states as much against as for. He hesitates, for example, to accept on its own merits King Richard's prophecy of civil bloodshed, made late in the third act of *Richard II*; his reason is that "Shakespeare has not given much validity to Richard's providential claims earlier in this act [III], and has allowed them to be refuted as soon as they are uttered."[26] The "providential claims" to which Kelly refers do not have the doctrinal support—in fact, they are basically fantasies of escapism—associated with King Richard's prophecy and, later, with that of Carlisle, both of which reflect the widely supported medieval and Renaissance doctrine of inherited guilt. I hope to show that Shakespeare deliberately planted, in *Richard II*, these two prophecies that look ahead to the ultimate fulfillment of God's wrath, in the third generation, upon the house of Lancaster. We should keep in mind, as previously noted, that Shakespeare had in the early 1590s already written the *Henry VI* plays. Therefore, in creating *Richard II*, he had at least as much inbred motive to look ahead, in terms of historical chronology, to the problems of the *Henry VI* plays, and in particular the Wars of Roses, as he did to the problems of the two *Henry IV* plays, as yet unwritten. In short, the materials of the first tetralogy were relatively fresh in his memory, as were one or more statements by Holinshed in support of the theme that the guilt incurred by Henry Bolingbroke in the usurping of Richard II's throne was paid for by his grandson, Henry VI.

Richard II's hard-hitting prophecy of the doom that will befall England if Bolingbroke dethrones him is, fundamentally, an orthodox pronouncement that a twentyfold payment, in terms of God's justice, is the inescapable punishment of the rebel and those who aid him against an anointed king. He addresses Northumberland, emissary of Bolingbroke:

And though you think . . .

. . . .

[That] we are barren and bereft of friends,
Yet know—my master, God omnipotent,
Is mustering in his clouds on our behalf
Armies of pestilence; and they shall strike
Your children yet unborn and unbegot,
That lift your vassal hands against my head
And threat the glory of my precious crown.

[R2, III.iii.82, 84-90][27]

Kelly, as is his habit, provides alternative conclusions as to the meaning of Richard's prophecy. "King Richard's words," he observes, "could perhaps be taken as a prediction of the whole [fifteenth] century of intermittent strife over the crown that was caused by Bolingbroke's usurpation," but on second thought he shortens the time element to a lifetime: "It seems just as likely, or even more likely, in view of Richard's later prediction to Northumberland in the fifth act, that Richard is warning that Henry [Bolingbroke] himself will go through much trouble . . . and that those who have aided him in his rebellion will undergo the punishment of divine justice, which will [also] be felt by their children."[28] Kelly estimates that the promise of punishment contained in Carlisle's prophecy, which I shall quote shortly, extends into "the wars . . . of Henry VI" and even to a time beyond them, but he adds: "The bishop is not speaking in terms of divine punishment here, but in terms of a human situation."[29] In Richard's prophecy, Kelly has acknowledged the intervention of "divine justice," but he chooses to limit its future viability (by my mathematics) to not more than fifty years. In summing up Carlisle's prophecy, he inverts the procedure: the statement is to prove viable for eighty or more years, but humans, and not God, will fulfill it. It seems unlikely that Shakespeare intended that the two prophecies, both treating the effect of the same event upon a future time, should be so divergently interpreted, especially with respect to the principal avenger, God or merely man.

As Kelly has implied above, the deposed King Richard confines the scope of his act V prediction (i.55-68) to the near future. In this instance, he has obvious reasons to put a chill in Northumberland. His act III prophecy, in which there is a tone of inspiration, has already taken account of Northumberland's children and grandchildren as well as those of Bolingbroke, and in act V Richard is impelled, from bitterness, to inform Northumberland that, as kingmaker and especially as king unmaker, he will be one of the first to pay his dues to God—and indeed he is, in his son's loss of life and then in his own untimely death. The prediction of act V does not, even slightly, moderate or alter the two earlier and long-range prophecies, the king's and Carlisle's. Richard is only venting an understandable grudge upon Northumberland and pommels him with a few cold facts about the short-term consequence of planting "unrightful kings."

The certainty of God's readiness to confound Bolingbroke if he usurp Richard's throne finds its most concise statement in York's caution to him: "Lest you mistake. The heavens are over our heads" (III.iii.17), to which Richard adds the dreadfully vitalistic image of "God omnipotent" (l. 85). The single weakness of Carlisle's act IV prophecy, at least when examined by literal-minded critics, is that he, unlike Richard and the old-timers Gaunt and York, makes no unmistakable mention of God as the ultimate avenger. The context of *Richard II*, however, is so rich in its veneration and dread of God—more so, I believe, than any other Shakespearean play—that it is difficult to read the prophecy of Carlisle (himself a man of God) without registering its providential substance. More important in the literal sense, Carlisle makes evident the source of his foresight at the outset of the prophecy; he is, he affirms, "stirr'd up by God," and hence his vision of the future is what God has foreseen, and has helped him to foresee. If this is so, it must be God's will.

Carlisle's prophecy, by his own testimony inspired by God, is a response to Bolingbroke's impulsive and premature decision, early in the deposition scene, to "ascend the regal throne"; this presumption unlocks Carlisle's accustomed reserve:

> I speak to subjects and a subject speaks,
> Stirr'd up by God, thus boldly for his king.
> . . . .
> . . . if you crown him [Bolingbroke], let me prophesy—
> The blood of English shall manure the ground,
> And future ages groan for this foul act;
> . . . .
> O, if you raise this house against this house,

> It will the woefullest division prove
> That ever fell upon this cursed earth.
> Prevent it, resist it, let it not be so,
> Lest child, child's children, cry against you woe.
>   [IV.i.132-33; 136-38; 145-49][30]

The statement that suggests "a human situation" to Kelly is the clause "if you raise this house against this house"; in his context of "the wars . . . of Henry VI," he evidently means "the house of York and the house of Lancaster"; at any rate, he concludes that the opposition of two noble houses will be entirely the doing of men ("a human situation"). I believe that the key to the meaning of the prophecy is the earlier clause "if you crown him," an act that only God can validate. It follows that, by crowning Bolingbroke, the persons addressed by Carlisle will *automatically* raise the present house of March (the house of Richard's heir, young Edmund Mortimer) against the house of Lancaster, led by Bolingbroke. This opposition, of course, is a major factor behind the confrontation at Shrewsbury early in Henry IV's reign. It is not until the next generation that the weak house of March, through a fortunate marriage, merges with the stronger house of York, and as a consequence, the Wars of the Roses become inevitable. All the catastrophes foreseen by the inspired Carlisle are to derive from the sacrilege of crowning Bolingbroke, for the usurpation is the critical act at issue. In consequence, God's warning, if we accept Carlisle as His spokesman, and few Elizabethans would deny a bishop that office, is focused on the condition "if you crown him," which opens the prophecy and conditions the whole. Whatever follows, including the opposition of houses, becomes, if the warning against crowning Bolingbroke is not heeded, the inescapable destiny planned by God (although ostensibly worked by men) and contingent on the act of crowning. God knows, moreover, as He so often did in the Old Testament, that His warning will pass unheeded. Partially for this reason, Carlisle's prophecy is a masterpiece of craftsmanship. Not only has it linked the act of usurpation with later generations; it also is an excellent illustration of the Old Testament wisdom of God: the illusion that the Lancastrian faction has been granted a choice tends to justify, at least in the minds of the unwary, the severity of the providential punishment forecast by Carlisle, in particular in that part of his prophecy (ll. 139-44) which I have not quoted and which stresses "horror" and "dead men's skulls."

Shakespeare's overriding implication is that King Richard, and especially Carlisle, in predicting events not in the relatively near future (for informed men are sometimes capable of doing so) but in a time a half century beyond theirs, are to be understood as possessing a divinely granted clairvoyance. By such a means Shakespeare has prompted his audience to look to the Wars of the Roses and a bit beyond, while he has established the principle of inherited guilt. The formal and sermonic character of the two prophecies, especially Carlisle's, as well as the objectivity and interdependence of their predictions, suggests convincingly that the attention Shakespeare gave to them was dictated by a purpose much beyond the demands of the immediate play, *Richard II*. They are not to be mistaken for ornamentations. A third emphasis on the much later period of time comes at the end of the deposition scene; Carlisle, about to leave the stage, provides the audience with a final and apparently deliberate reminder of the long-deferred catastrophe: "The woe's to come; the children yet unborn / Shall taste this day as sharp to them as thorn" (VI.i.322-23). The present crisis, Shakespeare seems to insist, may be relaxed now and then, but it must ultimately be resolved, a long time hence, in a yet greater crisis. To the recurring emphasis, in *Richard II*, upon the theme of inherited guilt and, in consequence, upon the much later reign of Henry VI, in which that guilt is to be called to account, Shakespeare's eight-part historical epic, crystallized for us in *An Age of Kings*, owes both the basic unity and much of the structure that bind its parts into a sequence of coordinated events. That such a link is intended finds support in the plain and undisputed fact that the *Henry VI* plays, in which the prophecies of *Richard II* are fulfilled, had been written and performed only recently and were, in the composing of *Richard II*, a compelling part of Shakespeare's background.

The most self-explanatory evidence that God's curse upon the house of Lancaster was intended by Shakespeare to carry over to a second or, more likely, a third generation is a statement contained in the closing segment of Henry V's soliloquy on the night before the battle of Agincourt. For those who bear the guilt of a major crime and are yet unpunished, "war," as Henry has just lessoned his fellow soldiers, "is [God's] beadle, war is His vengeance" (*Hen 5*, IV.i.163). Left alone,

Henry has become aware of the strong personal implication of this principle:

> Not to-day, O Lord,
> O, not to-day, think not upon the fault
> My father made in compassing the crown!
>
> [IV.i.288-90]

He then proceeds to impress upon God the private penance he has done in behalf of the murdered Richard II. Reflecting Shakespeare's use of Robert Fabyan's *New Chronicles* (1516),[31] Henry boasts of the "contrite tears" he has shed on "Richard's body"; of the prayers made "twice a day" by five hundred beadsmen, whom he has hired, "to pardon blood"; and of the hymns chanted by priests, at his own expense, "for Richard's soul." What, in Fabyan, was shown as a penance intended to free the souls of Richard II and Henry IV from purgatory has become, in the context of the soliloquy, basically a gentleman's bribe: Henry has requested that God take account of the good works done by him and thus, in keeping with the Church of Rome's doctrine that good works command God's favor, that He put off the time of the inevitable vengeance upon the house of Lancaster. Both in Henry V's direct appeal to God to overlook, for the present, "the fault [his] father made" and in his recital of the details of his penance, which can at best postpone the fulfillment of the curse, Shakespeare has reminded the audience, emphatically, that the crimes committed by Henry IV are yet to be paid for.

The theme of Nobilitas, like that of inherited guilt, emerges as a unifying motif of Shakespeare's double tetralogy: its qualities are valor and selflessness betokening perfect manhood. It is provided, for example, with an uncommon emphasis in *Richard II*, a play in which, paradoxically, that dual caliber of spirit is almost nonexistent. Its near-to-total absence in this play prompts considerable concern on the part of King Richard's uncles, Gaunt and York. They recall the valor and, in particular, the subordination of self-interest to the welfare of England that had characterized the "royal kings" of the Plantagenet family, "renownèd for their deeds." They are especially proud of their parental court, that of Edward III. York can rightly boast, for example, when addressing Bolingbroke:

. . . brave Gaunt, thy father, and myself
Rescued the Black Prince, that young Mars of men,
From forth the ranks of many thousand French.

[II.iii.100-102]

He is here comparing his young manhood with his encroaching age,
"Now prisoner to the palsey"; in his choice of illustration, however,
and by a habit shared with Gaunt, he has contrasted the selfless vigor
of his father's reign, a time of high exploits, with the self-interest and
decadence of Richard II's court. Gaunt and York establish in their
repeated commentary a pole of Nobilitas which the kings in the plays
of the double tetralogy are hard put to restore. Only Henry V has, in
this respect, a reasonable success. In consequence, the theme of Nobilitas, and especially the effort to restore it, extend through the *Henry VI*
plays and *Richard III* to the coming of Henry Tudor, and he only promises, and does not carry out, a full restoration of that high quality.

The *Henry VI* plays need not carry the stigma of a trio of potboilers
highlighted by bloody battles, witchcraft, treason, conspiracy, and
political murders. In terms of Shakespeare's eight-part epic, they are the
time of an almost brutal darkness (as God was thought by some informed persons to have intended); within this darkness Nobilitas shines
only fitfully, first in the selfless military valor of Lord Talbot and, later
and likewise briefly, in the stalwart rectitude of Duke Humphrey. Both
men, however, are important proof that the qualities of Nobilitas, even
in the most treacherous of times, are not easily stamped out. At
Bosworth Field the eight-part historical epic is to end, at its almost
darkest moment. Behind the shining but slight figure of Henry Tudor,
the more solid figures of Henry VIII and Elizabeth I, seen distantly, are
to hold the fulfillment of Nobilitas, but of a somewhat different kind:
the difference, as Shakespeare must have known, relates to objectives,
not to essence.

In Tudor England, as in biblical and medieval times, it was widely
believed that God exercised vengeance upon evildoers, especially those
of prominent status, and occasionally upon entire cities or nations.
Biblical history, with some support from Homeric legend, was the fundamental source of late medieval and Tudor doctrines about the justice
of God and, in particular, about His power of vengeance. The important

Yorkist chroniclers, such as John Hardyng, and the Tudor chroniclers available to Shakespeare stress this power; in fact, the power of vengeance is the single attribute of God to which the chroniclers give a strong and repeated affirmation. Although Hall, unlike Hardyng and Holinshed, was reluctant to regard the downfall of Henry VI as an effect of inherited guilt, he was not at all reluctant to observe God's vengeance upon the actual evildoer. He endorses, without qualification, the almost universal belief that God could, and would, strike down the murderer: "To slaie and destroye innocent babes [the two York princes] / . . . the whole world abhorreth, and the bloud from the earth crieth, for vengaunce to all mightie God."[32] He shortly affirms: "the very devyne justice and providence of God" struck down the principal murderer, Richard III.[33] In Shakespeare's English history plays, God's vengeance upon the evildoer himself (e.g., Beaufort, Suffolk, and Richard III), and not upon the heir, is an equally frequent and a much more supportable phenomenon than is the metaphysical justice by which God requires a later generation to pay for an ancestor's crime.

Shakespeare's audience, whether through the Tudor chroniclers or through oral tradition, undoubtedly shared a few scraps of knowledge on the topic of Henry VI's inherited guilt. The "regulars" of this audience, who had seen the Henry VI plays performed in the early 1590s, either at the Rose Theater, or later at Shakespeare's, almost certainly marked, in the prophecies of the new play Richard II, a unifying motif that illuminated for them, much more sharply than before, the at times sardonic justice behind the lot of Henry VI and his kingdom. In light of the closing couplet of the Epilogue of Henry V (1599)[34] and its stress upon the continuing stage popularity of the Henry VI plays, which it unmistakably assumes the present audience has seen, the probability is that, in the years immediately following the original production of Richard II (ca. 1595), the repertoire of the Lord Chamberlain's Men included, from time to time, all the completed plays of the two tetralogies. If so, Shakespeare's historical epic, with much of its unity supplied by Richard II, assumed organic form in the presence of an audience immediately contemporary with its composition. In this sense, his audience shared an experience probably unique among public playhouses.

Robert H. West's thesis on the mystery that surrounds Shakespeare's plays—since the mystery (as he sees it) is close to total—does not encourage him to comment in specific terms on the problem of providen-

tial justice: "We never know precisely what the cosmic fact is"[35]—
which, of course, is right. By contrast, Robert G. Hunter, while endorsing West's principle of the almost total mystery of Shakespeare's
cosmos, is determined to discover which particular God—Augustine's,
Pelagius's, Calvin's, or an impersonal force—is the controlling Deity of
each of eight plays, five of them Shakespeare's. When he and his protean
deities are not at their game of cosmic hide-and-seek, Hunter is better
capable of a valid and instructive insight. He states of the two *Richard
III* plays (of which *3 Henry VI* is part 1): "[Shakespeare] allows us to
perceive that a design formed by the assertion of human will [Machiavel-
lian, not Pelagian] coexists in tragedy with the mindless revolutions of
Fortune's wheel. But coexisting with both these patterns and transcend-
ing them both is a pattern determined by the exercise of the omniscient
and omnipotent will of God."[36] Although Hunter sees Calvin's God as
the Deity of the two *Richard III* plays, his reference to God as "omniscient and omnipotent" conforms exactly with the non-Calvinist God of
the Yorkist and Tudor chroniclers and just as certainly with Shakespeare's "God omnipotent." Hunter, in the same context, proceeds to
a second good point: the *Richard III* plays "suggest that chance and consequence . . . are appearances which conceal the reality of divine providential justice."[37] Later he explains that "chance and will" form "patterns [that are] perceptible . . . and [that] coexist with the overriding
design of divine providence."[38] As these statements indicate, in *3 Henry
VI* and *Richard III*, the observable action appears to be entirely the work
of men plus the distortion of accident, but behind that which is observed, is the unalterable and "overriding" plan of God, barely perceptible, if at all.

West makes a statement that, I believe, is as pertinent as Hunter's
statements to the function of Shakespeare's serious plays, in particular
the eight-part historical epic: "Shakespeare's tragic outerness is an awesome mystery in which man participates."[39] In the light of the
statements provided by both West and Hunter, let us consider the roles
played by Carlisle in *Richard II* and by Henry Tudor, Earl of Richmond,
in *Richard III*. Carlisle, "stirred up by God," makes a long-range prophecy, in which he details the catastrophe that will beset England in the
third generation, but only if Henry Bolingbroke usurps the crown. That
Carlisle is actually inspired is proven, as Shakespeare meant it to be, by
the exceptional accuracy of the prophecy. He has become, for the mo-

ment, a participant in the "awesome mystery" which is God or the outer world controlled by God. Through Carlisle's voice, God has issued His ultimatum to Bolingbroke, who disobeys it. God's plan, which will "override" all human effort to thwart its fulfillment, takes immediate effect (although its full impact will be withheld) and comes to a period midway in the fourth generation at Bosworth Field, where Henry Tudor kills the tyrant Richard III. In short, Carlisle is the agent through whom God warns the Lancastrian faction of His plan; Henry Tudor, as the slayer of Richard III, is likewise (and more clearly) God's agent.

In both instances, especially in preparing his audience for Bosworth Field, Shakespeare has suggested the divine function of a man. Both individuals are participants in God's plan. The apparent cause of the prophecy is Carlisle, and the apparent cause of Richard III's overthrow and death is Henry Tudor, God's "captain." The true cause, in each instance, is God. Throughout the eight-part epic, this particular technique of appearance and reality, in which the observable conceals the divine cause, is Shakespeare's method; of this technique he makes periodic use, especially in the punishment of the rebel and the murderer, who have violated divine law. Shakespeare has also intended us, by means of Richard II's and Carlisle's prophecies, to view the Wars of the Roses and the principal schisms from which they arise, but certainly not every detail touching on these wars, as the design of God.

The principal source that made possible the wide acceptance of the reality of God's vengeance, whether upon the evildoer or his heirs, was the Old Testament. The Elizabethan could find numerous statements, in his privately owned Geneva Bible, about the exercise of this power. When the Israelites in the wilderness became rebellious, "the wrath of the Lord was kindled against the people and the Lord smote the people with an exceeding great plague" (Num. 11.33). He might also have read, or have heard from the pulpit, that because Saul, who had already put to death the priests of Nob, broke a second commandment of God when he "soght and asked counsel of a familiar spirit," the Lord "slewe him, and turned the kingdome unto David" (1 Chron. 10.13-14). Or he may have shuddered at God's outcry against unbelievers: "thei [the Philistines] shall know that I am the Lord, when I shall laie my vengeance upon them" (Ezek. 25.17).

The practice of vengeance in England had a half-legal and ancient societal basis which was, at first, independent of biblical doctrine. Its

shape was that of the common vendetta. Only in later centuries, especially in England and France, were the principles of vengeance, as we
find them in both the Tudor chronicles and Shakespeare's plays, to
assume a biblically oriented function: the trial by combat, introduced by
the Normans into England, added to the punitive purpose of the Anglo-
Saxon vendetta the requirement of a judgment made by God upon the
guilt or innocence of the defendant. In England, the Christian God, according to J.W. Jeudwine, did not become all-knowing and all-
powerful, in the minds of the people, until "the idea of the king as
author of law and conservator of national military power" had been
firmly established.[40] Apparently for the reason that the Anglo-Saxons,
many of whom lived in remote villages, had no close-at-hand example
of a broad and absolute authority, they found it hard to imagine an all-
encompassing power even in God. The rules of the vendetta did not
allow for any kind of appeal to God's judgment. When a murder was
committed, and the payment in coin (the wergild) had not been made,
"the offender [usually self-confessed] must defend himself against
the next-of-kin with whom rested the obligations of revenge."[41] Customarily, no one beyond the family circle was, in any significant way,
involved.

The providential justice which is recorded by the late medieval and
Tudor chroniclers has a double origin: (1) the Anglo-Saxon vendetta, in
which God played no recognizable role; and (2) Old Testament history,
with its stress on a vengeful God. The vendetta, little by little, became
amalgamated, as my second chapter will attempt to show, with concepts
of God's justice. This blend of primitive response and Old Testament
pronouncement is the type of punitory justice that we find, ideally, in
Shakespeare's plays. Because human nature tends toward hot-blooded-
ness, as in *Romeo and Juliet* and *3 Henry VI*, variations from this ideal
are generally, but not always, at or near the pole of primitive response.
The ideal form of punitory justice, in which God is recognized as the
rightful judge and a man as His agent, is most prominently enunciated
by Shakespeare in the English history plays (in spite of the violent killings of *3 Henry VI*) and in several important tragedies which are founded
upon history.

The experience of structuring his eight-part historical epic upon a pattern of crime and divine retribution was not desultorily put out of mind
by Shakespeare when he came, almost immediately, to the writing of

his mature tragedies. There is no such abrupt demarcation. In these later tragedies (excepting one), he again sought his materials from historical books, for he had come to see in the shaping of history the large part played by Providence. Its dramatic potential apparently fascinated and challenged him. In plays that were, unlike the double tetralogy, only single entities, the theme of inherited guilt was no longer organically appropriate. Shakespeare, however, had found in God's alleged power of retribution an outer dimension more substantive than that provided by fairies and ghosts and not only because of God's unmatchable eminence. Equally important, behind God's power of retribution were three thousand years, much of this period in biblical accounts, of sustained, and not merely sporadic, documentation. In the mature tragedies, the theme of God's judgment upon the trespasser, no longer tied largely to inherited guilt, becomes both more complex and, in particular, more sophisticated than in the English history plays. In *Hamlet*, for example, a careful scrutiny of the play is essential if the reader is to perceive the comprehensive scope of its pattern of divine retribution. In *Macbeth*, the pattern is partially obfuscated and, at the same time, is accented by the interposition of demons, who hold a temporary ascendance over God. In both *Hamlet* and *Macbeth*—I here omit, for the moment, mention of the non-Christian tragedies—the crime of political homicide, because it is committed by a man of high estate, stands outside the dominion of the civic law (as in the English history plays). If it had done otherwise, the perpetrator's punishment—and in *Hamlet* the punishment of his postcrime associates as well—would not have evoked the direct response of the divine law.

My premise in this book is that concepts of God's judgment, being fundamental to the plays discussed, control the principal destinies of each play world. In the next chapter, I shall discuss these Christian concepts together with their medieval origins and developments. Before I do so, with reference to both medieval and Renaissance tenets, it is appropriate to call attention to two tragedies of pagan background—*Julius Caesar* and *King Lear*—that are controlled (whether predominantly or late and unexpectedly) by the intervention of divine but non-Christian judgments, for these judgments offer rudimentary contrasts with those of the Christian plays. In *Julius Caesar,* in fact, the control of the supernatural over the destiny of men is more overt—at least on the surface—than in either of the two Christian tragedies. It is, if anything, too explicit; from the moment that Antony evokes the image of "Caesar's spirit, ranging for revenge" (III.i.271) to Brutus's ultimate appeasement of that spirit through suicide "Caesar now be still. I kill'd not thee with half so good a will" (V.v.50-51), the supernatural destructive force, although much less subtle than in *Hamlet* and *Macbeth*, has a primitive immediacy not approximated elsewhere in Shakespeare.

This immediacy derives not from the armies of Antony and Octavius, for they are merely the police symbols of the destructive force, but from the stealthy and ambient encroachment of "Caesar's spirit" and the fear of that spirit as it preoccupies and disorients the minds of the conspirators. The fear is born, initially, of the mob, ignited as it is by the promise of "seventy-five drachmas" to "each several man" in accord with Caesar's will, for the spirit of Caesar, now renovated and vitalized in ten thousand plebeian breasts, has become a force beyond the powers of intelligence or pragmatism, or even distance, to withstand. Hearing that "Brutus and Cassius / Are rid like madmen through the gates of Rome" (III.ii.269-70), Antony bluntly explains: "Belike they had some notice of the people, / How I mov'd them" (III.ii.271-72). At that moment of shock—a moment in which Brutus's and Cassius's high prospects have collapsed, instantly, into the urgency of panicked flight—the canker of the inevitable totality of the dead Caesar's power is implanted, inextricably, within the two conspirators' minds. The flight from Rome is, in a sense, illusory, for they never escape the impression from which they have fled—an impression undoubtedly strengthened by the cold faces they encounter, separately, in exile, for behind the placidity of each unsmiling face both are certain to sense the knowledge of their political isolation.

At Sardis, where the two men ultimately meet again, the truth of the divisive power of Caesar's spirit is promptly confirmed. Not only is each of the conspirators isolated, politically, from power within the Roman world and largely on its fringes as well; they are both in imminent danger, as their waspish debate attests, of isolation from one another. In barbing their charges and countercharges with allusions to Caesar, they testify to their long and incessant preoccupation with the fear of both Caesar's spirit and Caesarism (the mundane counterpart of that spirit). Cassius, compelled to save an alliance which both desperately need, acquiesces, as they conclude the interview, to Brutus's ill-conceived decision to march to Philippi. What is happening to both

Brutus and Cassius is best affirmed, I believe, in Brutus's confrontation, late that night, with Caesar's Ghost, which is apparently the product of an unconscious search, deep within his psyche, for the truth; for Brutus, too, has doubts about the march to Philippi. He has just, for example, qualified his promise to treat young Lucius tenderly, tomorrow and thereafter, with the condition "If I do live" (IV.iii.263-64). Cumberland Clark has summed up the psychology behind Brutus's vision of the Ghost in poignant terms: "When the inward voice warns Brutus that his end is near, then his consciousness of the ever-presence of Caesar's spirit is so intensified that it brings him into closer contact with the Unseen and results in a visible manifestation."[42] The talk between Brutus and the Ghost is best understood, I think, in terms of an interior dialogue in which his conscious mind is confronted by the deeply embedded fear of Caesar's spirit within his psyche. When the Ghost, an embodiment of that fear, promises to meet Brutus—at Philippi—a second time, Brutus's response bespeaks the utter exhaustion of his two-year labors to withstand a destiny that, in his innermost heart, he has long known to be unavoidable: "Why, I shall see thee at Philippi then" (IV.iii.284). He has resigned himself, for the moment, to the certainty of the doom that he has been at great pains to avoid.

Only seconds later, as the Ghost vanishes, Brutus's will, as opposed to the general resignation that has benumbed him, has become abruptly alert: "Now I have taken heart, thou vanishest. / Ill spirit, I would have more talk with thee" (IV.iii.285-86). He very probably intends to give the Ghost the type of argument for marching to Philippi that was presented to Cassius. This statement may be true. But there appears to be a second and more impelling motive behind his uplift of heart. The Ghost, the product of a search for truth deep within his psyche, has just forced Brutus, in a time of exhaustion and unguardedness, to assent to an almost certain death sentence at Philippi. In short, the death instinct, long nourished by Brutus's unremitting fears of both Caesar's spirit and Caesarism and by his concomitant anxieties, has in the figure of the Ghost overpowered, for the moment at least, his will to survive and, if possible, to regain the ascendant. The life force, together with the wilting energies that sustain it, has been compelled to total withdrawal. Suddenly, as if by a painful resolve, Brutus's will to survive ("Now I have taken heart") is aroused, and the Ghost—the embodiment not only of his fears but also of the death instinct, which is structured by those fears—vanishes. The life force, alerted by Brutus's desperate exercise of will, now demands of him the renunciation of the destructive forces that have threatened, and are threatening, its will for survival, which is also his. Brutus, in consequence, would like to tell the Ghost that he looks for victory and not untimely death at Philippi. The energy that sustains the life force, however, is to prove inadequate, especially after he has lost, through a miscalculation by Cassius, the first battle at Philippi. Having seen the Ghost a second time, Brutus does not attempt to escape the certain imminence of death: "I know my hour is come" (V.v.20). The implacability of Caesar's spirit not only has enforced errors of judgment upon the conspirators;[43] it also demands of them, as if to mock the life force that stands up to it, the abasement of suicide.

Caesar's spirit, it should be understood, although it has a singularity of purpose, is a collective and not a single entity. From the moment that Antony releases the mob, this spirit has become a multiple force, enshrined ultimately in hundreds of thousands of Roman breasts, not only in Rome but also on the fringes of the Roman world. Even in distant Lydia, Brutus senses the chill in the "forc'd affection" of its inhabitants. Nor has either Brutus or Cassius, at any time, expressed a sanguine hope that he will escape the ambient menace of rejection, the slow encroachment of which has slowly stifled his will for life. Theirs is the tragedy of personal isolation. It is also the tragedy of those who are confronted by a dark Inevitability which, throughout the time of trial, offers not even the respite that comes from a single illusion of escape.

Because the external manifestations of divine judgment in *Julius Caesar*, such as Antony's apocalyptic vision of the demigod Caesar's spirit "ranging for revenge" (III.i.271-76) and, at Philippi, the several statements attesting to the fulfillment of that vengeance, are overtly presented, I have attempted—possibly to my hazard—to trace the struggle for supremacy (which, of course, is never in doubt) as it takes shape within Brutus's mind. Unlike *Julius Caesar*, the second pagan play—*King Lear*—is not based upon the formula of crime and judgment central to this book; for the unwarranted political homicide—the hanging of Cordelia—does not take place until the play's last scene and then at the same time that Edmund, on whose authority she is unlawfully hanged, is being punished, ostensibly by the gods, for treason, a crime of equal import. In fact, not only are the divine judgments of *King Lear* confined, with one exception, to the closing scene, in which four malefactors are justly brought to account, but the characters' perceptions of the gods as expressed throughout the first four acts do not—in their consensus—prepare us for these judgments. The gods are customarily seen—except belatedly by Albany (IV.ii.78-80)—as possessing an unprincipled power that is basically at odds with our Christian concepts of justice.

Lear, for example, at the outset of his play, invokes four gods— Helios ("the sacred radiance of the sun"), Hecate, Apollo, and Jupiter—primarily, it appears, to bolster the image of his authority in both the disowning of Cordelia and the later banishing of the faithful Kent. The invocations, in terms of the nature of the gods, establish them as symbols of power, and since Lear calls upon these gods to sanction wrongful acts, he hints at their readiness to countenance injustice as opposed to justice. The image of the gods as amoral is supported recurrently throughout the first four acts not only by the rapid political ascent of the wicked characters over the virtuous ones but also by the perceptions of the actors, in particular Lear and Gloucester. In the first storm scene, a lately humbled and wiser Lear sees the gods as either indifferent to right and wrong or, in one important instance, as supporting wrong against right, for he concludes that they have joined "with two pernicious daughters [Goneril and Reagan]" in tormenting him: "O, ho! 'tis foul" (III.ii.22-24). He sees in the gods an absence of ethical principle. Lear, attesting to his own "ethical reversal,"[44] for he has now come to think in terms of objectivity and not of blind self-advantage, is prompted to lesson the gods on what he holds to be their fundamental duty:

> Let the great gods,
> That keep this dreadful pudder o'er our heads,
> Find out their enemies now.
>
> [III.ii.49-51]

He advises them to direct their harassment to persons whose "undivulgèd crimes" are as yet "unwhipp'd of justice" (III.ii.51-53), specifically the murderer, the perjurer, and the lecher (ll. 53-55). To these he adds the "caitiff . . . / That under covert and convenient seeming / Hast practis'd on man's life" (ll. 55-57). In short, the duty of godhead, in the awakened consciousness of Lear, is to use its power for purposes of justice and not to misuse it, as the storm gods have just done, upon the heads and chilled bodies of innocent outcasts.

If Lear's denunciation of the gods as hostile and his prompt readiness to lesson them on justice attest to his manliness, Gloucester's appraisal of them, once he has been blinded, is shaped by an embedded conviction of their hostility, for his superstitions have taught him that a man's fortunes are what the gods have chosen to make them. His readiness to submit to their will is matched only by the self-pity that nourishes it: "As flies to wanton boys, are we to th' gods— / They kill us for their sport" (IV.i.37-38). Both men, however different in temperament, have observed in the gods' capricious satisfactions a total neglect of ethical principle. Lear would, moreover, agree—at least basically—with Gloucester's later charge that the gods have "great opposeless wills" (IV.vi.38), but with one important exception: within those areas in which the gods are indifferent, a man, Lear would argue, can shape for himself a tolerable existence. To both Lear and Gloucester, although one is resolute and the other infirm, the gods are amoral. They are, in short, pagan in their want of principle and not, by any definition, Christian.

Three or four comments by other characters suggest that the gods are not quite so amoral and capricious as Lear and Gloucester would have us think. The banished Kent's parting good wish to Cordelia ("The gods to their dear shelter take thee, maid" [I.i.181]) is, however, partially offset by France's observation that Cordelia has suffered the gods' "cold'st neglect" (I.i.254). Edmund's statement that he dissuaded Edgar from seeking Gloucester's life only by reminding him that "the revenging gods / 'Gainst parricides [do] all their thunders bend" (II.i.45-46) is, of course, a trumped-up falsehood. More germane to his sentiments about the gods, who in his mind are the amoral lackeys of his revered goddess Nature, herself amoral, is his petition to them to "stand up for bastards" (I.ii.22). Albany, quite late in the play, makes a statement that is ideally Christian in its conception of justice; it contains, however, a qualification that stamps it, at best, as transitional. Hearing of the treacherous Cornwall's death, he states:

> This shows you are above,
> You justicers, that these our nether crimes
> So speedily can venge!
>
> [IV.ii.78]

The phrase "This shows you are above, / You justicers" makes amply clear that Albany, caught up in a world of flux and betrayal, has long had doubts about the gods and their supernal justice. He must be "shown" evidence of it. His readiness to accept one piece of evidence as proof is a readiness, I believe, that an audience—especially an attentive one—is inclined to hold in abeyance. His optimism does, however, establish a bright crack of light on the dark and glowering face of the *Lear* heavens.

What, then, are we to think of the gods of the play's last scene? For they respond almost precisely to Lear's lesson on moral justice (III.ii. 49ff.) and show nothing of the amorality of which Lear and Gloucester have accused them. Is Lear perhaps the enlightened pagan to whom even the gods must ultimately conform? Or does the change lie in something altogether outside the gods' natures? The judgments of the final scene, moreover, suggest that Shakespeare, in depicting them, had in mind Lear's former instructions to the storm gods; the lecher, the murderer, and the treacherous "caitiff," identified by Lear, are also conspicuous victims of the judgments. The first of the present statements on divine judgment—that by Edgar—is constructed on a double entendre, for while one judgment is explicitly explained, the second judgment, which is now of more immediate concern, is only implied. To Edmund, just defeated in trial by combat, Edgar justifies the gods' blinding of their father Gloucester for adultery and leaves the implied judgment—one upon treason—to his brother's interpretation:

> The gods are just, and of our pleasant vices
> Make instruments to plague us.
> The dark and vicious place where thee he got
> Cost him his eyes.
>
> [V.iii.170-73]

Edmund (now mortally wounded) accepts this judgment upon his father's act of adultery and, rather than disclaim his own responsibility in the judgment, confirms that he was, indeed, the wicked "instrument" and, in turn, that he must be destroyed, for he had also plotted his father's ruin: "Th' has spoken right; 'tis true. / The wheel is come full circle; I am here" (V.iii.173-74). He means, of course, that the gods, being "just," have no choice but to demand of him his life. Albany makes the scene's third and concluding statement on the just retribution of the gods. He substantiates, upon his learning of the violent deaths of the murderess Goneril and the equally treacherous Regan, the broadened conviction that the gods, formerly held to be capricious and amoral, have now acted with perfect justice: "This judgment of the heavens, that makes us tremble, / Touches us not with pity" (V.iii.131-32). This time, importantly, Albany does not couch his acceptance of the gods' justice in terms that expose his previous misgivings. He accepts the orderly working of the divine law as an already established and unchallengeable fact.

What is significant, then, about the judgments of the final scene? We see the gods, of course, only through the characters' minds, and they, in turn, see them only through Shakespeare's mind. All four judgments—upon Gloucester, Edmund, Goneril, and Reagan—have been anticipated, in act III, scene ii, by the petition of Lear to the gods for justice. He has demanded of them that they turn from the indiscriminate punishment of unoffending outcasts and, instead, bring those both guilty of major crimes and as yet "unwhipp'd of justice" to account. The fundamental truth which the child-humbled Lear, in his first blush of incipient wisdom, has advocated will ultimately be grasped by the younger men, and in particular, by Edgar and Albany, the emergent leaders of England: until men find justice in their gods, they can have none among themselves. Nor does the transformation that we have noted derive from the gods; for godhead, of itself, is unalterable. The new conviction that holds the gods to be just is the communal work of well-ordered minds and is dictated, in particular, by the logic of survival: anarchy has barely been constrained and, lest anarchy again threaten England, an absolute and highly visible pattern of justice must be established; for without such an example of discipline, mankind, and in particular its lords and would-be rulers, will respond, each in his own way, to an overriding inner voice. Deities, and specifically the polytheistic pagan gods—so Shakespeare has posited—are as men, whether in time of flux and distraction or again in time of wisdom, have chosen to make them.

That the society headed by Albany and Edgar, as well as by Lear, had he lived, is culturally ready for Christianity is attested by its transmutation of its pagan gods into intelligences governed by principle and no longer by amorality and caprice. The times, however, are not, in the historical sense, ready; they lack some seven hundred years of the period of Christ. In the plays to which chapters will be given—eight English

history plays and two Christian tragedies—the concepts of divine justice
are, to say the least, inflexibly Christian. In them, since Shakespeare's
extramundane focus is principally on God's judgment upon a murderous
and self-seeking man of high estate (e.g., Claudius), we can best see how
His judgment works by an examination of either the instrument of that
judgment or, when God punishes by means of conscience, the human
object of it.

The next chapter will pause, both briefly and yet comprehensively,
to discuss important historical concepts of God's justice as they became
known to Shakespeare and to his fellow Elizabethans and, in consequence,
as they found repeated expression in close to one-third of his dramatic
canon. Several of these concepts have, indeed, infiltrated *King Lear* (e.g.,
the Christian-type judgment, the human instrument, and the trial by combat) and, with less definition, *Julius Caesar*, which stands closer to the
Christian plays only in its important act of homicide. The extraneous
concept of the pagan plays, in particular *King Lear*, becomes, of course,
a central focus both in the English history plays—whether in conjunc-
tion with, or apart from, the biblical device of inherited guilt—and in
Hamlet and *Macbeth*. In these plays, the theme of God's judgment—
foreseen by Shakespeare's audience at the moment when the act of criminal
homicide is committed—is central and crucial to the total dramatic structure, for the homicide triggers the political repercussions which, in turn,
produce (whether late or soon) the agent best fit, by kinship and pro-
ficiency, to execute the judgment.

TWO

The Justice of God:
Medieval and Renaissance

Shakespeare's plays provide examples of three types of punitive retaliation: the revenge of justice; the revenge of honor; and the revenge of passion. Of these three, only the first is granted a wide social acceptance, for only it comes under God's laws. The second is condoned if the subsequent injury is not in excess of the motive, and the third, being animalistic, has no societal acceptance whatsoever. The second category—the revenge of honor—is often a topic of burlesque in Shakespeare's plays, as it is in the Fluellen-Pistol confrontation or, in comedy, during the Cesario-Andrew duel; but when honor is too hot-headedly pursued, as with Tybalt, a whole city will be aggrieved. The third category—the revenge of passion—is used by Shakespeare to accent atrocity and, collaterally, to warn the spectator against the monster within him: a series of such revenges are found in *3 Henry VI*, the most bestial example being the York brothers' murder of young Prince Edward; but none appalls more, or is more admired, perhaps because we see embodied the passion of primordial giants, than that of Othello. The revenge of justice, the first and the only category worthy of commendation, always entails a judgment made by God. Take, for example, the executions of Cambridge and his fellow conspirators, who have plotted Henry V's death, as the case is presented by both Holinshed and Shakespeare: public officials carry out the punishments, but the beheadings have been ordered by the King, who acts under a law which, in the name of God and as the deputy of God, he has sworn to uphold. Revenge when sanctioned by God is justice.

Dozens of Old Testament passages, of which I have quoted but three (p. 32) so far, not only implanted the power of God's vengeance in the medieval and Renaissance consciousness but have illustrated for all

Christians the common principle underlying the revenge of justice: the evil deed deserving of retribution, they collectively affirm, is the deed held by God to be worthy of His punishment, which was customarily death. High on this list are murder and rebellion, but also included are heresy, adultery, and theft, as attested not only by God's acts but more specifically by the Ten Commandments. The second force in shaping the late medieval and Renaissance patterns of vengeance, especially as formulated in the post-Conquest trial by combat, was the Anglo-Saxon vendetta; it provided a mode, in particular the principle of the next of kin as avenger, and a firmly established tradition. Much as in the nineteenth-century American West, the vendetta was the principal law of Anglo-Saxon England, especially in the more sparsely settled areas; although it shaped fundamental aspects of the later trial by combat, it does not seem to have taken into account any kind of intervention by God. The avenger acted only as next of kin in behalf of his family and under protection of the communal law. "Every old collection of [British] custom," J.W. Jeudwine has remarked, "contains provisions regulating this privilege of settling criminal . . . matters by the sword as a privilege of the freeman."[1] At no place in these documents is there a mention that a judgment by God is entailed. The wergild, or money payment as compensation for murder, was designed to spare further bloodshed; but the practice of paying it, even though merciful, became very largely a mundane consideration. Local officials were thought, and the kings of England were known, to demand an ever larger share of the blood money.

The earliest mention of the wergild appears in the Dooms of Aethelberht, the first king of Kent, about the year 600: "If a man slays another, he shall pay as compensation [to the kindred] the ordinary wergild of 100s,"[2] which was, at that time, the body price of a freeman having no official status. As we learn from later edicts, the wergild was only a substitute for blood revenge and need not be paid. One of the dooms of King Edmund of Wessex, about 945, reads: "Henceforth, if any man slays another, [we order] that he by himself shall incur the blood-feud. . . . If . . . his kinsman abandon him, refusing to pay anything [i.e., the wergild] in his behalf, then it is my will that the whole kindred, with the sole exception of the actual slayer, be free of the blood-feud so long as they give him neither food nor protection. . . . And, if any one of the other kindred [that of the slain man] takes vengeance on any man besides the true slayer, he shall incur the enmity of the king . . . and he shall forfeit all that he has."[3] An examination of this passage makes clear: (1) that the family of the killer may refuse to pay the wergild; (2) that, if it refuses to pay the wergild and yet continues to harbor the slayer, each adult male of the family would remain an eligible (although secondary) target of revenge; and (3) that King Edmund, by his special dispensation, was attempting to restrict the blood feud to the two central persons, the slayer and the slain man's next of kin. A rash of uncontrolled vendettas, especially in the tenth century, when the Danes were powerful in England, would have placed Wessex, militarily, in a highly vulnerable position.

Two statements by Jeudwine, for long an authority on medieval tort and crime, may seem to stand in contradiction to the royal edicts that I have just quoted. His first statement reads: "The king or duke did not pretend to interfere with the right of private vengeance."[4] And the second one: "There was a wide exemption of boroughs from king and county jurisdiction."[5] Jeudwine's focus is on Britain at large and not specifically on the important medieval kingdoms of Kent and Wessex. He has attempted a generalization which includes those areas, such as Wales, Scotland, and the northern half of England, where government up to the time of the Plantagenet kings was much less centralized than were the governments, whether Anglo-Saxon or early Norman, of southern England. In such outlying areas, the local vendetta remained free of royal intervention, nor was a blood feud that extended over several generations a danger to a kingdom's stability. Hence, in much of Britain, the "right of local jurisdiction" over the vendetta was a powerful tradition and was able to resist the encroachment of sophisticated restraints, especially those imposed by the King.[6]

Sister Mary Bonaventure Mroz, in her study of divine vengeance, has argued that the wergild was "an inducement to forego the recognized right" of blood revenge.[7] The wergild could be a viable substitute for physical retaliation only upon proof of guilt, nor without this proof could there be a "right of blood revenge." Therefore, when the guilt is known and the wergild is either not offered or, being offered, is refused, the subsequent duel between the next of kin and the offender (customarily a murderer), in view of the already established guilt, is not to be confused with the later and more formalized trial by combat, which presupposed the need of a judgment by God as to guilt or innocence. In *Romeo and Juliet*, for example, the duel between Romeo and Tybalt exemplifies, although much out of its traditional milieu, a climax of the Anglo-Saxon blood feud and not, by definition, a trial by combat, for Tybalt's guilt has been witnessed and therefore established. Under the Anglo-Saxon system, the murderer's guilt, when alleged but not proven, was customarily tested, like that of the suspected arsonist or thief, by one of two ordeals, water (usually boiling) or hot iron.[8] These two ordeals, unlike the Anglo-Saxon duel, were thought to induce a judgment by God. The trial by combat, the purpose of which was to determine guilt or innocence, was to become the third and most publicized ordeal, but not until the Normans, who brought it from the Continent, had become firmly established in England.

A law of William the Conqueror attempts to establish trial by combat, long practiced in Normandy, as a means of determining guilt in England. The principal conditions of William's law, while attesting to the enmity between Saxon and Norman, appear to be just: "If an Englishman challenges any Frenchman to a combat for theft or manslaughter or for any cause in which combat or judgment is customarily had between two men, he shall have full leave to accept the challenge. . . . Furthermore, if a Frenchman challenges an Englishman to combat, for [one of] the same causes, the Englishman shall have leave to defend himself by combat, or by [the ordeal of] iron, if that suits him better."[9] William seems to have allowed for the possible superiority of the Norman, who could well have had experience in trial by combat, and hence permitted the Englishman the choice of an alternate ordeal. William's is the first mention known to me of trial by combat as one of the ordeals in England. The trial by combat, since it was an ordeal, was not, in the legal sense, a means of blood revenge. Its purpose was to determine, through a judgment by God, which of the two combatants was guilty. A well-known confrontation, found in both Holinshed and Shakespeare, illustrates this purpose. Is Thomas Mowbray guilty of treason and murder as charged? Or has Bolingbroke, the accuser, perjured himself and thus committed an equally serious crime? A trial by combat, by its very nature, overruled all precedent testimony and was thought to invoke God's judgment upon the accuser—and not the accused—if the former had falsified.

Norman law, while condoning for a time the Anglo-Saxon blood feud, sought to discipline it by a system of appeals. Sister Mary B. Mroz explains: "An appeal for murder of a father is denied when the appellant has an elder brother living, because 'by such elder brother should this appeal have been brought.'"[10] If the appellant was qualified and the guilt of the murderer uncontested, the appellant could proceed in his vengeance, as in Anglo-Saxon times, unless the court chose to impose and carry out the punishment, as ultimately became the rule. Where guilt was not established, however, trial by combat had become a standard practice by the year 1120. Among the laws of Henry I, the third Norman king, there are several references to trial by combat as an ordeal. Of the crime of homicide, Henry's Law LXXXVII states: "If any one can prove by judgment of hot iron, or battle [trial by combat], or the production of lawful witnesses or oath-helpers . . . that he was assaulted and forced to commit homicide in self-defence," he will have satisfied the court, "and justice . . . shall be done."[11] The purpose of the Norman system of appeals was twofold: (1) it placed, as far as possible, a restraint upon the often undisciplined vendetta by ascertaining that an appellant was technically qualified to proceed against an offender, whether actual or alleged; and (2) it supervised the trial of alleged guilt, whether by hot iron or trial by combat, and thus assured the defendant of God's judgment, and not that of a biased country mob, upon the right or wrong of his actions.

During the reign of the Plantagenet kings, the trial by combat was the most noted of the three ordeals, although each of them came under strong papal opposition. The years 1220 and 1221 provide records of several trials in which the ordeal by battle was used. One case recorded in the "De Banco Roll of 1220" was unusual, for it involved seven potentially guilty men. William Smallwood, "a confessed felon, . . . [had] turned approver" and, in consequence, was obliged to "appeal and vanquish [by combat] a certain number of persons—often five—in order to secure a pardon."[12] He implicated six others, among them Adam, "son of the priest," who was said by William to have been his partner in three homicides and one robbery: "And this he offers to prove by his body, and he takes as his first opponent Adam."[13] Adam "denies the entire charge [offering defense] by his body." The report abruptly closes: "William . . . is vanquished and hanged."[14] The court, as we see, imposed and executed the punishment.

In murder cases, a large number of appellants were widows. When the jury (established by Henry II) failed to reach a decision as to the accused's guilt or innocence, the chosen ordeal was often trial by combat. In a footnote to item LIV of the Magna Carta (1215), R.T. Davies, a modern editor, explains how the combat involving a female was handled: "In criminal cases the duellum had to be fought between the appellant in person and the accused. But in certain cases . . . the appellant might fight by proxy. These privileged cases included women, men over sixty, and those who had lost a limb, etc."[15] A woman's appeal posed an uncommonly potent danger to the defendant. His opponent by proxy was customarily a man of some skill in combat: a knight, for example, "who was [the woman's] relative or had been hired to fight."[16] The fact that "the use of champions was greatly extended as time went on"[17] suggests that some women may have found the Norman system of appeals a ready way to be avenged upon a hostile neighbor. A woman, however, could not be an appellant if she had a husband or a grown son.

The trial by combat, called a wager only when property, and not guilt, was at stake (for example, the duel between King Hamlet and King Fortinbras), was to assume a reputation in the twelfth and the thirteenth century in western Europe, and especially in England, much in excess of its original status as an alternative ordeal often fought, in Norman times, by a pair of rustics. The legends of King Arthur and Charlemagne, with their emphasis on knighthood and trial by combat, were almost in entirety the product of the twelfth century. As an ordeal, over which God was the judge, the trial by combat had been intended by the Norman kings both as an alternate to the existing ordeals, boiling water[18] and hot iron, and as a means of upgrading the questionable legal status of the blood feud, upon which they had imposed a system of appeals and, when a combat was called for, the allegedly immaculate judgment of God. In the meantime, knights had been hired, customarily by the county court, or assizes, to take part in the trial by combat in behalf of unqualified appellants. The knight's principal peacetime responsibility, as recorded by Ramón Lull, was "to mayntene and deffende wymmen / wydowes and orphanes / and men . . . not puyssaunt ne stronge."[19] The trial by combat, although still an ordeal, had become romanticized much beyond its intended function. Quite likely a handsome widow of status did find a champion as readily at the manor as at the courthouse. Such at least is the testimony of the great medieval legends, for all literature, however exaggerated, has a basis of raw and

unembellished actuality. Trial by combat became the medieval experience most honored by the great Renaissance epic writers—Ariosto,
Tasso, and Spenser. Shakespeare made recurrent use of it, as I shall
shortly note, but (if I may exempt *The Two Noble Kinsmen*) restored to
it much of its somber factualness.

Only a few accounts of a knight's actually having taken part in trial
by combat have come down to us, and these are confined mainly to combats which, because of advance notoriety, were fought in London before
the King. Of the three witnessed by Richard II, one survives only in
a skeletal form and another (the Bolingbroke-Mowbray confrontation)
is stopped before a blow is struck. The remaining trial by combat, in
1380, features John Anneslie, knight, who is champion in his wife's behalf, and Thomas Katrington, Esquire, who allegedly sold for his own
profit a French castle belonging to Mistress Anneslie. When the King,
marking the exhaustion of the two men, had stopped the combat, Anneslie showed an unexpected renewal of courage and offered "great
summes of monie" if the King would allow the combat to continue.
Why so impetuous? Why so courageous? He had just noted that "the
esquire through excessive heat, and the weight of his armor, did marvel-
louslie faint."[20] Sir John Anneslie, opportunist that he was, comes out
no worse, and no better, on the moral scale of knighthood than the
average medieval knight. The sometimes unheroic character of trial by
combat, when fought by two flesh-and-blood knights, finds a stress in
the account recorded by the twelfth-century monk Jocelin, who on a
trip to Reading acquired his information firsthand from one who had
been vanquished. Henry of Essex, knight, in the time of Henry II, had
the misfortune to be argued into a trial by combat, near Reading, by
his persistent cousin Robert de Montfort, also knight, on the charge of
"treason to the king." Specifically, he had "cast down," in a battle
against the Welsh, "the standard of the lord king and proclaimed his
death,"[21] not knowing that the King had been rescued. In the trial by
combat, Henry did the best he could against Robert and exchanged perhaps one blow for five. When the combat was over, the Reading monks
at the family's request agreed to bury Henry, who revived on the way
to the burial ground and, abjuring knighthood, became "a professed
monk." Was Henry, like Falstaff at Shrewsbury, feigning death? And
had Robert an ulterior motive, probably self-advancement, in mind?

The trials by combat just summarized are typical of human motives and attitudes undeserving of praise, even though the reader may appreciate the naive candor of Henry in relating his story. Unless we turn to legend, it is difficult to find a commendable example of trial by combat, especially one that, in addition to worthy knights, patently illustrates a judgment by God, upon which the trial was habitually predicated. It is my opinion that in the trial by combat between Walter Scott's Ivanhoe and his enemy Bois-Guilbert, staged in a medieval setting, we have an ideal combat more acceptable than those described by Ariosto or Spenser, partially because Ivanhoe is closer to a real-life study than is the Renaissance epic hero. The intrinsic merit of Scott's trial by combat, although a bit unlikely, is that it expresses the intention of that ordeal with emphasis and remarkable clarity. Wounded and weak, and his horse worn with travel, Ivanhoe insists upon the combat, there being no one else to defend Rebecca from being burned at the stake. The Grand Master, in the meantime, has described trial by combat as an "appeal to the judgment of God." Ivanhoe, upon entering the lists, supports this interpretation: "It is the judgment of God—to his keeping I commend myself." When, on the first encounter, Ivanhoe is unhorsed and Bois-Guilbert, although unhurt, reels momentarily and then tumbles from his saddle and two minutes later is pronounced dead, the ordeal has come (despite an impression of manipulation) to its ideal fulfillment. The closing pronouncement confirms the perfection of Scott's trial by combat: "This is indeed the judgment of God," said the Grand Master, looking upward—"*Fiat voluntas tua!*" The revenge of justice attains its ideal form only when God, and not the human agent, is seen as the destroyer of evil.

To Christine de Pisan, a brilliant and yet pragmatic French woman, who flourished about 1400, a perfectly just trial by combat was impossible (or, at best, accidental), for it was silly to suppose that the much weaker man could defeat the stronger. Her central argument against trial by combat, which she terms "champ de battaile," conforms with the objection of a long line of popes: "For to trowe [trust]," writes Christine, as translated by William Caxton, "that the feble shalle overcome the stronge / & the olde the yonge . . . / by the strengthe of goode right / . . . is but attemptyng of god."[22] She warns against the presumption of "temptyng that god shulde doo myracle."[23] She gives an example that has its twentieth-century parallel in the Sacco-Vanzetti case: two brothers "accused of thefte" were compelled "to deffende hemself in champ of bataylle where . . . they were overcome."[24] Later "was founde the theef that had doon the dede. . . . [T]he two brethrene that . . . were dystroyed were nothing gylty thereof." This injustice, she adds, had happened "dyverse tymes in dyverse landes."[25]

Since Church officials and many prominent lay persons shared Christine's views on trial by combat, she is prompted to explain why it had persisted: "It is a thynge whiche is in usage in the dedes of noble men & in thexercyce of armes & knyghthode," and she adds: "The custome shall not yet faylle in all places."[26] Chivalry, she contends, has its own values, most of them foolish. Sometimes the motive behind the trial by combat is "pride, presumpcion or folye . . . for to gete worshyp [honor]" or to prove that "myn owne lady . . . is fayrer / than hys."[27] Particularly at fault, says Christine, is the "statute" of knighthood which holds that a man shall be "deshonoured . . . without that he soone accepteth the gage of him that casteth hit unto him."[28]

An important view of William Segar, who rose through several heraldic ranks to become, after eighteen years, "Garter king of arms, chief herald of England, in 1603,"[29] is in marked disagreement with those of Christine de Pisan. Of the now defunct trial by combat, he contends: "Every small disequalitie [of rank, weapons, age] ought not make difference chiefly where God is Judge: before whom is no difference of persons."[30] The main value of Segar's two books lies in the facts presented, not in the author's opinions. In the earlier book (1590), ascribed to Segar on the basis of internal evidence, he can produce only seven trials by combat (one of them, in reality, a wager) that had been recorded in the four and a half centuries preceding the Tudor era; the last of these took place in 1441, and in this instance, "after the third blowe given, the King [Henry VI] staied the fight."[31] The earliest combat listed by Segar is noteworthy because it may be the only wager by combat fought on English soil and thought to have been historical and not legendary: "*Edmond*, of the rase [*sic*] of West Saxons, fought in combat with *Canutus* King of *Denmarke*, for the possession of the Crowne of *England*. In which fight, both princes being wearie, by consent departed [divided] the land betwixt them. Anno 1016."[32] Wager by combat, despite being recorded but once, was of more than just momentary interest in England. Edward Coke, in the *Institutes* (ca. 1630), states that the wager by combat was favorably regarded by the

Plantagenet kings as a means "for . . . saving of christian bloud." Edward III, he tells us, challenged the French king to such a combat in 1342, the prize being "the right to the kingdome of France." For the same prize, adds Coke, Richard II challenged "Charles the French king for saving of Christians guiltlesse bloud, and to put an end to that bloudy and lingring war."[33] Both challenges were refused. Coke, together with Segar, favored the reinstatement of the wager by combat. He contended that God had shown approval of the wager, and a tacit repudiation of war itself, "by the single battail between David and Goliath."[34]

That Shakespeare had an exceptional knowledge of both the trial by combat and the wager is repeatedly illustrated in both the English histories and the tragedies. His knowledge of protocol, for example, as shown in the ceremonies preceding the Bolingbroke-Mowbray trial by combat (R2, I.i and I.iii), is remarkably close to Segar's authoritative outline of these complex ceremonial functions.[35] In Shakespeare's plays, it is sometimes difficult to classify a combat as strictly one of trial or one of wager for the reason that the combatants are men of high estate. In the Edgar-Edmund duel, for example, both a judgment upon individual guilt and the lordship over England are at stake. The clear intent of the duel, however, is to prove by combat the alleged crimes of the "manifold traitor" Edmund; in consequence, the purpose is that of trial by combat, to which the idea of wager is, at best, an adjunct. Albany sees in Edmund's defeat and imminent death, when linked with the deaths of the two sisters, "this judgment of the heavens." Elsewhere, Shakespeare, primarily for dramatic effectiveness, turns an important battle into what, without the battle, would be a wager by combat. Prince Hal's victory at Shrewsbury over Hotspur is the single decisive episode of the battle, and had the duel been fought prior to the general engagement, as Hal has requested, no blood but that of Hotspur need to have been spilled. The same interpretation is true of Richmond's victory over Richard III and Macduff's victory over Macbeth; each of these victories both decides and abruptly terminates the battle and, like Hal's, determines the lordship over the kingdom. These two combats, however, have a second purpose: in each a man's guilt is on trial—specifically the guilt of a king, whose guilt (because he is king) cannot be brought before a court of justice by customary methods. The hiatus, in which other action is suspended and the king and his antagonist hold center stage, becomes the moment of God's judgment upon the king.

Of the duels just mentioned, the Bolingbroke-Mowbray confrontation is an excellent illustration of the protocol of trial by combat; the Hal-Hotspur duel, although stripped of ceremony, is a de facto wager by combat, for it both determines the lordship over the kingdom and spares further bloodshed, which might have been in excess of that already past; and the Edgar-Edmund engagement, although the protocol in the interest of economy is held to a minimum, is basically an orthodox trial by combat. Moral guilt, absent in the Hal-Hotspur duel, tends to complicate the classification of the remaining two single combats which terminate a general battle. Although the moral issue is important in the duel between Richard III and Richmond, the fact that a king opposes a would-be king, while no one else in either army has a claim to royal status, tends to emphasize the political issue over the moral one; the latter cannot be fully dismissed, however, because of the huge weight of evil which Richard has brought to Bosworth Field. By contrast, the Macbeth-Macduff confrontation is not between two claimants of the throne, nor is Macduff in the royal line. His clear purpose is to make Macbeth pay in kind for the murder, at Fife, of his wife and children. The moral issue, and not the throne, is the dominant focus. Macduff's position is that of appellant. For these reasons, the duel assumes the status of trial by combat, although the idea of a wager, since Macduff is a lieutenant of Malcolm, the rightful heir, is not totally absent. In his mature years Shakespeare rarely descended to pat, uncomplicated formulas. The Hamlet-Laertes duel highlights the poet's ingenuity. Apparently a fencing match, the duel is in actuality a murder plot. Personal motives, moreover, are abruptly confounded by a higher destiny, which turns them to its advantage; not only must Hamlet die for having been Heaven's scourge, but so must three other persons, including Laertes, each for his particular guilt. The aborted duel becomes, as will later be shown, the occasion of God's final judgment upon the court of Claudius. Indeed, in the light of Shakespeare's textual evidence (which is founded upon medieval doctrine), the outcome of each of the combats cited by me (excepting the wager between Prince Hal and Hotspur) rests upon a divine judgment.

Shakespeare's acceptance of the infallible justice of the trial by combat is most succinctly summed up in *2 Henry VI*. Having observed the combat in which the armorer Horner is slain by the unskilled appellant Peter, King Henry confirms the justice of the outcome: "By his [Horner's] death we do perceive his guilt [treason]." Of Peter, he adds: "And God in justice hath reveal'd to us / The truth and innocence of this poor fellow" (*2 Hen 6*, II.iii.100-101).[36] In short, Peter's accusations have been vindicated by God, for had he lied, God would have given Horner the victory.

The intervention of God was not thought to be confined to the judgment He made when presiding over one of the three medieval ordeals. Both His will and His capacity to judge and to punish were held to be infinite in their applications. Thomas Beard, an Elizabethan recorder of more than five hundred testimonies of God's judgments upon men, sums up a widely held opinion of his times: "And unto him [God] belongeth the direction and principall conduct of humane matters, in such sort, that nothing in the world commeth to pass by chance or adventure, but onely & alwaies by the prescription of his wil."[37] Not only were God's powers over man without limit; once they had been willed, they were not reversible. Edward Hall, the Tudor chronicler, stresses the unbending resolve of God: "God knoweth what he had predestinate & what he had ordained before, against whose ordenaunce prevayleth no counsaill, and against whose will avayleth no stryvinge."[38] Although God's mercy was emphasized by St. Augustine and, in later times, by his many adherents, and again upheld by Richard Hooker, who argued the Anglican theme of "salvation through Christ,"[39] it is God's power of vengeance that most occupied the Elizabethan, schooled (as he was) in the New Testament admonition: "Vengeance is mine: I wil repaye, saith the Lord" (Rom. 12.19). John Donne, in a sermon, elucidates this power which God claimed as only His: "No attribute of God is so often iterated in the Scriptures, no state of God so inculcated, as this of Judge and Judgment."[40] Shortly he adds: "God knows what is evill, he knows when that evill is done, and he knows how to punish . . . that evill."[41] This doctrine, a staple of the Elizabethan mind, finds repeated affirmation in Shakespeare's history plays and tragedies, especially upon violation of the Sixth Commandment: "Thou shalt not kill."

God, as the Old Testament instructs, had multiple means of imposing His punishment upon those who broke His law. The predominant stress on the human agents of God's vengeance is a late medieval refinement. The old instruments of God's wrath were inanimate forces of nature: the Flood of Genesis 7 and the brimstone and fire (probably huge thunderbolts) that "rained on Sodom and Gomorrah," recorded in Genesis 19.24-28. As Sister Mary B. Mroz explains, "God wreaks upon the sinner the just vengeance of His wrath, through ministers of His own choosing. All creation [human, subhuman, and inanimate] stands ready to carry out His judgments."[42] Thus Abimelech (Judg. 9), for "the shedding of his brethrens blood," is killed, as God intended, by a millstone which a woman (standing above him) drops upon his head;[43] Jezebel is trampled to death by horses (2 Kings 9.33); and Hatto, a tenth-century archbishop of Mentz, for having burned down a barn full of beggars, is eaten, at God's commandment, by "rats & mice."[44] The means of vengeance most often employed by God of the Old Testament is the plague, which He used on frequent occasions against Egypt and Israel as well as against the Near East enemies of Israel. Thomas Beard even contends that the French pox of the late Renaissance was a plague, hitherto unheard of, visited by God upon continental Europe and much of Asia "for the greater punishment of the disordinate lust of men."[45] To Beard it was a "terrible and hideous scourge of Gods wrath."[46]

In late medieval and Renaissance times, the instrument of God's punishment, partially because of the three-hundred-year experience of trial by combat, was customarily held to be a man, not something subhuman or inanimate such as a force of nature. The twofold Tudor and Stuart doctrine which, in a seeming contradiction, held that revenge belonged only to God but at the same time insisted, as argued by Coke and other statesmen, that it likewise belonged to the magistrate, meant simply that the magistrate in executing the law, which was based on Old Testament instruction, was acting as God's agent; "For revenge," Coke put it, "belongeth to the magistrate, who is Gods lieutenant."[47] In cases involving murder, treason, or theft, the magistrate was an instrument of God year in, year out, as opposed to the appellant and his one day of service in the trial by combat. Both the magistrate and the medieval appellant, if his accusations were honest and not proven to be falsely sworn, were thought to be ministers of God, good men in the service of His will. Opposite in character to the minister, and sometimes even more useful to God, was the scourge.

The earliest examples of the scourge of the Old Testament God, as I have indicated, were floods, brimstone, and plagues, for each of these inanimates have naturally destructive characteristics. In medieval times, John of Salisbury (ca. 1150) classified tempests, whirlwinds, earthquakes, and destructive fires, both collectively and individually, as "the divine scourge."[48] No less terrifying than inanimate forces was the man appointed by God to be His scourge against the wicked. Such a scourge must either be born evil or made evil by God or he will be unfit for the task of human destruction; and, being evil, he too must be destroyed, as were, for example, the biblical tyrant Zimri, who "was the Lords rod to punish the house of Baasha,"[49] and the most renowned scourge of history (prior perhaps to the late 1930s), Attila the Hun.[50] Remarking on tyrants, John of Salisbury concludes: "For there is prepared a great fire wherewith to consume the scourge after the Father has employed it for the correction of his children."[51] Having read approximately sixty-five Elizabethan and Jacobean tragedies, I have not found a single avenger in them, even of those born to be good men, who does not experience, after his task is fulfilled, the avenging stroke of God.[52] Although the severe Tudor laws against private blood revenge were a factor in the stage avenger's untimely death, the obsession with his mission of even the good avenger, such as Hieronimo or Hamlet, tends to transform him, as Hamlet is brought to realize (*Ham*, III.iv.173-75), from a minister into a scourge; as such, he too must be destroyed.

In Western history, including that of the Old Testament, tyrants who have served God as His scourge are virtually beyond count. By contrast, noted ministers of God's justice are extremely few, mainly because the minister, usually a man of the law, has rarely attracted the attention bestowed upon the lawless. "Public magistrates," writes the medievalist Mroz, "are recognized as the foremost human agents of divine vengeance."[53] Such magistrates in medieval and Renaissance England included the bailiff, the local or itinerant judge, even the hangman—all of them unnoted persons. A man of God, a self-denying man intent upon a tyrant's destruction, might also qualify as God's minister. Indeed, as John of Salisbury suggests, he might be chosen by God for the purpose of getting rid of the tyrant and reestablishing the political stability of the state: "God . . . appointed as His instrument the martyr Mercurius, who, at the command of the Blessed Virgin, pierced the tyrant [Julian the Apostate] . . . with a lance, and compelled the impious wretch as he was dying to confess that the Galilean, namely Christ, . . . was victor and had triumphed over him."[54] The kings of late medieval England, as they appear both in the Tudor chronicles and in Shakespeare's plays, supply two clear-cut examples, one of the scourge and the other of the minister: Richard III and Henry of Richmond, respectively. Of the persons murdered by Richard, all were not wicked, but it can be—and, indeed, has been—argued in support of the Tudor myth that his murder of the two Yorkist children, Edward V and his brother, Richard, was essential to God's plan to put the Tudor monarchs upon the English throne. In Henry of Richmond's slaying of King Richard, whether directly or by proxy (for, on this point, Shakespeare and the chroniclers are not in agreement), and in his political marriage to Elizabeth of York, the Tudor chroniclers and Shakespeare are of one voice: Richmond is the minister of God. By means of Henry's efforts, "God . . . had delivered them [the English] from miserable captivitie & restored them to libertie and fredome."[55] In particular, Henry had delivered England from the scourge Richard.

Among the instruments through which God was thought by the Elizabethans to exact punishment upon the wrongdoer was the human conscience, in which had been implanted, at an early age, His commandments. Timothy Bright, a well-known Elizabethan authority on mental abnormality, attests to this belief: "A molestation riseth . . . from conscience, condemning the guiltie soule of those engraven laws of nature [God's commandments], which no man is voide of."[56] He elsewhere tells us that a sense of painful guilt comes not from a "breach of humane laws . . . but of the Law divine & the censure [is] executed with the hand of God."[57] La Primaudaye, in *The French Academie*, published in London in 1618, states of the crime that might have gone unpunished: "There is no sinne that can avoide punishment, and that findeth not a Judge even in him that committed it, to take vengeance thereof by meanes of the affections which God placed in man to that ende."[58] In "The complaynt of Henrye duke of Buckingham," first printed in the 1563 edition of *The Mirror for Magistrates*, the Duke recalls the pangs of conscience experienced by both Richard III and himself before, and after, the murder of the two young princes:

So gnawes the griefe of conscyence evermore
And in the hart it is so diepe ygrave,
That they [offenders] may neyther slepe nor rest therfore,
Ne thynke one thought but on the dread they have.

[ll. 225-28][59]

Having studied the power of conscience as an instrument of divine
vengeance, in particular as this power was known to Shakespeare and
his contemporaries, Sister Mary B. Mroz concludes: "Human nature
. . . may, by God's ordination, wreak its own vengeance," especially by
means of an "accusing conscience."[60] In Shakespeare's plays, the conscience as an instrument of God's vengeance—especially if we hold in
mind that it is constructed mainly of the commandments laid down by
God—is second in importance only to the working of His vengeance
through a human agent. Richard III, Cardinal Beaufort, and in particular Lady Macbeth are destroyed by conscience. Macbeth, in contrast
to the Lady, escapes the ultimate perils of conscience only by resorting
to, and focusing his mind upon, a determined course of action, a mode
of escape attempted by Richard III up to his last and most atrocious
murder and its recoil upon him.

The Tudor monarchs looked upon rebellion as the most heinous of
crimes and vigorously condemned it. More objective minds, without
disagreeing with the Tudors, saw rebellion as God's most effective
means of punishing a wicked prince and sometimes his wicked subjects.
In an interpretation of a passage from Raphael Holinshed's Chronicles,
Mary B. Mroz has stated: "The Peasants' Revolt [against Richard II in
1381] is permitted by God in divine retribution for evil doings, 'speciallie the sinnes of the whole nation.'"[61] A later passage by Holinshed
suggests that the rebellion of 1399, led by Henry Bolingbroke, was
thought to have been God's means of punishing Richard II and his
degenerate associates, but in particular the King: "Furthermore, there
reigned abundantlie the filthie sinne of leacherie and fornification, with
abhominable adulterie, speciallie in the king, but most chieflie in the pre-
lacie. . . . Against [Richard] . . . the wrath of God was so whetted and
tooke so sharp an edge, that the same did shred him off from the sceptre
of his kingdome."[62] Although God was alleged to use rebellion as a
means of punishment—in this instance, the dethronement of Richard
II—He appears not to have condoned it any more than He approved of

the tyrant whom He used as a scourge and then destroyed. The history of the ill fate of rebels is an ancient one. Just as the tyrant of the Old Testament—of whom Saul and Joash, King of Judah,[63] are illustrative—is ultimately destroyed by God, so are those destroyed who rebel against their king. When Abimelech, by force of blood, had ruled over Israel for three years, "God sent an evil spirit betwene Abimelech and the men of Shechem," who as fellow Israelites had helped him to usurp the throne. The Shechemites, now in revolt against him, "reviled Abimelech," who in battle two days later "slewe them, . . . toke the citie, . . . and sowed salt in it" (Judg. 9.1-6; 22-45). Abimelech, not long after, is killed by the falling millstone at Thebez. "Thus God [requited] the wickednes of Abimelech. . . . Also the wickednes of the men of Shechem [who had twice rebelled against the throne] did God bring upon their heades" (Judg. 9.56-59). This biblical example of the fate of rebels finds a late medieval parallel in the civil wars between Henry IV and his former allies, the Percy family, who had put him on the throne and then, like the Shechemites, rebelled against him. All principal leaders of the Percy rebellions are killed in warfare against King Henry or are captured and then executed. Of Henry IV, on the eve of the battle of Shrewsbury (1403), Edward Hall writes: "He doubted not but God would bothe aide and assiste hym, against untrue persones and false forsworne traytours."[64] The King's confidence, of course, was adequately rewarded. A page later, Hall describes the "wretched" death of Owen Glendower, a principal Percy ally, when besieged in Wales by the royal army: "[Glendower] received a finall reward mete and prepared by Goddes providence for suche a rebell and sedicious seducer."[65]

In light of the fact that only four years earlier Henry Bolingbroke had personally led a rebellion against the English throne, and had done so successfully, we may be surprised that he is depicted by Hall as overridingly confident that rebels are necessarily despised by God as "untrue . . . and false traytours." At that earlier time, however, he had entertained—as shown by both the chroniclers and Shakespeare—no doubt about the wrongness of rebellion in itself. His uncle York, as treated by Shakespeare, admonishes him upon the bold manner of his return from exile to England: "Even in condition of the worst degree, / In gross rebellion and detested treason" (*R2*, II.iii.108-109), nor does Bolingbroke, at this early time, deny the wrongness of dethroning an ordained king. His cause as a rebel—unlike the later cause of the

Percies—had been hallowed by a powerful offsetting factor. Bolingbroke's intentions against Richard II had chanced, at that particular moment in history, to be instrumental to those of God: Richard must be punished for enormous crimes (rapacious taxation and murder) against both his countrymen and the divine law. Hence, the instrumentality of Bolingbroke's cause to God's plan may be thought to have assumed, almost imperceptibly, a strong providential priority while God delayed judgment upon its manifest wrongness, for rebellion was thought, in medieval and Tudor times, to encompass "all [the] sinnes against GOD and man."[66] The present interpretation, in that it sees rebellion—however odious—as the sanctified instrument of a kingdom's political and moral rehabilitation, has the advantage, moreover, of suggesting why God has compromised Bolingbroke's punishment by deferring the greater part of it to his descendants. The many rebellions against him, once he is king, are to be conceived—fittingly, I think—as God's method of chastising Bolingbroke, in his lifetime, with a few lashes of his own brand of civil disobedience. They are not intended to overthrow him. The instrument of rebellion—whether used by God to destroy a king or merely to punish him—is not unlike the scourge of conscience; much as God rebukes a man through a violated conscience, He likewise can, and will, rebuke a king through the outraged and rebellious minds of that king's subjects. For, in the collective conscience, as in the individual conscience, the punitive stimulus is prompted by the presence of the divine law.

The rebel who becomes king ceases to bear the epithet of "rebel," at least officially. Other than Bolingbroke, the majority of noble-born rebels in Shakespeare's history plays—Worcester, Vernon, Oxford, Salisbury, Kent, the younger Mowbray, Archbishop Scroop, the elder Hastings, Northumberland, Cambridge, Lord Scroop of Masham, and Thomas Grey—are summarily executed, knowing their penalty is irrevocable. Henry V, once Cambridge and his colleagues are led to execution, attests to the watchful Providence that sustains a king against rebellion: he ascribes the discovery of their defection to "God," Who "graciously hath brought to light / This dangerous treason" (*Hen 5*, II.ii.185-86).

On occasion, in the English history plays, a kinsman questions the justice of a brother's or father's punishment for treason and seeks to avenge it. Archbishop Scroop, it is said, "bears hard / His brother's death at Bristow, the Lord Scroop [of Wiltshire]" (*1 Hen 4*, I.iii. 270-71) and a principal motive of young Thomas Mowbray, in *2 Henry IV*, is to avenge his father upon Bolingbroke, now king. The crime of political homicide, however, has a much more compelling claim, as treated by Shakespeare, than does death for treason upon a kinsman's right of vengeance, in particular since the murder has, unlike punishment for treason, not an iota of sanction from the law. Three conditions are, in all instances, whether in the history plays or in the tragedies, fundamental to this right of vengeance, for Shakespeare was expertly aware of the heroic revenge tradition which, present in most of his sources, corresponded closely to the formalized trial by combat and differed from that combat only in the total absence of legal recognition and procedures: (1) the victim must have been unjustly killed; (2) the process of constitutional law must be inadequate or unavailable; and (3) the avenger, acting as agent of God, must be next of kin or, at the very least, the nearest of kin capable of the execution of vengeance.

The tradition that I have just outlined is an ancient one. Most interesting are the variations in its formula, for they are reflections of the values of each civilization. The principal example set by the Old Testament God lies not in the instruments He used, since He had infinite alternatives, but in the unflagging precedent He set against the act of murder lest His Sixth Commandment go unheeded. Revenge for the murder of a king, even a wicked one, was inevitable and usually swift: "Amen [Amon], the sonne of Manasseh, was slaine by his owne servants, but the Lord stirred up the people of the land to revenge his death, & to kill all them that had conspired against their king."[67] As vulnerable to God's wrath as the regicide was the king, "to whom," as Thomas Beard has said, "the sword of justice is committed by God to represse wrongs and chastise vices," should he murder, and not protect, those under his command.[68] Of the rulers of Israel, Abimelech, for having killed all but one of his brothers (Judg. 9.5), and Saul, for having "slaine the Lords Priests" (1 Sam. 22.21), are brought by God to violent and untimely deaths. The history of Judah is replete with kings who murdered those whom they should have protected. Among others Jehoram and Joash incur the wrath of God and are destroyed. Of Jehoram, who as king put to death his brothers and other princes of Judah, it is written: "The Lord smote him in his bowels with an incurable disease. . . . his guttes fell out [and] he dyed" (2 Chron. 21.4,

18-19). Two generations later, the high priest Zechariah, when slain by Joash, cries out: "The Lord loke upon it, & [avenge] it!"—a supplication fulfilled by the servants of Joash (2 Chron. 24.22-25). In contrast to the Old Testament, the ancient Greek legends provide strong testimony that, in Homeric times and later, the next of kin—and not ignoble human instruments—was the chosen agent of God. Pyrrhus, as a consequence of a prophecy made by the seer Helenus, protégé of Apollo,[69] is persuaded to sail from Scyros to Troy for the double purpose of destroying the city and avenging his slain father, Achilles. Once the city is razed, he completes, through the sacrifice of the Trojan Polyxena, the appeasement of his father's ghost.[70] In a Greek legend I need not summarize, Orestes at Apollo's command avenges the clandestine murder of Agamemnon, his king and father. The early medieval Nordic legends, which are partially historical, include the tale of Amleth, who avenges his father Horwendil,[71] and the later Nordic account of the vengeance taken upon Helle,[72] King of Britain, by the Danish princes Siward and Biorn in behalf of their murdered father.[73] These legends stress the avenger's part without a mention of God and are, therefore, in their treatment of the theme of vengeance, basically similar to the Anglo-Saxon vendetta.

The common denominator of these three traditions—biblical, Greek, and Nordic—is that the victim, a man (or men) of high status, has been unjustly killed. The Hebraic mind emphasizes the role of God as the avenger; the ancient Greek tradition, the closest to the late medieval practice of vengeance in England, observes a balance between the part of God and the part of His agent, who is customarily the next of kin; and the Nordic semihistorical legend shows its pagan, sometimes nihilistic world view by stressing vengeance as the responsibility of man alone and not of God. The heir to these ancient traditions is the Hamlet portrayed by Shakespeare. A better example, however, of the late medieval avenger, because less cosmopolitan than Hamlet, is Henry Bolingbroke, whether Shakespeare's or Holinshed's: he answers perfectly, in his resolve to avenge the unlawful murder of his uncle Thomas, Duke of Gloucester, to the three conditions that I have established, but only because the aging John of Gaunt has rejected the responsibility of next of kin to Thomas.

In Shakespeare's two historical tetralogies—in particular in *Richard II*, in which he appears to have established, with immaculate care, the principal themes of his eight-part historical epic—no idea of high significance is so apparent as is the intervention of God in human affairs. This theme is first given stress in the second scene of *Richard II*. John of Gaunt, without an awareness of God's widely accredited power of intervention, could not have advised his sister-in-law, the Duchess of Gloucester, in respect to the clandestine murder of her husband, in words such as these:

> Put we our quarrel to the will of heaven;
> Who, when they see the hours ripe on earth,
> Will rain hot vengeance on offenders' heads.
>
> [*R2*, I.ii.6-8]

He specifies that "God's substitute [the King] . . . / Hath caus'd his death" and then concludes: "God's is the quarrel . . . / Let heaven revenge." Four acts later, when King Richard has been deposed and is imprisoned at Pomfret, and Bolingbroke is king, the Duke of York accepts the new political order—in terms that authenticate Gaunt's philosophy—as the product of God's intervention: "Heaven hath a hand in these events, / To whose high will we bound our calm contents" (*R2*, V.ii.37-38). The fulfillment of God's retribution upon Richard, as foreseen by Gaunt and confirmed by York as Heaven's "high will," helps to substantiate the validity of the play's two long-range prophecies (King Richard's and Carlisle's), as quoted in chapter 1, which state, collectively, that Bolingbroke's crimes against King Richard must, in their turn, be paid for, but not until "God omnipotent," having withheld for a half century His second important act of vengeance, shall confound the kingdom in a prolonged civil strife ("the woefullest division . . . / That ever fell") and strike down Englishmen "yet unborn and unbegot." Shakespeare has shown Gaunt's prediction of God's vengeance upon King Richard and its fulfillment within the scope of a single play and has planted in that play the two substantial and long-range prophecies that project the fulfillment of their predictions to a time within the second half of the eight-part historical epic. By thus substantiating prediction and fulfillment in the immediate plot, he has established a credible link between Bolingbroke's crimes in *Richard II* and God's long-predicted punishment of those crimes in *2-3 Henry VI*. The credibility of this long-deferred payment of guilt finds additional support in Gaunt's assertion that the forces of divine retribution are ac-

tivated only when "the hours [are] ripe on earth." Plutarch's doctrine
of "the delay of the Deity," for which he provides several good reasons,
is not as convincing as is the simple Old Testament statement by God
that, when He is so minded, He "visits the iniquitie of the fathers upon
the children" even as late as the fourth generation (Exod. 20.5). For this
delay, the biblically oriented Elizabethan asked of Him no pertinent
motive.

Nor is God's deferred vengeance against the house of Lancaster untouched upon in the plays immediately preceding *1-3 Henry VI*. Indications of His vengeance, as well as the fear of it, are recurrent in both
Henry IV plays. Shrewd pragmatist though he is, Henry IV senses, on
occasion, the imminence of an outer force; he admits, for example, an
awareness of the "secret doom" prepared for him by God and thinks
that Hal's reprobate conduct may be "the rod of heaven" by which he,
as king, is chastised because of his former "mistreadings" (*1 Hen 4*,
III.ii.4-11). A few critics have suggested—and I agree—that the dis-
orienting effect of repeated rebellions upon King Henry and, somewhat
later, his fatal and debilitating illness, which Shakespeare terms "apo-
plexy," are signs of God's vengeance upon him. That he escapes the full
force of vengeance, divinely worked, may be explained, in part, by a
theory advanced by Plutarch: God examines each soul, he contends, to
find if "it may turn to repentance, and He gives time for amendment
to those whose vices are not ineradicable and incurable."[74] That Henry
is repentant is evident in his speech which concludes *Richard II*, in two
or three observations made by him in his own two plays, and in particular in the next-to-last words that he speaks to Prince Hal: "How I
came by the crown, O God, forgive" (*2 Hen 4*, IV.v.219). Long aware
of the imminence of God's judgment upon him, he is, as testified, in
the next and closing line—the urgent supplication that God "grant . . .
true peace" to Hal—equally aware that the main thrust of God's judgment has not, as yet, been fulfilled. This discomforting knowledge is his
final torment.

My interpretations of Shakespeare's history plays and certain of his
tragedies will be structured upon a three-part formula: (1) the crime of
political homicide when committed by a man of such status that he cannot be brought to justice by means of constitutional law, but only by
divine judgment; (2) the genesis or political repercussions of the crime,
or both, for the former may manifest important extenuating circum-

stances and the latter, in all but one play, produces the agent, or agents, of the punishment; and (3) God as the prime mover of the punishment upon the murderer and, on two occasions, upon his offending associates as well. I have included all essentials; basically, however, the formula is the crime, its genesis or political repercussions and, most important, the exercise of divine judgment.

In the English histories, which precede in time the tragedies and will be discussed first, the murder of one or more men of high status is the usual catalyst that excites the basic resources of the play into action. Without the murder there would be no significant story and probably neither a thesis nor a plot. In addition, an analysis of the impact of the unjustly slain man or men upon the events of the play tends to create (and this pertains to the tragedies as well) a number of new interpretations, which I believe to be valid. Nor is the theme of Nobilitas, briefly discussed in chapter 1, an isolated phenomenon, especially when the two historical tetralogies are viewed as an eight-part epic of the Plantagenet family (which divides into Lancaster and York); for the history of England from 1398 to 1485, as it is known to us today, is inseparable from a history of that family. Whenever self-interest and self-indulgence are allowed to corrode Nobilitas, the family and, with it, the nation fall upon difficult times: murder within the family is committed with schismatic consequences that are beyond the cure of political craft. Under Henry V, the qualities denoted by the term *Nobilitas*, in particular valor and selflessness, are restored to a level approaching that of Edward III's reign; but the restoration, especially in terms of an ordered hierarchy, is to prove more apparent than real: the March and Yorkist faction, providing substance (however unwittingly) to the providential prophecies made in *Richard II*, finds itself no longer either enforced or contented to concede the Lancasters' right to the throne. Time and, apparently, the manifold resources of God are on the Yorkist side, at least until the moment when Richard III, by usurping the throne of Edward V, is permitted to jar the divine pendulum.

THREE

Thomas of Gloucester:
The Sword of Retribution

To the reader of Shakespeare's *Richard II*, the repeated mention of "Gloucester" or "Woodstock" is apt to evoke nothing more than the name of a nobleman who has been murdered. In his 1946 edition of the old play *Woodstock* (ca. 1591), A.P. Rossiter is mindful of the difficulties to which a reader or spectator of *Richard II* is subjected if he has no prior knowledge of the enmity between Thomas Woodstock, Duke of Gloucester, and his nephew King Richard: "The whole matter of the death of Gloster, with the king's complicity and Mowbray's part, must have equally been involved in difficulty, from which readers of Shakespeare depend [as they still do today] on editorial notes from history-books to relieve them."[1] F.S. Boas was one of the earliest critics to have stressed this difficulty: in speaking of *Richard II*, he wondered "how its hearers or readers could be . . . much moved by its opening scenes, of which the recent murder of Gloucester is the pivot, when the Duke himself was nothing more to them than a name."[2] At the same time, he offered a viable solution to the problem as it related to the Elizabethan audience: "The conclusion . . . that Shakespeare knew the anonymous piece [*Woodstock*] . . . and could count on the audience's familiarity with it, would go far to explain some puzzling features in his own work."[3] Confronted by the historical fact that, without the murder of Gloucester, the events of King Richard's last years could not have been put into momentum, Shakespeare almost certainly depended on the familiarity of his audience with the Duke of Gloucester and, especially, the circumstances that allegedly surrounded his death. For this purpose a knowledge of Holinshed's *Chronicles* would have provided a more accurate set of facts than does *Woodstock*, which in contrast stands closer to the spirit of Gloucester as depicted later by Shakespeare.

That Shakespeare's audience did have a knowledge of the exceptionally stageable *Woodstock* has been established within the past fifty years through the researches of Wolfgang Keller, Paul Reyher, J.D. Wilson, and ultimately Rossiter.[4] Their findings, and particularly those of Rossiter, have shown not only that Shakespeare, in writing *Richard II*, depended on his own assurance of the audience's knowledge of *Woodstock* and, in consequence, made a number of allusions to the materials of that play without sensing a need to elaborate upon them but also that he made an occasional use of the materials himself in the form of verbal borrowings[5] and, equally much, in the favorable traits of character that he ascribed to Gloucester. Nor need we be misled by Shakespeare's unhistorically affable image of Gloucester as long as we know that it is the Gloucester of *Woodstock*—and not the pigheaded and contentious duke of Holinshed's *Chronicles*—to whom the characters of *Richard II* hark back.

A main point is that a pragmatic knowledge of the deeply rooted enmity between King Richard and the Duke of Gloucester brings to the opening scenes of Shakespeare's play a much more adequate reading than does the glamorized background offered by the old play *Woodstock*; therefore, I propose to look at Holinshed's *Chronicles* first. In the year 1388, when Gloucester controlled the infamous Parliament that sentenced to death Richard's principal advisers, including Robert Tresilian, the Lord Chief Justice, he is said to have been "a sore and a right severe man, might not by any meanes be removed from his opinion and purpose, if he once resolved upon any matter."[6] From this relatively early time, when Richard was only twenty-one years of age, until 1397, the pigheaded Gloucester was to remain the King's most tenacious political enemy. An incident over the city of Brest, which Richard had returned to the Duke of Brittany in 1397, gave rise to the clash of wills that was to be fatal to Gloucester and, ultimately, to Richard himself: "In this twentith yeare of his reigne king Richard . . . delivered [Brest] unto the duke of Britaine, by reason whereof no small sparke of displeasure arose betwixt the king and the duke of Glocester," who stubbornly opposed the yielding of "'anie strong hold gotten with great adventure by the manhood . . . of your noble progenitours.'"[7] Shortly thereafter, the Duke of Gloucester with the assistance of "the earles of Derbie, Arundell, Marshall, and Warwike" conspired "to take king Richard . . . and commit [him] to prison." The Earl Marshal, better known to us as Thomas Mowbray and soon to be appointed, by Richard's favor, the Duke of Norfolk, "discovered all their counsell to the king."[8]

What followed is today comparatively well known. Gloucester was kidnapped by the King's associates and was smuggled across the seas to Calais, "whereupon the king sent unto Thomas Mowbraie, earle marshall . . . to make the duke secretlie awaie."[9] That Mowbray "prolonged time" is to his credit; but the King's threat against his life, if he did not carry out the "commandement," had the direct effect of procuring Gloucester's death.

Of equal importance to a judgment of Gloucester's posthumous impact upon the play *Richard II* is his historic relation to the common people, particularly those of London. Obstinate as he was, he had sought and won the favor of the Londoners, who were, at this point in history, in severe need of a champion against a king who, among other extravagances, entertained ten thousand favorites a day at the royal palace and sustained the cost at the people's expense.[10] Holinshed reports that the King, in the year 1397, complained of Gloucester's "procuring trouble at home, by stirring the people to rebellion."[11] A second statement by Holinshed confirms the people's sense of debt to Gloucester: "The Londoners were right sorie for the death of the duke of Glocester, who had ever sought their favour . . . [and] would have beene contented to have joined with the dukes [Lancaster and York] in seeking revenge of so noble a mans death."[12]

When Gaunt, in *Richard II*, speaks of his deceased brother as "my brother Gloucester, plain well-meaning soul" (II.i.128), the epithet finds no support in Holinshed's cantankerous portrait; it derives, instead, from the image of Gloucester as delineated in the play *Woodstock*. Because he wears a coat of uncut frieze and has an attitude of conciliation and candor, even of compassion, the Gloucester of the old play is dubbed "Plain Thomas," although he is more widely known by the surname Woodstock, derived from his place of birth. The Woodstock of the play bluntly draws the contrast between himself and the King's capering favorites: "In these plain hose I'll do the realm more good / Than those that pill the poor, to jet in gold" (*Wood*, II.ii.35-36).[13] Meanwhile, King Richard is fearful of the dynamic love in which Woodstock is held:

> . . . for whilst he keeps the country
> There is no meddling, he's so well beloved
> As all the realm will rise in arms with him.
>
> [IV.i.80-82]

Placed at a pole opposite to Robert Tresilian,[14] whom Rossiter has dubbed the Lord Chief Injustice, Woodstock stands for justice and not rebellion as an instrument of the people's politics. Hence it is an irony of the old play that, through rebellion, his murder by King Richard is avenged. The rebellion, led by the Dukes of Lancaster and York, carries out the *wish* of the people as it had been expressed by Holinshed: "The Londoners" were "contented to have joined with the dukes in seeking revenge of noble [Gloucester's] death." There was historically, of course, no such rebellion. As Holinshed, in contrast to the fiction of *Woodstock*, has made clear, an opportunity for rebellion, fully fledged, had been prepared for the historical Henry Bolingbroke; for the people, aroused by Gloucester, had but the need of a second vigorous leader.

An uncommonly elucidating statement is found in Holinshed concerning an event that took place shortly after the news of Gloucester's death, in August 1397, had reached London: "Here the dukes [Lancaster and York] and other fell in counsell, and manie things were proponed. Some would that they shuld by force revenge the duke of Glocesters death, other thought it meet that the earles Marshall [Thomas Mowbray] and Huntington, . . . as cheefe authours of all the mischeefe should be pursued and punished."[15] The present-day reader may be relatively certain that Bolingbroke, at that time Earl of Derby and soon to be Duke of Hereford, was among the "other[s]" who attended this meeting. His father was the Duke of Lancaster, who was present; moreover, Bolingbroke had, for some twelve years, been notoriously prominent in English politics. That we soon find him in pursuit of Thomas Mowbray attests to the likelihood that he was one of those who advocated that the "cheefe authours of all the mischeefe should be pursued and punished." At the Shrewsbury Parliament, January 1398, "Henrie duke of Hereford accused Thomas Mowbraie duke of Norfolke of certaine words which he [uttered] in talke hadst betwixt them, as they rode togither latelie . . . betwixt London and Brainford, sounding highlie to the kings dishonor."[16] In light of the specific charges reported elsewhere by Holinshed and later employed by Shakespeare in the opening scene of *Richard II*, a good guess can be made as to Bolingbroke's major accusation: Mowbray had a responsible part, despite his implications that the blame is King Richard's, in the murder of Gloucester. Had not Mowbray been declared one of the "cheefe authours of the mischeefe" and therefore to be rightly "pursued and punished"? Bolingbroke, it is evident, had found an opportunity to put the process of revenge into momentum. The game of dominoes would begin with Mowbray.

Almost assuredly the Elizabethan audience was aware of much of the historical background which I have summarized. To them the opening scene of *Richard II* was fraught with broader implications than the modern reader is aware of: for those who had seen *Woodstock* at the theater there was the precedent, however wrong historically, that the dukes of England had avenged, in a bloody civil war, the murder of Gloucester; and for those who knew something of Holinshed, the knowledge that revenge had been planned would illuminate, with specific consistency, the opening scenes of *Richard II* and, in particular, the role that Bolingbroke is about to enact in Shakespeare's play. In short, Shakespeare's audience would hold the play to be revenge oriented from its outset. To the Elizabethans, in contrast to modern views of the play, Bolingbroke's manifest function was that of the avenging agent of God, for he was close kin to Gloucester, and Gloucester's murder, being a flagrant sin against God, could not with honor go unavenged.

Shortly after the first scene, which is set at Windsor Castle, has opened, Bolingbroke makes his three charges of treason against Mowbray and, lest he forfeit the attention of King Richard, withholds for last the most damaging accusation:

> Further I say, and further will maintain
> . . . .
> That he did plot the Duke of Gloucester's death,
> Suggest his soon-believing adversaries,
> And consequently, like a traitor coward,
> Sluic'd out his innocent soul through streams of blood.
>
> [*R2*, I.i.98-103]

The phrase "suggest his soon-believing adversaries" is a thrust, although oblique, at Richard, who had been Gloucester's principal political enemy. At the same time, it suggests Mowbray's role in the contriving of the duke's death to have been that of a comparatively oily politician: the informer who, by means of "suggesting," hoped to evade the burden of direct responsibility. Nor will Bolingbroke relent even when confronted by his father, Gaunt:

Throw down, my son, the Duke of Norfolk's gage.
         . . . When, Harry, when?
Obedience bids I should not bid again.

                                              [I.i.161-63]

Bolingbroke is not to be moved from his resolve by his father or the
king. The trial by combat, reluctantly ordered by Richard, is exactly
what Bolingbroke desires. According to the testimony of the Earl of
Westmoreland in *2 Henry IV*, there is no way that Mowbray could have
escaped unpunished from the lists at Coventry; he informs Mowbray's
son:

> The Earl of Hereford was accounted then
> In England the most valiant gentleman.
> . . . .
> But if your father had been victor there,
> He ne'er had borne it out of Coventry;
> For all the country, in a general voice,
> Cried hate upon him.
>
>   [*2 Hen. 4*, IV.i.131-32; 134-37]

The confidence of victory belongs to Bolingbroke, and should he fail,
Mowbray is all but assured of a public lynching.

More significant than Bolingbroke's confidence of destroying Mowbray, and thus achieving the first step of his revenge, is the oath which
he makes in behalf of his murdered uncle and with which he culminates
his charges against Mowbray:

> [Gloucester's] blood, like sacrificing Abel's, cries
> Even from the tongueless caverns of the earth,
> To me for justice and rough chastisement;
> And, by the glorious worth of my descent,
> This arm shall do it, or this life be spent.
>
>   [*R2*, I.i.104-108]

No modern critic, to my knowledge, has looked upon *Richard II* as a
play of revenge. Bolingbroke, beyond the initial statement of vengeance,
supplemented by a later one, never commits himself as to what his fun-

damental motives are. His resolve of vengeance, although manifest in the oath that I have quoted, has customarily gone unnoted by critics. But is it of such small account? In each of Shakespeare's most immediate sources, *Woodstock* and Holinshed's *Chronicles*, Gloucester's death was actually avenged, or else, as I have already noted, the vengeance was planned. Near the end of his account of Richard II's reign, Holinshed looks back and states: "The duke of Glocester, cheefe instrument of this mischeefe [the disharmony within the realm], to what end he came ye have heard. And although his nephue the duke of Hereford tooke upon him to revenge his death, yet wanted he moderation and loialtie in his dooings, for the which both he himselfe and his lineall race [especially Duke Humphrey and Henry VI] were scourged afterwards, as a due punishment unto rebellious subiects."[17] What Holinshed has stated in this passage, namely, that Bolingbroke "tooke upon him to revenge [Gloucester's] death," is the interpretation of history which Shakespeare has sought to recapture in his play; nor, in showing this revenge, does Shakespeare exaggerate an iota the importance of Gloucester's place in history. For it is Gloucester's murder, of which King Richard's is an effect, that marks the commencement of the irremediable schism that is to make inevitable the breakup of the Plantagenet dynasty and thus alter, with the accession of the Tudors, the shape of England's institutions. Although Richard, in the theater, monopolizes center stage (in part, as willed by the director), Bolingbroke—a Plantagenet but not of the hallowed line of Plantagenet kings—becomes, from the moment of his oath of vengeance, the dominant mover of events in the play. The oath of vengeance, moreover, is spoken with a candor and intent not to be found in the politically compromised statements that follow Bolingbroke's return from exile. In short, he means what he has said: he must avenge the crime against his uncle. This resolve, as well as a related and secondary one, controls the action, as opposed to the considerable inaction, of Shakespeare's *Richard II*.

Not only did the Elizabethan audience possess a knowledge of Gloucester that helped to justify the strenuous reaction of Bolingbroke to his uncle's death; there was, moreover, a contemporary parallel that, without fully justifying revenge, made the Elizabethan theatergoer more aware than we are today that the spirit of Gloucester demanded it. Lily B. Campbell has stated the circumstance quite well: "In the minds of many Elizabethans the blood of Mary Stuart cried from the ground against Elizabeth as did that of Thomas of Woodstock against Richard II."[18] Much of the religious fervor of those who would avenge Mary attaches to the oath made by Bolingbroke; he provides his resolve to avenge his dead uncle with a strong biblical sanction: "[His] blood, like sacrificing Abel's, cries . . . for justice and rough chastisement." The voice of the martyr, and in death, Gloucester has become a martyr, demands to be heard. Those unjustly deprived of life, moreover, as my second chapter has shown, were thought to be the special wards of God, and in consequence, they were to be avenged by Him. Sister Mary Bonaventure Mroz, in her careful study of divine vengeance in medieval and Renaissance England, constructs her central thesis on a premise that is the mark of all civilized nations: "Lawful vengeance, in the strict sense, must be the vengeance of the divine law."[19] Tudor England, probably because its collective mind, like that of ancient Greece, was more responsive to the fundamentals of justice and was less cluttered with sophistications than is that of the twentieth-century world, accepted this premise as the foundation of its criminal laws. The demand for vengeance—whether murder, theft, or bodily harm was the issue—came not only from the violated person, his family, and the populace at large but also from God in behalf of that person. In turn, the magistrate who carried out the law did so not only in the service of the violated person, his family, and the populace or the state but just as importantly in the service of God, Whose commandment had been broken. There is, in consequence, a binding correlation between Bolingbroke's resolve of vengeance in behalf of his murdered uncle and the inscrutable part that God, the first lawmaker, was thought to exercise in that vengeance; for King Richard and his associates are in violation of God's Sixth and, excepting His prohibition against false idols, His most dreaded Commandment: "Thou shalt not kill" (Exod. 20.13).

That the spirit of Gloucester shapes, on the mundane level, the thoughts of men in *Richard II* is evident in two ways: throughout act I and part of act II, and again at the beginning of act IV, the characters are repeatedly mindful, both in word and in action, of the crime against the dead duke; second, through the instrumentality of Bolingbroke, Gloucester's demand for vengeance is both initiated and fulfilled. At the same time, as early as act I, scene ii, God's part in that vengeance is expressed so emphatically as to leave little doubt that He is thought to be the prime motivator behind it. Not only has Gaunt stated that, when murder is committed, the forces of divine justice "rain hot vengeance on offenders' heads," he also proceeds to explain why he (and *theoretically* any man) cannot undertake vengeance upon a king:

> God's is the quarrel; for God's substitute,
> His deputy anointed in His sight,
> Hath caus'd his [Gloucester's] death; the which if wrongfully,
> Let heaven revenge; for I may never lift
> An angry arm against His minister.
>
> [I.ii.37-41]

Gaunt is here affirming the doctrine of a king's divine right and, in so doing, has made it clear that God is recognized as the only qualified avenger of Gloucester upon King Richard for the reason that no subject can rightfully make, and execute, judgment upon his king. In the ideal sense, which omits the requirement of an agent, this observation is correct. That God is the prime motivator of the vengeance, although not necessarily the only avenger, is supported in the play by recurrent testimony as to His powers over human events, including His capability of vengeance. Bolingbroke, by providing a biblical sanction for his task of vengeance, has tacitly affirmed that God has an important part in it. York notes, early in act V, that the citizens, on Richard's return to London, had cast dust upon his head and then explains that "God, for some strong purpose, steel'd / The hearts of men" (V.ii.34-35) lest these men have sympathy for their captured king; he immediately concludes, speaking of Richard's overthrow and Bolingbroke's accession, that "heaven hath a hand in these events" (V.ii.37) and that the new political order must be accepted because it is the effect of Heaven's "high will." Bolingbroke, although he clearly indicates God's part in the vengeance, thinks customarily in terms of his own strength. His father and his uncle York, by contrast, tend to see only God's function in the control of human destiny, as when York must warn Bolingbroke to temper his high ambitions "lest you mistake. The heavens are over our heads" (III.iii.17), to which Bolingbroke replies, probably honestly at the time, that he has no intent to oppose "their will." The older and more experienced men, as elsewhere in Shakespeare, are the spokesmen of tradition: they see God as the principal architect of human events, as well as ready to avenge misdeeds. In his elder years, a repentant Bolingbroke will come to share, although less manifestly, his father's and his uncle's awareness of the uncompromising power of God's will.

The prevalent testimony of the play *Richard II* is that God is the prime motivator of events until act V, although the events appear to be moved by men. Even emotions, foresight, and impules of the moment are said to be controlled or prompted by God. York, as just noted, blames the unkindly reception given King Richard, when led a captive through London by Bolingbroke, on the premise that "God [has] steel'd the hearts" of the onlookers; before Carlisle can deliver his prediction of civil wars in the third generation, he has to be, as he tells us, "stirr'd up by God" (IV.i.133); and, in a sequel play, when a much-chastened Henry Bolingbroke, now on his deathbed, marvels at Hal's indiscreet impulse in having taken the crown from his pillow, he is able to identify the source behind that significant impulse:

> God put it in thy mind to take it [the crown] hence,
> That thou mightst win the more thy father's love,
> Pleading so wisely in excuse of it!
> [*2 Hen 4*, IV.v.179-81]

In the trial by combat between Mowbray and Bolingbroke, although an abortive one, we expect God's presence, for the only reason for such a trial was to ask a judgment of God, and we may assume that, for His own inscrutable purpose, He chose to put King Richard, and not the combatants, at center stage. He has chosen, it seems, to put King Richard on trial, for neither combatant bears as much guilt as does the King. Blind to consequences, Richard then proceeds to mete out the banishments that are to assure his own defeat.

Having opened the play *Richard II* with the resolve to avenge Gloucester ("This arm shall do it, or this life be spent"), Bolingbroke, even though he is later careful to conceal his ultimate intents, is dogged in execution. He has taken upon himself, as Holinshed reports, "to revenge" his uncle's murder, and this intention includes the resolve "to drive King Richard to resign his crowne." The banishment of Mowbray for life, as recorded by Holinshed and then by Shakespeare, completes the first phase of vengeance; but whatever Bolingbroke's satisfaction, it must have been compromised by the fact of his own six-year exile. Even so, he has not calculated wrongly: his confrontation with

Mowbray, and indirectly with Richard, over the matter of his uncle's murder, has won for him and his mission a considerable patronage, an achievement already recorded by Holinshed:

> A woonder it was to see what number of people ran after him in everie towne and street where he came, before he tooke the sea [for France], lamenting . . . his departure, as who would saie, that when he departed, the onelie shielde, defense and comfort of the commonwealth was vaded and gone.[20]

As this episode in *The Chronicles* attests, the favor of the people, once belonging to Gloucester, had descended to Bolingbroke, the most vigorous of the direct descendants of Edward III. Nor does Shakespeare neglect the humble posture that Bolingbroke, undoubtedly mindful of the dangers that beset the pigheaded and willful Gloucester, was thought to have assumed in his historic role as the exiled champion of the people. King Richard speaks the lines:

> Ourself, and Bushy, Bagot here, and Green,
> Observ'd his courtship of the common people,
> . . . .
> As 'twere to banish their affects with him.
> Off goes his bonnet to an oyster-wench,
> A brace of draymen bid God speed him well
> And had the tribute of his supple knee,
> With "Thanks, my countrymen, my loving friends";
> As were our England in reversion his
> And he our subjects' next degree in hope.
>
> [*R2*, I.iv.23-36]

In this portrait of Bolingbroke there is not a trace of the unrestrained candor shown in the opening scene. For the first time we see in him the posture of humility that is to be his mask until he dethrones the King.

What is behind this mask is a subject of controversy. It is my opinion that the mask conceals both the avenger and, as time unfolds, the partner of destiny whose plans, beyond the fulfillment of his sworn vengeance, are both so crucial and so uncertain that he must trust to that habit of silence which, as if subserving his remarkable luck, is to become a political asset that both chills and disarms. Although not an outright opportunist, as Shakespeare depicts him, he has the knack (from God perhaps?) of finding himself at the right place at the right time. Even his banishment has been fortunate, for the confiscation of his estates in his absence, while alienating hearts from King Richard, has gained for Bolingbroke not only a refurbished and very ample recognition but also the unexpected sympathy of hundreds of his high-ranking countrymen, including Northumberland, once Richard's friend.

The single act that makes inevitable the overthrow of Shakespeare's Richard is the confiscation of the Lancastrian estates only moments after John of Gaunt has died. Ironically, it is Richard's fear of Bolingbroke, "our subjects' next degree in hope," that prompts this crime, for which the need of financing "our Irish wars" is at best a commendable gloss. Richard has heard his cousin's oath of vengeance; he has witnessed, probably more than once, the persistence of his cousin's temperament; and he has been compelled, in fear of retaliation, to banish Mowbray for life and, out of that same fear, to reduce Bolingbroke's sentence of exile from ten years to six. Mowbray's punishment has been, at best, a partial satisfaction to Bolingbroke. Should Bolingbroke inherit the Lancastrian estates, the wealthiest in England and powerful in arms, Richard (as he well knows) will be the next object of his cousin's wrath, and dethronement is the least of his dire expectations. Had not Bolingbroke, for example, likened Gloucester's blood to Abel's and thus assumed a divine sanction for his mission? Jean Froissart has explained, in part, Richard's rationale in confiscating the patrimony of Bolingbroke: the King assumed that "a banysshed man" had no rights of inheritance.[21] More pertinent to the core of the issue is a statement by Holinshed: "The king meant his [Bolingbroke's] utter undooing."[22]

The early months of Bolingbroke's exile have had, for him, two effects which have counterbalanced one another: he has been put out of contact with his supporters in England; on the other hand, he has won sympathy because of his exile, not only among the commoners, but also from persons of estate. As yet, however, he has remained, as an exiled subject, ill equipped to confront and to defeat an anointed king, who retains the support, however grudgingly, even of Bolingbroke's own father, the wealthiest landowner in England. The news of both his father's death and, more unexpectedly, the confiscation of the Lancastrian estates has left Bolingbroke with one of two choices: either he must accept the status of a penniless exile or move against Richard before the sudden sympathy for his latest misfortune has begun to cool. Of the political repercussions of the confiscation, Holinshed reports: "diverse of the nobilitie, aswell prelates as other, and likewise manie of the magistrats and rulers of the cities, townes, and communaltie, here in England" wrote to Bolingbroke, now in Paris, and urged him to replace Richard as king and save England from "utter ruine."²³ In short, a widely unforeseen event has tipped the balance of power in England from King Richard (whose high office, and not his performance, has commanded allegiance) to Bolingbroke, the political heir of Gloucester. Holinshed proceeds to explain: "through the earnest persuasion of Thomas Arundel, late Archbishop of Canterburie," likewise exiled by Richard, the historic Bolingbroke "got him downe to [Brittany]" and, joined by several compatriots, was soon ready to sail to England.²⁴ Importantly, Holinshed (Shakespeare's principal source for the materials cited in this paragraph) makes no mention that Bolingbroke, at this early time, had any private intent of taking over Richard's throne. The revolt of the nobles, alluded to by Holinshed, is dramatically illustrated in Shakespeare's play. Only minutes after the confiscation of Bolingbroke's patrimony, we are shown the revolt of three lords— Northumberland, Ross, and Willoughby—whose disaffection is symbolic of the general revolt. Not only are these three lords sympathetic to Bolingbroke; more specifically, they fear for both their own security and, in particular, the welfare of their heirs (II.i.235-45).

King Richard's confiscation of Gaunt's property, as shown by Shakespeare in act II, scene i, follows immediately upon the Duke's death—precisely, at lines 159-62. At lines 285-88 of the same scene, Northumberland reports that Bolingbroke's "eight tall ships" are en route from Brittany and "shortly mean to touch our northern shore." Historically, Gaunt died early in February 1399—Jean Créton, a French chronicler, gives the date as February 3—and his son Henry Bolingbroke was not to make the unauthorized return from exile until July. Meanwhile, King Richard had left England in late May and arrived, again according to Créton, who had accompanied him, at Waterford, Ireland, on June 1. Few critics have had reason to comment on the triple chronology of Shakespeare's scene at Ely House (II.i). Of these, Robert Ornstein makes, I believe, the most adequate comment: "Shakespeare has the report of Bolingbroke's return come at the very close of the scene in which Richard seizes Gaunt's estates. Perhaps Shakespeare telescopes time only to achieve a striking effect."[25] This "striking effect," in my mind, is intended to highlight the dispatch with which Bolingbroke has responded to the act of confiscation.[26] On the other hand, he may be hovering off the English coast for a purpose that Shakespeare has chosen to withhold. On this view Ornstein comments wisely: "Yet this handling of events leaves open the possibility that Bolingbroke led an army to England [for an undisclosed purpose] and then discovered that Richard had given him a perfect excuse for rebellion."[27] In either case, Bolingbroke has now a second powerful motive for vengeance upon the King and his associates. He insists, however, that he "comes but for his own." So earnest is his explanation of his return (II.iii.113-36), which is made to York, now Lord Governor, that both the audience and most readers tend to accept the breaking of the exile as prompted entirely by the confiscation of his patrimony, which has made of him, in his own words, "a wandering vagabond" seeking reparation. York, after hearing out his nephew, sets the keynote for this acceptance:

> My Lords of England, let me tell you this:
> I have had feeling for my cousin's wrongs,
>
> . . . .
>
> But in this kind to come, in braving arms,
> Be his own carver and cut out his way,
> To find out right with wrong—it may not be.
>
> [II.iii.140-45]

The reprimand, which is part of the official statement of the Lord Governor, does not obscure York's genuine acknowledgment of the rightness of the stated cause, namely, that Bolingbroke's bold return to England is prompted solely by the needs of survival.

What precisely does Bolingbroke seek? only his property? or vengeance, as I maintain? Or is it the throne, as many critics believe? Or does he ride on the crest of his luck, whatever the outcome? E.M.W. Tillyard, among several remarks on Bolingbroke, has stated: "He is made the first mover of the tournament [trial by combat] and he wants to do something about Woodstock's murder. But he has no steady policy and having once set events in motion is the servant of fortune."[28]

John Palmer, much like J.D. Wilson, has contended that Bolingbroke "waits upon his fortune"[29] and thus has recognized a more adjustable dependence upon fortune than has Tillyard. By contrast, Derek Traversi observes in Bolingbroke a "purposeful advance . . . towards the ends he has proposed to himself."[30] Like H.N. Hudson and many twentieth-century critics, including Brents Stirling, he holds that Bolingbroke, a master of calculation, aims "to seize the crown."[31] Muriel Bradbrook has remarked, both wryly and perceptively: "Bolingbroke's character . . . is largely built up from what he does not say."[32] This statement identifies the Bolingbroke mask, the man and the enigma, behind which lies, speculatively, a half dozen inscrutable machinations. Most of the critics who contend that Bolingbroke aims to take over the throne make the mistake, I believe, of thinking that he has this intention at the time he lands at Ravensburgh. They tend to "build up" his purpose—in contrast to his character—"from what he does not say" and are guilty of the same mistaken inference as are York and King Richard from within the play. Robert Ornstein comes close to the truth when he writes: "Bolingbroke . . . gives himself to his destiny by refusing to think about the consequences of his acts."[33] This statement is akin to the thinking of Wilson and Palmer, namely, that Bolingbroke "waits upon his fortune"; it also projects, as a corollary, the idea that only when a man fits himself to the task at hand, deferring until propitious the greater task, and hence has no fear of incurring an untimely remorse, which might henceforth enslave him to the past—only then can he be a partner of destiny. A memory of the past, for Bolingbroke, is customarily a spur to action and, until he has become King, never a topic for remorse. He remembers his confiscated property, but of his dead father, since he cannot restore him to life, he never indicates a thought. Above all, he does not forget, as will be further illustrated, his oath in behalf of Gloucester: "This arm shall [avenge him], or this life be spent." In this, as in other ventures, Bolingbroke moves a calculated step at a time.

Holinshed, as I have noted, placed major stress upon Bolingbroke's intent to avenge his uncle Gloucester upon the king's faction; and Shakespeare, in turn, emphasizes both the intent of vengeance and the problem of the confiscated estates. The calculating mind of Bolingbroke, as Holinshed (and especially Shakespeare) understood, was almost certain to note the dangers inherent in brashly accepting the offer of the kingship made by the illuminaries of England and noted by Holinshed. A principal danger, which is affirmed in the rebellions of the *Henry IV* plays and, later and at large, in the *Henry VI* plays, lay in the doctrine of primogeniture, a right which on Richard's death or deposition would belong to his natural heir, historically eight-year-old Edmund Mortimer. Bolingbroke's personal experience of being dispossessed, and the large sympathy shown in his behalf, must have impressed upon him the many times greater danger of dispossessing a kingdom's heir. Even though only a small minority of critics has seen a revenge motif in *Richard II*, and then one that is not more than secondary in importance, vengeance is the only identifiable theme which, resolved upon with candor by Bolingbroke, extends through the play, and does much to unify it, from the opening scene until late in act IV. E.M.W. Tillyard is correct when he says of him, although without elaboration: "He wants to do something about Woodstock's murder." It is right to add, however, that Bolingbroke is provided, as Shakespeare treats him, with a second motive for vengeance that must have been more personally compelling than the first. It has to do, as we might expect, with the confiscated estates. Both motives direct him, although first through underlings, to King Richard.

That Bolingbroke's role, as treated by Shakespeare, is fundamentally that of an avenger is substantiated by his second statement on vengeance, customarily unremarked by critics. To the partial completion of the punitive resolve contained in this statement, Shakespeare will shortly devote an entire scene (III.i). Bolingbroke must, he contends, go directly from Berkeley to "Bristol Castle," for ensconced in that castle are

> Bushy, Bagot, and their complices,
> The caterpillars of the commonwealth,
> Which I have sworn to weed and pluck away.
> [II.iii.165-67]

These are the men, Bagot excepted, whom two scenes later he is to accuse of having "fed upon my signories [estates], / Dispark'd my parks and . . . / From my own windows torn my household coat [of arms]" (III.i.22-24). The crimes against Bolingbroke and the Lancastrian estates, and not the offenses against the King and Queen, which serve chiefly as a generalized preface, are the heart and brawn of Bolingbroke's accusations (III.i.16-27) made at Bristol. Upon concluding them, he orders King Richard's partners in plunder "dispatch'd" and thus makes good upon his "sworn" intent.

Bolingbroke never repeats his oath to avenge Gloucester made in the first scene; on the other hand, he says nothing and does nothing that would abrogate the oath. He moves upon Richard, who has returned to Wales from Ireland, with machinelike precision. What has amazed students of the play is the immense army that he musters with no apparent effort. The Lancastrian forces and those of the northern ally Northumberland are said by the historian Charles Oman to have rendezvoused with Bolingbroke somewhere between Ravenspurgh and Doncaster.[34] Many thousands of soldiers, however, are later to be added to the rebel army on its march south and westward toward Bristol. When Sir Stephen Scroop hints at the gravity of this situation (III.ii.91-92), King Richard, who only minutes earlier has found comfort in God, as well as His angels, and in the belief that "heaven still guards the right," is allowed by Shakespeare to envision Bolingbroke as his copartner in God's service: "If he serve God, / We'll serve him too, and be his fellow so" (ll. 98-99). This concession by the King, who is by his office "God's deputy," identifies Bolingbroke as a servant of God equal in status to the King himself ("his fellow"). Scroop then offers a description of Bolingbroke's army, and we are induced to picture not a disciplined band of warriors but rather a pilgrimage of innocents trudging to the relief of a ravished shrine:

> White-beards have arm'd their thin and hairless scalps
> Against thy majesty; boys, with women's voices,
> Strive to speak big, and clap their female joints
> In stiff unwieldy arms against thy crown.
> Thy very beadsmen learn to bend their bows
> Of double-fatal yew against thy state;
> Yea, distaff-women manage rusty bills
> Against thy seat: both young and old rebel,
> And all goes worse than I have power to tell.
>
> [III.ii.112-20]

Shakespeare's purpose is to show that most of England has now rebelled against its king. The image shaped in our minds, however, is that of innocents in the service of a mission sanctified by God. In the images (Richard's and Scroop's) just cited, Shakespeare has provided Bolingbroke's objective with indications of divine approbation, until now ironically the comfort of Richard in his fantasies, and this approbation is, of course, most evident in the presence of the King's beadsmen in Bolingbroke's rebel army. Although these are but indications of a divine presence, we are perhaps better prepared to accept York's later explanation of Richard's fall and Bolingbroke's accession: "Heaven hath a hand in these events" (V.ii.37), to which he adds that its "high will" must be accepted. The favor of Heaven—so it is suggested—has begun to shift, almost imperceptibly, from Richard and his fantasy world to Bolingbroke.

John Palmer has seen no "fixed purpose" in Bolingbroke and discredits those who view him as "bent on obtaining the crown from the outset."[35] Traversi and other capable critics, coming after Palmer, have argued once again for Bolingbroke's "purposeful" intent "to seize the crown." In short, when critics have argued that Bolingbroke has a "fixed purpose," that purpose has invariably been said to be directed, in a customarily Machiavellian fashion, at obtaining the throne. Shakespeare has offered almost no textual evidence, aside from the Bolingbroke mask (into which much may be read), that will sustain such a long-term purpose. He is at pains, by contrast, to stress two solid motives for vengeance (Gloucester's murder and the confiscated estates), quite likely because they have a justification not shared by a conspiratorially premeditated usurpation. Given a choice between a prosaic villain and a prosaic soldier of fortune, Shakespeare chose the latter image for Bolingbroke, whose "fixed purpose" on the march to Bristol, and almost certainly on the march to Flint Castle, is the fulfillment of his sworn vengeance but who, as the abrupt return from exile indicates, retains a flexible capability both within that fixed purpose and beyond it. He knows, moreover, that the task of fulfilling his vengeance in behalf of Gloucester will automatically restore to him the Lancastrian estates, for his plan of vengeance takes its shape from the dictates of his pragmatic mind. The punishment must be such that Richard, who has dared to set himself above the statutes of England, cannot repeat lawless acts of the type now to be avenged; hence, the ultimate purpose of the vengeance is to destroy the last vestige of Richard's political hold over England. In this, Bolingbroke acts as much in the public interest, which serves to justify the final phase of his vengeance, as in his own. Beyond the fulfillment of his vengeance, coupled with the automatic regaining of the Lancastrian estates, there is no adequate testimony in the play that Bolingbroke has a significant predetermined plan; he must, however, have had in mind certain options, each of them bearing upon Richard's successor.

Whether or not Bolingbroke places his personal interests above those of England, whether or not he finds, as events unfold, a communion of these two interests, he must have observed that the road to vengeance, because of the unfortunate conditions in England, would culminate in a sizable dilemma once Richard had been dethroned. The first part of the dilemma arises from the self-evident administrative inadequacy of King Richard's eight-year-old heir at a time when England is in dire need of a stable and competent government. Even if we allow for Shakespeare's error, as testified in *1 Henry IV*, and accept the older Edmund Mortimer, uncle of young Edmund, as Richard's heir apparent,[36] Bolingbroke would be confronted with the same political dilemma. For the uncle, as his deportment at Glendower's Welsh castle and his failure to show up at the crucial battle near Shrewsbury bear witness, possesses not an iota of the stuff of kingship. Bolingbroke has seen, in Richard II, the disaster that attends the rule of an indulgent and self-serving king. To put Richard's rightful heir on the throne, no matter which Edmund Mortimer, must have appeared to Bolingbroke a flagrant disservice to England, even now at the utmost brink of economic and moral bankruptcy. Equally unwise, as time will forcibly illustrate, is the other principal option, namely, that Bolingbroke, in whose silent strength are found some of the qualities of kingship, defy the irrevocable law of primogeniture, by which God selects the heir, and place himself upon the throne. This course may have been the more agonizing for Bolingbroke to confront—and yet the more persistent. He has, as he knows to his hazard, the overriding support of the people, not only his huge army of volunteers, but also those tens of thousands who, in their need, cried: "God save thee, Bolingbroke! . . . Jesu preserve thee!" as he rode victorious into London. The issue has narrowed to a basically unanswerable question: "Whose will must be obeyed—the people's or that of God?" For in this instance, and at this time, the two wills are diametrically opposed. Although Palmer's view that Bolingbroke, in pursuing "his infant fortune, . . . had acted . . . undesignedly"[37] and my view that revenge is his dominant long-term motive are on the surface very different, we reach much the same conclusion. It is correct, I firmly believe, to accept in full Bolingbroke's own explanation, made dispassionately years later, of how he came unlawfully to the throne:

> . . . then, God knows, I had no such intent,
> But that necessity so bowed the state
> That I and greatness were compelled to kiss.
>
> [*2 Hen 4*, III.i.72-74]

He is also aware, as becomes transparently evident during his "death-bed" reflections, that in dispossessing King Richard's rightful heir, he has isolated himself from God's favor.

Taking over the throne is, as I have suggested, only a corollary of Bolingbroke's twofold motive of vengeance, although a highly important one. The original oath of vengeance, made in behalf of Gloucester and provided with a biblical sanction, has committed him to a task from which he cannot, in private honor, back off. Upon default of his father, Gaunt, and that of York, who "loved his ease and lytell busynesse,"[38] the task of avenging Gloucester has become, according to Norman law, the familial obligation of Bolingbroke. The chivalric code, as exemplified in the Norman trial by combat, recognized God as the supreme Judge and Avenger. If an offender, such as King Richard, was of such status that he could not be brought to ordinary process of justice, God was thought to retain these two high offices, unqualified by local officialdom, and to have need only of an agent. Holinshed, Shakespeare's principal source, illustrates God's role of Judge and Avenger as it applied to Richard II and his court: having made judgment upon the "lechery [and] adultery" of Richard's court "whereby the whole realm . . . was infected . . . the wrath of God was dailie provoked to vengeance for the sins of the prince and his people"; as punishment for such conduct, we are then told, God "did shred him [Richard] off from the scepter of his kingdome."[39] Whereas Holinshed looked upon Bolingbroke, in the dethronement of Richard, as a "rebellious subject," who together with his "lineall race" was "scourged afterwards," Shakespeare's view of him is less severe: as an agent of God he is not morally condemnable until he orders the former king's murder, which appears not to have been God's will.

Lest the deposition scene (*R2*, IV.i.154-318) be regarded primarily—and, I believe, wrongly—as a self-interested coup d'état on the part of Bolingbroke, Shakespeare is careful to preface it with charges of conspiracy against the Duke of Aumerle, historically liaison officer to King Richard at the time of Gloucester's murder. Hence the focus is on guilt and not on self-advantage. Bolingbroke, who has not quite finished dealing with Richard's lieutenants, supervises the formal charges:

> Now, Bagot, freely speak thy mind—
> What thou dost know of noble Gloucester's death;
> Who wrought it with the King, and who perform'd
> The bloody office of his timeless end.
>
> [IV.i.2-5]

Bagot, who has turned state's evidence, replies: "Then set before my face the Lord Aumerle." The charges against Aumerle, in Holinshed's account, are placed at a distance after, and not before, the deposition scene. The transposition made by Shakespeare well serves his dramatic purposes: the accusations directed by Bagot and then by Lord Fitzwater and other lords against Aumerle—namely, that as Richard's deputy he had a direct part in Gloucester's murder—not only escape anticlimax by being placed immediately before, and not after, the deposition scene; more important, being so placed, they are intended to impress unmistakably upon the audience that the principal cause behind Richard's dethronement, which is to follow, is the autocratic and hence lawless murder of his uncle, for Aumerle's responsibility in it is clearly subordinate to that of King Richard. This being so, the dethronement is to be viewed as the climactic act of Bolingbroke's revenge, which has now been politically and publicly justified—indeed, in Parliament itself.

To Holinshed's statement that Bolingbroke pursued revenge even to the taking of Richard's "guiltlesse life,"[40] Shakespeare seems not to have responded. The murder of Richard, in Shakespeare's play, can be explained in terms more immediate than those of vengeance—specifically, in terms of the rebellion of January 1400. Ironically, having suggested to Exton the murder of the imprisoned Richard, Bolingbroke (now Henry IV) arrives at the same point of guilt at which Richard stood at the outset of the play. The murdered Richard has become, as it were, the murdered Gloucester, whose "blood like sacrificing Abel's

crie[d] . . . for justice and rough chastisement." The cycle has been renewed, and other men will appoint themselves to avenge Richard upon
Henry Bolingbroke. When King Richard's coffin is set before him,
Henry IV shudders at the knowledge of what Exton, as his instrument,
has done: "They love not poison that do poison need, / Nor do I thee"
(V.vi.38-39). Whereas Richard had played Cain to Gloucester's hapless
role of Abel, it is now Henry who has assumed the role of Cain. In com-
manding Exton, "With Cain go wander thorough shades of night /
And never show thy head by day or light" (ll. 43-44), whom is he rejecting? Only Exton? More than Exton, I think: he has used the phrase
"with Cain go wander." Since Henry is responsible for the murder of
Richard, Exton being but his instrument, and the idea of murder has
proven revolting to his nature, he has sought to reject, together with
Exton, that part of himself which is Cain and at which he is now ap-
palled.

With the murder of Richard, Henry IV finds that he has perpetuated
a cycle of which he himself must be the next victim. That he does not
become the next victim is (as Shakespeare depicts him) a matter of good
fortune and possibly of God's grace, and not the intent of his fellow
men, such as Northumberland and Douglas. An irony is that, in having
completed a mission in behalf of Gloucester, and having somewhat inadvertently taken a step beyond that mission, Bolingbroke has established
for posterity another Abel, namely the murdered King Richard, who
must demand the blood of another Cain. Once that Cain (unprotected
by the biblical mark) has been butchered, namely, Henry VI, who inherits the guilt of his grandfather, he too will become another Abel
demanding blood revenge. The threefold cycle will be completed at
Bosworth Field.

Behind such cycles of retribution and the slack and flow of the larger
currents of history, Renaissance man, like his medieval forebears,
recognized that, while men might seem to be the cause of them, the
principal impetus is derived from God. Jean Créton, the Frenchman who
accompanied Richard II on the Irish campaign in 1399, warns offenders
of the long accepted reality of divine power: "He who willingly doeth
evil or injury to another is often seen to be greatly punished by God,
who is powerful above the present race of men as well as the past."[41]
Of the omnipotence of God, the Tudor chroniclers later bear witness:
"God knoweth what he hath predestinate," writes Edward Hall,

"against whose will avayleth no stryvinge."[42] Holinshed provides a focus more pertinent to this chapter: "For it is a heavie case when God thundereth out his reall arguments either upon prince or people."[43] King Richard, he adds, has felt God's "thunder," accompanied by the bolt, "for the fowle enormities with which his life was defamed."[44] The punishment of Bolingbroke, however, who stepped beyond the role of God's minister and became both a usurper and a murderer, must wait. At the moment, there is no worthy candidate who by nearness of kinship to Richard, as well as strength of arms, is able to undertake the burden of God's agent; for, as my second chapter has made clear, the working of God's vengeance is conditioned customarily upon the availability of a qualified champion. The murder of Gloucester, of which the dethronement, the usurpation, and King Richard's murder are effects, is the most costly homicide, in terms of bloodshed, in the annals of England; for the crimes against Richard, as well as the usurpation, were likewise crimes against divine law, and once Gloucester had been avenged, demanded a retribution which, coming late and compounded by two generations of distrust, was to take the shape of repeated and bloody civil wars. Indeed, England was to revert—at least ostensibly— to the savagery that, on a much smaller scale, had marked the Anglo-Saxon vendetta.

A bare outline of Shakespeare's eight-part historical epic, not excluding the four historically earlier plays, is largely an abstract of jarring hostilities. We know, however, that such an overall impression is incorrect. The skeletal framework of clandestine murders, vengeance, civil discord, and force of brute arms is relieved, and upgraded, by often capable poetry, put out of mind at times by sparkling interludes of comedy, provided with an overall unity by the theme of inherited guilt, humanized by the alternating bloom and decay of Nobilitas, and near the end deprived of its forbidding aspect by Richard of Gloucester's ironic and explosive humor. We are currently reminded, as we have been in *Richard II*, of the judgment of God. It asserts itself more tentatively in the *Henry IV* plays and in *Henry V* than in the other plays, possibly in recognition of the improved level of Nobilitas within the ruling family. Even in these plays, as will be shown, God's dreaded judgment arising from the guilt incurred by Henry IV is clearly enunciated, or is unmistakably implied, at crucial intervals.

FOUR

Richard II and the Delay of Providence

Despite the fact that Gloucester's murder gave impetus to a long and bloody period of English history—the Age of Retribution—it is invariably the murdered Richard II, and not Gloucester, who comes to mind. This calling to mind, as we find it in the *Henry IV* plays, is understandable. Richard was the second king of England who came to the high office by means of unqualified primogeniture, and hence was held to be appointed only by God.[1] Theoretically, he could not be removed from that office by any mere human. Gloucester, despite his powerful political leverage, was the sixth son of Edward III—no nonentity, certainly, but *not* a man whose violent death could of itself propagate the crucial issues that, for decades, marked the aftermath of King Richard's murder.[2] The period of history to which I refer, although initiated by the murder of Gloucester, reached its climax, very early in the period, with that of Richard. Gloucester's murder called for vengeance only upon the King and his close associates; the dethronement and murder of Richard, by contrast, coupled with Bolingbroke's usurpation, were thought by the Tudors to have evoked God's vengeance upon all England.[3] It would come, however, only when "the hours" for it were "ripe on earth."

J.D. Wilson and Karl Thompson have interpreted Shakespeare's portrait of Richard II as that of a martyr king, whose death, of itself, would demand a heavy payment. Wilson calls him an "exemplar of royal martyrdom."[4] Although Thompson in his article "Richard II, Martyr" attempts to identify the living Richard as a martyr, he is careful to qualify his interpretation: he tells us that, in not fighting back against Bolingbroke, Richard "affects . . . the pose of the true martyr."[5] This qualification has some truth in it. King Richard, in likening himself to Christ and his enemies to Judases, does establish the posture of a man who has sacrificed his total worldly comfort in the service of a high principle. But one is inclined to ask: What high principle? There is no high

principle, religious or political, in which he has actively, and for the betterment of his fellow men, engaged himself. There remains, however,
within the play a significant principle as well as the illusion, mainly
Richard's, that he has sacrificed himself in behalf of that principle. He
himself embodies the essence of it through the good fortune of his birth;
but except as the principle relates to his private welfare, he falls short
of grasping its total significance. The principle is the divine right of
kings and, especially, the idea that it is not subject to violation. Ironically, Richard seems to make use of it as a suit of armor that will cow
Bolingbroke into awe and submission (see R2, III.ii.47- 62) rather than
as an ideal that, in behalf of his successors, he must defend at any cost.
The living Richard simply does not have the toughness of mind fundamental to the true martyr.[6]

The historians, including Jean Froissart (who had met and talked with
King Richard), have customarily portrayed him as a person of charm and
graciousness. Despite a partiality for the house of Lancaster, Edward
Hall (Holinshed's source for certain later episodes of Richard's reign)
speaks sympathetically, and even kindly, of the deposed king: "If there
were any offence, it ought more to be imputed to the frailtee of his wanton youth then [than] to the malice of his heart."[7] Holinshed, in turn,
evaluates Richard as a victim of "evill counsell" who was "otherwise
a right noble and woorthie prince" and adds: "He was seemelie of shape
and favor, & of nature good inough."[8] The impression that Richard
was a likable man, though weak of will, was to be attested by the many
rebellions undertaken in his behalf, all but one after he was dead. M.M.
Reese sums up the impression left by the dead Richard: "But time and
martyrdom washed away the traces [of mismanagement], and only the
charm and the pathos stood in people's memory."[9] The martyrdom
had been bought with heartache.

The fact that Richard, in his last days, appeared to have become a
helpless innocent pathetically sacrificed to the ambition of a ruthless cap-
tor (Bolingbroke) undoubtedly touched the hearts and the consciences
of many of his countrymen. To the potential forces of retribution he had
become, even while yet in prison, a martyred king, for his punishment
seemed to outweigh his offenses. In his behalf the Duke of Exeter and
others undertook the abortive rebellion of January 1400; this attempt
was followed, not long after Richard's death, by two rebellions even

more abortive. In the year 1402 "sir Roger Claryngdon knight and eight gray Friers," accused of organizing a campaign of slander in behalf of Richard against Henry IV, were "strangeled at Tiborne." A major charge was that they had circulated "tauntyng verses against kyng Henry."[10] Shortly after, the Earl of St. Paul, husband of Richard's half sister, led an invasion of the Isle of Wight, again in the name of Richard.[11] There was a fourth minor uprising—as contrasted to the three major rebellions of Shrewsbury, Gaultree Forest, and Bramham Moor—upon news that "king Richard was yet living in Scotland."[12] Such abortive attempts to unseat or embarrass Henry IV affirm a deep popular regret over the untimely dethronement of Richard, whose better qualities outlived, in the minds of many fellow Englishmen, his inadequate conduct as a king.

In Shakespeare's history plays immediately subsequent to *Richard II*, we can note three distinct responses toward the dead Richard. To the forces of retribution (led by Northumberland, Hotspur, and Richard Scroop, Archbishop of York) he has become a martyr worthy of avenging. To the Lancastrians, especially Henry IV, he is the example of a man unfit to be king—certainly no martyr. Ultimately, to the March and York claimants to the throne, he is called to mind mainly for his pivotal place in history—a king deposed in defiance of divine law—and not for any personal attributes, favorable or otherwise. To these responses—especially the first and the third—the dead Richard owes his power to shape issues central to the later plays of the eight-part historical epic.

A change of heart, once Richard is dead, is particularly evident, as shown by Shakespeare, in the altered attitude of the Percy family both toward Henry Bolingbroke and toward Richard, who had foreseen with clairvoyance such an alteration:

> Northumberland, thou ladder where withal
> The mounting Bolingbroke ascends my throne
> . . . .
> Thou shalt think,
> Though he divide the realm and give thee half,
> It is too little, helping him to all.
> And he shall think that thou, which knowest the way

To plant unrightful kings, wilt know again,
Being ne'er so little urg'd, another way
To pluck him headlong from the usurped throne.
                              [*R2*, V.i.55-56; 59-65]

As Richard has foreseen, Henry IV is to have but two choices: for the
Percies' help in putting him on the throne, he must either share his
kingdom with them, and share it generously, or completely ignore
them. On this problem the third scene of *1 Henry IV* is focused. By
denying the petition of the Percies that he ransom Edmund Mortimer
("On the barren mountains let him starve"), Henry has rejected them.
In the episode that follows, we hear from the Percy family what only
a reader with the greatest foresight might have anticipated: a favorable
estimate of Richard. Nor is this favorable attitude toward the man
whom the Percies have helped to dethrone prompted only by their now
bitter hatred of Henry IV. A second factor, customarily unnoted, is at
work. Worcester's remark that Edmund Mortimer had been proclaimed
by Richard "the next of blood" evokes from Northumberland an unexpected remorse over Richard's fate: "The unhappy King—Whose
wrongs in us God pardon!" The response that then comes from
Worcester provides a strong hint of the sequence of attitudes that have
refocused the thinking of the Percy family; of Richard, he observes: "for
whose death we in the world's wide mouth / Live scandaliz'd and
foully spoken of" (*1 Hen 4*, I.iii.153-54). Hotspur, taking up the essence
of Worcester's remark, illuminates the dilemma that has forced upon
the Percies an unsought change of attitude:

　　　　Shall it, for shame, be spoken in these days
　　　　Or fill up chronicles in time to come,
　　　　That men of your nobility and power
　　　　Did gage them both in an unjust behalf

　　　　. . . . .
　　　　To put down Richard, that sweet lovely rose,
　　　　And plant this thorn, this canker, Bolingbroke?
　　　　　　　　　　　　　　　　　[I.iii.170-76]

Understandably disenchanted with Henry IV, the Percies are also aware
that the public has entertained second thoughts on the matter of Richard

and Henry. Those who dethroned Richard are "foully spoken of." Hotspur's praise of him as a "sweet lovely rose" not only attests to the present attitude of the Percy family; in its context, it points to the factors behind that attitude: public sentiment and the fear of what the "chronicles" based on that sentiment will report. In short, it is no longer the public fashion to denigrate King Richard.

Unhappily for the Percies, they ride the crest of popular sentiment in behalf of Richard to a crushing defeat at Shrewsbury. The generalship of Hotspur, who accepts battle even though much of the rebel army is absent, is to be questioned more than is the caliber of public sentiment as it relates to the former king. Sentiment favorable to him remained strong in 1403; as late as 1406, for example, "prudente policie" on Henry's part was required to quash the rumor that Richard was "yet living in Scotland." Had the rumor not been suppressed, "it had kendeled," according to Hall, "a great flame."[13] Historically, as reported by both Hall and Holinshed, Bolingbroke's crimes against King Richard, by exacting sympathy, were to make a martyr of a king who, in life, had evidenced no substance of the martyr. It is this image of the dead Richard that Shakespeare is at pains to stress.

That fond recollections of Richard are a principal force behind the rebellions of the *Henry IV* plays is most evident in part 2. In the third scene the Archbishop of York provides persuasive testimony of an awakened love for the dead Richard:

> They that, when Richard liv'd, would have him die
> Are now become enamour'd of his grave.
> Thou that threw'st dust upon his goodly head,
> When through proud London he came sighing on
> After th' admir'd heels of Bolingbroke,
> Criest now "O earth, yield us that king again,
> And take thou this!"
> [*2 Hen 4*, I.iii.101-107]

The posthumous attitude of the commoners toward Richard, although shaped, in part, by a distrust of Henry IV, finds a parallel in that of Marc Antony toward his dead wife Fulvia: "What our contempts do often hurl from us / We wish it ours again" (*Ant*, I.ii.120-21). Even before the Archbishop of York has appeared on stage in *2 Henry IV*, Shakespeare has been careful to establish the memory of Richard as a principal inducement in mustering the people against King Henry. We are told by Morton, in the opening scene, that the Archbishop has provided a spiritual sanction for the rebellion that he heads:

> [He] doth enlarge his rising with the blood
> Of fair King Richard, scrap'd from Pomfret stones;
> Derives from heaven his quarrel and his cause;
> Tells them he doth bestride a bleeding land,
> Gasping for life under great Bolingbroke.
>
> [*2 Hen 4*, I.i.204-208]

The fact that the blood of Richard, when shown to the commoners, has power to "enlarge" the rebel army is evidence of the devotion in which his memory has been held. In death he has attained a power for which he was temperamentally unfit when alive: he can assemble and move armies against his arch tormenter.

The passage that I have just quoted contains more of note than its testimony of the dead Richard's martyrdom. The Archbishop is said by Morton to derive "from heaven . . . his cause" and hence is character-ized as an agent with a divine sanction to destroy Bolingbroke. In a util-itarian and immediate sense, his aim is to avenge "a bleeding land" against the Lancastrian king. But the motive of which an agent is prin-cipally aware, as I hope to show in my discussion of the play *Hamlet*, need not be exactly the same as that held by God. The "blood" of Rich-ard "scrap'd from Pomfret stones" and the hundreds of volunteers who respond to it suggest (in Morton's context) that the vengeance to be taken on Henry IV, on an absolute and hence nonutilitarian level, is to exact atonement for Richard's murder, which is symbolized by the blood "scrap'd from" the site of the assassination. The two blood images tend to unite the two victims of Bolingbroke (the land and the dead Richard) in a bipartite motive, since both demand vengeance. But the Archbishop of York, who has no identifiable kinship with the dead king and proves to be defective as a military leader, is not a qualified agent of God despite Morton's sanctified portrait of him. Has Shakespeare perhaps teased his audience with a prospect of divine judg-ment, although the time is yet a half century from "ripe"?

Opposed to the public's favorable response, as shown by Shakespeare, toward the dead Richard is that of the Lancastrians, especially Henry IV;

his harsh view of Richard has been shaped partly by psychological factors. The disfavor in which Henry has found himself, as evidenced by the repeated rebellions against him, has prompted in him a rooted preoccupation as to the right or wrong of the usurpation. Years later, in *2 Henry IV*, he is to look back and recall "the indirect crook'd ways" by which he came to the throne. In the meantime, in part 1, he is aware of a persistent sense of guilt. At the outset of the "royal interview," in which only father and son participate, he suggests that the prodigally inclined Hal has been "mark'd / For the hot vengeance and the rod of heaven / To punish my mistreadings" (*1 Hen 4*, III. ii.9-11). He is oppressed, he fears, by God's "secret doom" and thus implies his trespasses against God. As the interview progresses, it is manifest that Henry, in order to justify both the usurpation and the murder to himself and thus to mitigate his pain of guilt, has constructed an image of King Richard that is one of unqualified ineptitude. Prince Hal, in his boisterous and vain conduct, Henry insists, has patterned himself, even though only half-consciously, upon the example of Richard:

> For all the world
> As thou art to this hour was Richard then
> When I from France set foot at Ravenspurgh.
>
> [III.ii.93-95]

In Henry's formula of kingship, Richard stands for the trivialities which a king of England must avoid. He is called to mind as "the skipping king" who daily "mingled his royalty with cap'ring fools." His friends were "shallow jesters and rash bavin wits"; he had, in short, "enfeoff'd himself to popularity" (III.ii.69). The King then directs the lesson at Hal:

> And in that very line, Harry, standest thou;
> For thou has lost thy princely privilege
> With vile participation.
>
> [III.ii.85-87]

Henry has shaped an image of Richard as being exactly what a monarch of England should not be. To no small extent, he is correct. The reader is aware, however, that Henry is intent upon justifying his right in having taken the throne from Richard and his heirs, and hence denigrates him, and that the need for justification arises from a nagging and persisting sense of his past malefactions.

For Henry, comfort and strength of mind are found in a Lancastrian ideal of kingship, and his own policy of aloofness has become the cornerstone of this ideal:

> Thus did I keep my person fresh and new,
> . . . .
> Ne'er seen but wond'red at, and so my state,
> Seldom but sumptuous, show'd like a feast
> And won by rareness such solemnity.
>
> [III.ii.55-59]

The ideal unfortunately has been built upon a calculated effort to assume a posture exactly the opposite of that of King Richard. Too mindful of Richard and his excesses, Henry has formulated for his Lancastrian heirs a cult of abstinence. "After the excesses of Richard's reign, the Lancastrians reject fatness and imprudence in both man and the commonwealth."[14] In this reaction, which becomes with Henry IV an overreaction, Richard's vengeance arrives at a subtlety not found in the repeated rebellions. Henry's overriding conviction that the usurpation was justified because of the self-demeaning conduct of Richard has brought him to the wrong concept of the ideal king. Had he not sought to rule by means of aloofness, had he been less inclined to keep his former supporters at a distance, had he preserved but a small portion of the comradeship or "vulgar company" of which he accuses Richard, the house of Lancaster might have been much less vulnerable to the charge of usurpation and hence to civic retributions. A doctrine of abstinence, if too highly valued, can be as destructive to a dynasty as can its opposite trait, excess.

Henry has thus been humbled by three forms of adversity: (1) the repeated rebellions against him; (2) his self-enforced habit of abstinence (an overreaction to Richard's mode of extravagance) and its effect of isolating him from his fellow men; and (3) the reprobate conduct of Prince Hal, whom he likens to Richard. Long conscious of the mildness of such punishment when measured against his "mistreadings" (an overt euphemism, since he dare not name his crimes against King Richard), he is to make his deathbed scene, years later, a kind of confessional, even though the emphasis of his words, addressed to Hal, is pragmatic. In the closing speech of *Richard II*, he had likened both Exton and, by implication, himself to Cain for their part in Richard's murder and had resolved to "wash this blood off from my guilty hand." It is fitting, therefore, that his final speech (*2 Hen 4*, IV.v.178-220) of his own two-part play should include a confession of his earlier crime, the usurpation; for introspection has taught him the wrongness of this act. Not only does he admit the "indirect crook'd ways" of his accession, but he speaks of "the soil of [my] achievement" and "an honour [the crown] snatch'd with boist'rous hand." And having advised Hal how to suppress the discontent of men opposed to the Lancastrian dynasty ("busy giddy minds / With foreign wars"), he is mindful that the usurpation has offended not only his fellow men but, much more importantly, God: "How I came by the crown, O God forgive." He knows that the four or five rebellions against him, as well as his recent fatal illness, are only a fraction of the punishment that is his due and that God has long withheld. Therefore, his last words spoken to Hal—the prayer that, God granting, Hal as king of England "may . . . in true peace live"— are not simply the fond gesture of a parent. Henry is, above all else, mindful of the biblical admonition— so often alluded to by churchmen and chroniclers—that God, at His pleasure, will visit the unabsolved crimes of the father upon the child (Exod. 20.5).

The Pope, we are told by the chronicler Robert Fabyan, had ordered Henry IV, who had asked his counsel, to do penance for having usurped the throne and for having murdered Richard II and had recommended, in particular, "contynuel prayer & suffragies of the churche."[15] The King did not carry out the terms of this penance. His son Henry V, however, who wished to free the souls of both Richard and his own father from purgatory, "in most habundaunt maner perfourmyd it: he buyldyd iii houses of relygyon."[16] Meanwhile, according to Hall and Holinshed, "[Henry V] caused the body of kyng Richard the second to be removed with all funerall pompes . . . from Langely to Westminster, where he was honorably enterred with Quene Anne his firste wife in a solempne toumbe . . . set up at the costes . . . of this noble prince kyng Henry."[17] Of this and other information supplied by Fabyan and

Hall, Shakespeare has made a reconstruction which points up much more emphatically the Lancastrian sense of guilt than do the pages of the chroniclers. In the quiet dawn just before the battle of Agincourt, Henry V soliloquizes:

> Not to-day, O Lord,
> O not to-day, think not upon the fault
> My father made in compassing the crown!
> I Richard's body have interrèd new,
> And on it have bestowed more contrite tears
> Than from it issued forced drops of blood;
> Five hundred poor I have in yearly pay,
> Who twice a day their wither'd hands hold up
> Toward heaven, to pardon blood; and I have built
> Two chantries, where the sad and solemn priests
> Sing still for Richard's soul.
>
> [*Hen 5*, IV.i.288-98]

This passage is Shakespeare's most complete statement of the Lancastrian dread of God's vengeance for the crimes committed by Henry Bolingbroke against King Richard. Nor are the plea to God to delay His vengeance and the elaborate emphasis on penance prompted entirely by the imminence of battle; as the context makes manifest, the atonement was begun at the outset of Henry V's reign, two years before Agincourt, and will be sustained until it has ended. A heartfelt repentance, however, is not to prove a sufficient payment for the murder of a divinely appointed king, whose throne has been usurped. At best, it might postpone that payment. The most significant statement of the soliloquy is Henry's plea that God "think not [today] upon the fault / My father made"; for it revitalizes the theme of inherited guilt, so forcibly stressed in the prophecies of *Richard II*, first by the King and then by Carlisle, both of whom foresaw, as I have shown in chapter 1, God's vengeance upon a later generation if Bolingbroke dare to ascend Richard's throne. Carlisle's warning against the usurpation and its dangers had reached its climax in a memorable statement, especially pertinent to later times: "Prevent it, resist it, let it not be so / Lest child, child's children, cry against you woe" (*R2*, IV.i.148-49). The apprehension of Henry (a "child") is doubly justified, for his death in the impending battle could spell defeat for the English army.

When Shakespeare wrote *Richard II*, he was certainly more mindful of the already written *Henry VI* plays than he was of the yet unwritten and probably unplanned *Henry IV* plays and *Henry V*. In consequence, *Richard II*, with its promises of God's vengeance upon later generations, is, in an important sense, more of a piece with the *Henry VI* plays than with the later three plays of its own tetralogy. The foreboding prophecies of *Richard II*, with their focus upon a third generation, were Shakespeare's method of justifying the tumult, brutality, and excessive bloodshed of the *Henry VI* plays, especially part 3; by establishing cause, prediction, and effect, he was able to provide these later plays with a relevance to past events and hence a substance, thus upgrading them as works of art. When he came to the writing of the intervening plays, in which the curse of inherited guilt, in conformance with historical sources, must remain unfulfilled, he was at pains to remind the audience, from time to time, that the prophecies of *Richard II* were not just theatrical ploys but had a substance as yet unrealized. Henry V's succinctly stated dread that God may be ready to strike, relative to the other indications of the delayed vengeance that I have cited, is the most evident link—and a very essential one—between the prophecies of *Richard II* and the turbulent bloodletting of the *Henry VI* plays, in particular the murders of three Lancastrian heirs, each of a different generation. Shakespeare, although he had no evidence from the Tudor chronicles that Henry V, at Agincourt, had expressed a fear of God's imminent judgment, has been careful to implant a reminder, at this critical point almost midway in the eight-part historical epic, that the theme of inherited guilt, as well as the dread of that guilt, is still a vital stimulus.

As the chroniclers available to Shakespeare attest, the naked fact of Richard's deposition and Bolingbroke's accession, and not the emotional response to them, was to engender a crucial issue over which, in the third generation, the Wars of the Roses were fought. The payment of blood had been evoked at the time of Richard's deposition and subsequent murder: "The citizens of Burdeaux [Richard's birthplace] toke this matter very sore . . . Besechyng God devoutly on their knees, to be the revenger and punisher of that detestable offence and notorius crime."[18] According to Hall, God responded (somewhat belatedly) to this prayer by imposing distrust and bloodshed upon the English people, for many of their parents had shared in Bolingbroke's crimes. Eighty-five years after Richard's death, at the time of the triumphant return of Henry Tudor from Bosworth to London, the people were to chant praises to God, "whiche had delivered them from miserable captivitie & restored them to liberty and fredome."[19] Almost a century of retribution had ended.

In the composition of *Richard II*, Shakespeare had been careful to establish the Tudor hypothesis, as he found it in both Hall and Holinshed, namely, that the payment for Richard's deposition and the unrightful accession of Bolingbroke is, as forecast in the play, the Wars of the Roses. The speaker, Carlisle, has been (as he reminds us) "stirred up by God":

> And if you crown him [Bolingbroke], let me prophesy—
> The blood of English shall manure the ground,
> . . . .
> And in this seat of peace tumultuous wars
> Shall kin with kin and kind with kind confound;
> . . . .
> O, if you raise this house against this house,
> It will the woefullest division prove
> That ever fell upon this cursed earth.
>   [*R2*, IV.i.136-37; 140-41; 145-47]

As payment for Bolingbroke's usurpation and his murder of Richard, the entire kingdom of England must undergo the punishment of God before it can be salved of its wounds. That interpretation derives from the chronicles of Hall and Holinshed as substantiated by modern critics, including M.M. Reese and Irving Ribner.[20] These critics and others, however, tend to focus on the deposition, which I believe can be justified by Richard's extravagant abuse of power,[21] and not on the usurpation, which supplanted Richard's line of heirs, as the crime to be avenged. Fifty years later, when British tempers had cooled, only the fact of the usurpation was to count, not the emotional biases engendered by it. Central to this fact was the neglecting of Richard's natural heir, at the time a child. This violation of a divine right, and not the deposition or murder of Richard, becomes in the mid-fifteenth century the crux of the confrontation between Lancaster and York. Importantly, the violation of a royal family's primogeniture was held to be the ultimate crime against God.

In act II of *1 Henry VI*, the principal seed that is to germinate ultimately into the Wars of the Roses is planted in the mind of young Richard Plantagenet. His dying uncle, Edmund Mortimer, Earl of March, tells him of the unhappy fate that has befallen his own right to the throne once held by Richard II. The pivotal point of the discussion (II.v.63-97) is the deposition of King Richard and the subsequent usurpation of the throne by Bolingbroke even though Mortimer (the younger and correct Mortimer this time) had the right of succession, which now belongs to young Richard, his nephew and heir to the dukedom of York. To the fact that he is heir (on his mother's side) to the Mortimer (unmarried and childless) who had been heir to Richard II, Richard, Duke of York, is to owe his substantial primogeniture, for on his father's side his claim in descent of Edward III is inferior to that of Henry VI. Once Henry's political favorites are "at jars" with the Lord Protector, York will be ready to proclaim his right to England's throne:

> Then will I raise aloft the milk-white rose,
> With whose sweet smell the air will be perfum'd,
> And in my standard bear the arms of York.
> [*2 Hen 6*, I.i.249-51]

Bolingbroke's usurpation—made possible, of course, by his dethronement of King Richard—has altered the course of history, as it was known to Shakespeare, far beyond what any act or decree might have done if Richard had remained on his throne. Had he continued to reign and had he not produced a male child, the younger Edmund Mortimer, the great grandson of Edward III, would have succeeded him as monarch. Whether the deposition (as some argue) or the usurpation is the central fact, the consequent rejection of the lawful claimant has thus, some fifty years later, propagated a crucial political confrontation. Shakespeare's Richard has foreseen the dark consequences of the fracture in primogeniture almost as clearly as has Carlisle. "God omnipotent," Richard had warned his enemies, when at Flint,

> . . . shall strike
> Your children yet unborn and unbegot
> That lift your vassal hands against my head
> And threat the glory of my precious crown.
>
> [III.iii.87-90]

These words sum up, in large measure, the legacy of inherited guilt bequeathed by the usurper Bolingbroke, but made possible by the intolerable autocracy and self-indulgence of Richard II, to England of the mid-fifteenth century.

FIVE

The Later Gloucesters:
Humphrey and Richard

Among the titles of English peers, none has been more ill omened than that of Gloucester. When King Edward IV, in the last of the *Henry VI* plays, presents the dukedom of that title to his brother Richard, he is met with a sharp retort: "Let me be duke of Clarence . . . / For Gloucester's dukedom is too ominous" (*3 Hen 6*, II.vi.106-107). Richard is mindful of the unhappy fates of two former Gloucesters: Thomas of Woodstock and, more recently, Duke Humphrey. Indeed, of Duke Humphrey's sudden demise, almost certainly by means of murder, Edward Hall has written: "The name and title of Gloucester hath been unfortunate and unluckie to diverse, whiche . . . have been erected . . . to that stile and dignitie, as Hugh Spencer, Thomas of Woodstocke . . . and this duke Humphrey."[1] The trait of dogged aggressiveness, especially in matters of politics, appears to have been the common, and ultimately mortal, abnormality of each of the Gloucesters: Thomas and Humphrey, no less than Richard, accumulate a formidable array of noble-born enemies. The master politician, however, both of English history and Shakespeare's dramaturgy, is Richard of Gloucester. Holinshed has provided a concise glimpse of this man's irrepressible craft: once Richard had observed that the crown was within his reach, he took delight in the art of "a deepe dissembler" who could "kisse whome he thought to kill."[2] Had Duke Humphrey (uncle of Henry VI) been as clever a "dissembler" as was Richard and had he remained alive but a few more years, the latter might have found no opportunity to seize the crown.

Of the sons of Henry IV, the most militant and, as some historians hold, the most cantankerous was Humphrey, Duke of Gloucester. The historian Charles Oman, basing his facts largely upon C. Kingsford's *Chronicles of London* (1905), a collection of minor chronicles of the fifteenth century, as well as upon the *Proceedings of the Privy Council*,[3] ar-

rives at some unpleasant conclusions about the character of Duke Humphrey. Oman holds him to have been a man of "selfish, arrogant, and
captious temper" who, at the time of his appointment to Lord Protector, "had already roused many enemies."[4] A second statement by
Oman, although having some truth, also shows a twist of illogic and
bias: Humphrey "had built up for himself a party in the city of London,
apparently by demagogic arts. It was his affability to the commons . . .
which won him the ill-deserved title of 'Good Duke Humphrey.'"[5]
On one major point Oman is in agreement with the sixteenth-century
chroniclers Edward Hall and Raphael Holinshed, who also attest to
Humphrey's popularity with the commons of London; but neither Hall
nor Holinshed comes to Oman's conclusion that the title of "Good
Duke Humphrey" was "ill deserved." Hall, in fact, praises the capable
administration of Humphrey: he "had valeantly and pollitiquely by the
space of XXV yeres governed this Realme."[6] Shakespeare, of course,
owes his debt to Hall and Holinshed, and not to Oman, in the writing
of the *Henry VI* plays. In *2 Henry VI*, somewhat at odds with Oman's
portrait, Humphrey emerges as both the pivotal and the most stolid
figure in the political confrontation. His very presence assures the stability of young Henry VI's kingdom; his untimely death opens the way
to the Wars of the Roses.

A strong foundation of truth underlies Oman's statement that concludes his unfavorable account of Humphrey, Duke of Gloucester: "The
removal of the duke was, in reality, a very unwise and shortsighted
step. . . . His place as first prince of the blood was taken by his cousin,
Richard Duke of York."[7] Of this fact Hall, as well as Holinshed and
Shakespeare, was aware: as long as Henry VI remained childless, Humphrey was the King's nearest kin of blood. But something more than
the technical matter of Humphrey's removal from the line of succession
was involved. At stake (in the judgment of the Tudor chroniclers) was
the security and wise direction of young Henry's kingdom. Hall has
stated the matter concisely: "If this Duke had lyved, the Duke of Yorke
durst not have made title to the crowne: if this Duke had livyd, the
nobles had not conspired against the king, nor yet the commons had not
rebelled: if this Duke had lyved, the house of Lancastre had not been
defaced and destroyed, which thynges hapned all contrary by the de-
struccion of this good man."[8] In short, Duke Humphrey, as he had
become known to Shakespeare, was held to be a man of integrity and

strength of mind, not merely a person next of blood to the King. His death is not only to be avenged; it is to result in a vacuum of authority utterly detrimental to the house of Lancaster and damaging to England at large. It is to have two significant effects: a private one and a public one, in both of which God's judgments will be apparent.

In the opening scene of *2 Henry VI*, the Marquess of Suffolk, who has bartered the English territories of Maine and Anjou in exchange for Henry's French bride Margaret, is dubbed a duke by the delighted monarch. Turning to the peers, Humphrey, Duke of Gloucester, storms in rightful indignation:

> O peers of England! Shameful is this league,
> Fatal this marriage, cancelling your fame,
> . . . .
> Razing the characters of your renown,
> Defacing monuments of conquer'd France,
> Undoing all, as all had never been!
>
> [*2 Hen 6*, I.i.93-98]

With this statement Shakespeare puts in motion the political confrontation of the play. Suffolk, whom Humphrey terms "the new-made duke who rules the roast," together with the Dukes of Buckingham and Somerset, stands for expediency. Humphrey, in whom Tillyard (using his Machiavellian formula) has observed the strength of the lion and the loyalty of the pelican, but no element of the fox,[9] is the champion of an England strong both at home and on the Continent.

The doom of Humphrey, masterminded by Suffolk and Cardinal Beaufort, is shortly to be sealed. Humphrey's duchess, Eleanor Cobham, on the charge of having sought to destroy the King, is arrested and exiled to the Isle of Man. In consequence, Duke Humphrey, although innocent of complicity, is brought into disgrace. Young Henry VI, compelled by circumstance and the imperious presence of his Queen, commands his uncle to hand over his staff of office: "Henry will to himself / Protector be." Once the lion of England but now politically incapacitated, Duke Humphrey finds himself surrounded by a snarling wolf pack: Suffolk, the Cardinal, Buckingham, and even Richard, Duke of York, who is an unlikely ally except for his well-kept secret of obtaining the throne. What Humphrey observes, before he is led off to prison

and subsequent murder by apparent strangulation, is an England beset
by transverse patterns of self-interest; he turns to Henry VI and sums
up the anarchy that has now beset the English court:

> Thus is the shepherd beaten from thy side,
> And wolves are gnarling who will gnaw thee first.
> Ah! that my fear were false! ah! that it were!
> For, good King Henry, thy decay, I fear.
>
> [III.i.189-94]

At times cantankerous, especially when crossed by Cardinal Beaufort,
and openly disdainful of the oily self-interest of Suffolk, Duke Humphrey is no paragon of diplomacy. His strength is his iron-minded
presence; it has for years held in check his antagonists' personal ambitions which, unleashed as they are now, are to destroy the house of Lancaster. Humphrey has been the final bulwark against God's inevitable
retribution in behalf of King Richard. The retribution had been forecast,
as I have shown, by both the King and Carlisle in *Richard II*, and sixteen
years later, the inevitability of it, often alluded to, was to be reaffirmed,
at Agincourt, by Henry V:

> Not to-day, O Lord,
> O, not to-day, think not upon the fault
> My father made in compassing the crown!
>
> [*Hen 5*, IV.i.288-90]

Henry V and, more recently, his youngest brother, Humphrey, have
shared a common responsibility: to hold off God's judgment upon their
house for their father's crimes. Concluding his comments on the consequences of Humphrey's death, Hall has written: "God knoweth what
he [God] had predestinate & what he had ordained before":[10] the evident suggestion is that the demise of Humphrey is essential to a larger
plan withheld by God.

The removal of Humphrey (as treated by Shakespeare) has opened a
conspicuous breach in the office of authority. Even before he is actually
murdered, although he has been imprisoned, both the Cardinal and Suffolk take on themselves the function of self-appointed Protectors. Their
two blunders are so asinine as to suggest that God has blinded them to

reality. To have York out of way, the Cardinal grants him the regency of Ireland and, with it, an army. Humphrey, whose virtues have been those of a statesman and not a politician, would assuredly have observed the stupidity of such a grant. York, in soliloquy, is prompt to grasp the circumstance of his advantage:

> Well, nobles, well, 'tis politicly done
> To send me packing with a host of men.
> . . . .
> 'Twas men I lack'd, and you will give them me:
> I take it kindly; yet be well assur'd
> You put sharp weapons in a madman's hands.
>
> [*2 Hen 6*, III.i.341-42; 345-47]

The assignment to Ireland has thus become, for York, a politically strategic windfall. Without it, he would have remained powerless.

The second major blunder is shortly to surface, immediately after the murder of Humphrey. Suffolk, who has plotted the murder with the assistance and encouragement of the Cardinal and Queen Margaret, has thoughtlessly underestimated the reaction of the commoners. Richard Neville, Earl of Warwick, breaks upon the presence of King Henry VI:

> It is reported, mighty sovereign,
> That good Duke Humphrey traitorously is murd'red
> By Suffolk and the Cardinal Beaufort's means.
> The commons, like an angry hive of bees
> That want their leader, scatter up and down
> And care not who they sting in his revenge.
>
> [III.ii.122-27]

Like Warwick, the mob is anxious to "do some service [for] Duke Humphrey's ghost" (III.ii.231) and that service is the immediate death or exile of the Queen's favorite, Suffolk.

Holinshed, in a paraphrase of Edward Hall, has written: "The decaie of the house of Lancaster . . . of likelihood had not chanced if this duke [Humphrey] had lived. . . . This is the opinion of men, but Gods judgements are unsearchable, against whose decree and ordinance prevaileth no human counsell."[11] The idea that the "unsearchable" judgment of God is poised to assert itself and thus to bring about "the decaie of the house of Lancaster," even if Humphrey were not dead, and that God will, in the meantime, make judgment in behalf of Humphrey is affirmed in the play by young King Henry VI:

> Some violent hands were laid on Humphrey's life!
> If my suspect be false, forgive me, God;
> For judgment only doth belong to Thee.
>
> [III.ii.138-40]

In stating that judgment belongs to God and only to God, Henry has voiced a basic philosophy of the English chroniclers and, to a very large extent, that of Shakespeare's serious plays: the controlling destiny—both in individual matters and those of nations—was thought by most men of knowledge to be the "unsearchable" judgment of God, "against whose will," as Hall has stressed, "avayleth no stryvinge."[12] In matters of homicide, especially those in which the law may be insufficient or unenforceable, Shakespeare's thesis is perhaps best stated by John of Gaunt: "God's is the quarrel; . . . Let heaven revenge" (*R2*, I.ii.37, 40), for God, and not man, was held to be the absolute Judge and Avenger.

The judgment of God descends first upon the Cardinal and then upon the Duke of Suffolk and, in each instance, attests to the "unsearchable" and yet positive character of that judgment. When we first hear of the Cardinal's ailment, he is said to be tormented by the painful "secrets of his overcharged soul." The nature of the ailment is not unlike an infirmity that the Elizabethan pathologist Timothy Bright has described: "A molestation . . . riseth from conscience, condemning the guiltie soule of those ingraven lawes of nature, which no man is voide of."[13] To the medieval and Renaissance mind, the "lawes of nature" were identical with the dictates of God, a serious breach of which might become mentally and spiritually unbearable. Sister Mary Bonaventure Mroz, in her work on medieval vengeance, confirms this notion: "Human nature . . . may, by God's ordination, wreak its own vengeance," ordinarily by means of an "accusing conscience."[14] Shakespeare shows the conscience-torn Cardinal to the audience in act III, scene iii. Bedridden, he is in a state of frenzy, "blaspheming God and cursing men on earth"; meantime, he imagines that he is haunted both by the image of death and by "Duke Humphrey's ghost" with its hair, as he supposes, raised "upright, / Like lime-twigs set to catch my wingèd soul" (*2 Hen 6*, III.iii.15-16). The fact that he is haunted by the ghost of Humphrey, actually an illusion, attests to the power of the dead Humphrey over the consciences of those who have murdered him. Although God has a highly important role in retribution as treated by Shakespeare, He cannot be objectified as readily as can the dead man who demands that retribution. The episode of the Cardinal's death attests to the joint power of God's dictates and the ineradicable fear of the object (in this instance, Humphrey's ghost) most symbolic of their transgression.

Of the Duke of Suffolk's death, Holinshed has written in a paraphrase of Hall: "Gods justice would not that so ungratious a person should so escape."[15] In Shakespeare's play, as in Hall and Holinshed, Suffolk never reaches the place of exile for which he has set out; while en route by ship to France, he is captured by a man-of-war, historically owned by the Duke of Exeter, "Constable of the Towre," and taken to Dover Beach. The man-of-war's lieutenant, mindful that Suffolk "smil'dst at good Duke Humphrey's death," orders him decapitated. In this act, the lieutenant, who argues his complete loyalty to Henry VI's England (IV.i.71-103) and scorns those who have betrayed it, has performed a duty both as a public servant and as an instrument of God. The medievalist Mroz, in her study *Divine Vengeance*, confirms the right of the fifteenth-century public officer to avenge a murdered man: "Public magistrates, wielding the delegated authority of the Almighty, are recognized as the foremost human agents of divine vengeance."[16] Among recent critics, H.A. Kelly sustains my general viewpoint: he sees the deaths of both the Cardinal and Suffolk as an effect of "the punishing hand of God."[17]

The most complete statement of the principle behind the deaths of Cardinal Beaufort and Suffolk is that of E.M.W. Tillyard: "The judgment of God, invoked by Henry VI, is quick in striking two of Gloucester's murderers."[18] The principle of invocation, judgment, and retribution, applied by Tillyard to Humphrey's murder, is to have, as an effect of that murder, a more comprehensive application. Upon the first report of Humphrey's death, the Cardinal had feigned his innocence and, making use of a ready-at-hand idiom, explained the death as an effect of "God's secret judgment" (III.ii.31). In attempting to gloss over the murder, he may have spoken more truly than he thought. If God is to work retribution upon England for Bolingbroke's double trespass of usurpation and murder, then it becomes fundamental to God's intent that Duke Humphrey be removed from his high office. Without him, and only then, can the house of Lancaster be made vulnerable to the now unavoidable crisis of Richard of York's claim to the throne.

On an ethical basis only, Humphrey may seem undeserving of being struck down, in the prime of life, by God. But if his untimely death is intended by God, there is a moral justification: the usurpation of the throne by his father, Henry IV, has not been expiated. All four of Henry IV's sons died young, perhaps by God's plan, but none so violently as Humphrey, who is the last to perish. Fulfilling the theme of inherited guilt, the remaining descendants of the male line stemming from Henry IV are to come to violent ends: Henry VI is murdered in the Tower of London, and meanwhile, but of the fourth generation, Edward, Prince of Wales, is butchered by the Yorkists on the battlefield at Tewksbury. To the medieval mind, these deaths—in many quarters at least—were held to be signs of God's wrath against the house of Lancaster. Some fifty years earlier, had not the "citezens" of an entire city—that of English-held Bordeaux—petitioned "God devoutly on their knees to be the revenger and punisher" of those who had deposed and murdered King Richard II? In a medieval frame of reference the answer to this petition—if there is a precise answer—was to be the Wars of the Roses, which brought defeat to the house of the usurper: "Thei shal knowe that I am the Lord when I shal laie my vengeance upon them."[19] The house of Lancaster, for defying God, must be humbled.

Shakespeare, in his version of the Wars of the Roses, has implanted the strong implication that Richard, Duke of York, not only seeks the throne, to which he holds the claim of primogeniture, but also, together with his sons, is intent on avenging the wrongs done another Plantagenet, Richard II. The patriotic lieutenant who orders Suffolk's execution speaks, apparently for Shakespeare, of an important effect of Duke Humphrey's death:

> And now the house of York—thrust from the crown
> By shameful murder of a guiltless king [Richard II]
> And lofty proud encroaching tyranny—
> Burns with revenging fire.
>
> [IV.i.94-97]

Freed from constraint by Humphrey's death, the house of York (such is the implication of this speech) is eager to act, collectively at first, as the avenging agent of God's long-withheld punishment upon the house of Lancaster. Its purpose is both pragmatic and punitive.

That Shakespeare looked upon the Wars of the Roses as an instrument of God is, I believe, explicit within the context of the double tetralogy. Not only have Richard II, at Flint, and the Bishop of Carlisle, at Westminster Hall, the latter by his own testimony divinely motivated, foretold that "God omnipotent" is to punish Bolingbroke's usurpation by imposing "tumultuous wars," which will "confound kin with kin," upon a later generation; even more explicit are pronouncements, in *Henry V* and *2 Henry VI*, that war—whether foreign or civil—is an instrument of God's judgment upon wicked men. In a carefully articulated statement, Henry V at Agincourt has enunciated, for Shakespeare, an important function of war: "Now, if these men have defeated the law and escaped native punishment, though they outstrip men, they have no wings to fly from God: war is His beadle, war is His vengeance" (*Hen 5*, IV.i.158-62). In *2 Henry VI*, at the outset of the Wars of the Roses, we are to find a very similar statement. Mindful of Bolingbroke's usurpation, Shakespeare's audience and today's informed reader are of one opinion: the time is now ripe for God's punishment of that usurpation. What then of the statement made at the outset of the Wars of the Roses—at St. Albans? Young Clifford, in an attempt (however vain) to restore the battle courage of his fellow Lancastrians, invokes war: "O war, thou son of hell, Whom angry heavens do make their minister" (V.ii.33-34). His identification of "war" as the "minister" of the "angry heavens" is, in terms of meaning, identical with Henry V's statement that "war is [God's] beadle"; in both statements, war has been ascribed a divine and punitive instrumentality. Having established war as the instrument of an "angry" God at St. Albans, Shakespeare does not retract that impression, for the blood of ensuing battles is likewise testimony of the divine anger. The Wars of the Roses, on Shakespeare's evidence, may be understood as the instrument (other than the human agent) through which God has chosen to punish the Lancastrian usurpers.

The Wars of the Roses, as treated by Shakespeare, are to become, at Wakefield and Tewksbury, an arena of vengeance and unwarranted bloodshed. In Shakespeare's *Henry VI* plays, parts 2 and 3, out of sheer malice and sometimes in the name of God, the two Cliffords, young Rutland, Richard Duke of York, Edward Prince of Wales, and ultimately King Henry VI are not merely slain; they are ignominiously butchered. This type of bloodshed has been termed "the revenge of passion" and contrasts with orthodox vengeance, which was held to be "a vindication of God's honor against sin."[20] As delineated by Shakespeare in *3 Henry VI*, the avengers, in self-exaltation and undisciplined brutality, call to mind Timothy Bright's victims of "choler adust," who are possessed by "rage, revenge, and furie."[21] Denuded of restraint and reason, the participants of Shakespeare's play are self-degraded into animalism—part of the long-deferred punishment, as implied by Shakespeare, for the spilling of King Richard's blood. Meanwhile, out of the animosities and the bloodshed of the Wars of the Roses, and spawned by that discord, emerges the last of the controversial Gloucesters, ultimately to become the third and last Yorkist king, Richard III.

To an Elizabethan audience, mindful of the dogmas of the times, the eleven murders committed or superintended by Richard of Gloucester were certain to demand the retribution of God upon the murderer. This is a viewpoint eventually grasped by Richard, but not until he has found in the art of murder a boisterous and seemingly unparalleled delight. The first victim, Edward, Prince of Wales, is "pitiously manquelled" at Tewksbury by Richard and his two older brothers. Hall and Holinshed, in their chronicles, behind which stands Thomas More's *History of Richard III*, attest to the wrath of God which, as customary, is held to be inevitable: "The bitternesse of which murder, some of the actors, . . . in their latter dayes, tasted and assayed by the very rod of Justice and punishment of God."[22]

Richard's next victim, whom he impetuously dogs down in the Tower of London, as depicted by Shakespeare, is Henry VI, who has been deposed. Once Henry has prophesied, in the context of Richard's substantial ill fame, the outrages he is yet to commit and has concluded that all England "shall rue the day that ever thou wast born," Richard in indignation retorts: "I'll hear no more. Die, prophet, in thy speech. / [Stabs him] / For this, among the rest, was I ordain'd" (*3 Hen 6*, V.vi.57-58). The word "ordain'd," as I noted in my introduction, is used by Shakespeare—especially in the *Henry VI* plays—with God as the understood agent. In light of the prophecies in *Richard II* (both the King's and Carlisle's) which have foretold God's vengeance on the usurping house of Lancaster in the third generation, it would cut the grain of Shakespeare's logic, I believe, to question Richard's claim that he is a divinely ordained scourge, for he emerges at exactly the right time. Of the victims included "among the rest," he has recently had a part in the murder of Henry's Lancastrian heir, Edward, and, in the future, will murder those men who are to come under Queen Margaret's curse. Undoubtedly, Shakespeare has equipped Richard with the claim of a divine ordination to kill other men for the purpose of expelling any misgivings among his audience as to the hunchback's part in God's design, which is to punish not only the house of Lancaster but also that of York; for in its acts of perjury and in the bloodiness of its methods in war, it too has offended God. In the meantime—in the historical accounts—Richard's murder of Henry VI is to expose him, in turn, to certain retribution: "Bothe the murtherer [of this holy man] and the consenter [Richard also?] had condign and not undeserved punishment, for their bloudy stroke and butcherly act."[23] Unsure of who struck the death blow, Hall has affirmed that "constant fame" suspected Richard, Duke of Gloucester.

Standing over the corpse of Henry VI, Richard ponders his next murder, the style of which, like those that follow, will reflect less of the butcher and more of the Machiavellian and will thus fulfill his earlier resolve: "I'll set the murderous Machiavel to school" (III.ii.198). His brother Clarence, who, like Henry VI and Prince Edward, comes between Richard and the throne, will be the next to be dispatched, but with craft and subtlety:

> Clarence, beware; thou keep'st me from the light,
> But I will sort a pitchy day for thee;
> For I will buzz abroad such prophecies
> That Edward shall be fearful of his life;
> And then to purge his fear, I'll be thy death.
>
> [V.vi.84-88]

Richard's high ambition, which (supernaturally devised or not) is to enhance his effectiveness as a scourge, does not, in his early murders, put a clog upon his innate delight in the complex skills of knavery. To muffle the Duke of Clarence once and for all, Richard has cunningly circulated a prophecy of dubious origin. At the outset of the play *Richard*

III, Clarence complains that a wizard has told Edward IV that "by G / His issue disinherited should be," and concludes: "And, for my name of George begins with G, / It follows in his thought that I am he" (*R3*, I.i.56-69). Once Clarence is "mew'd up," his almost immediate murder is to bring to light the Machiavellian irony of his brother Richard, deftly chronicled by Hall: "That Prophesie lost not hys effect, when after kyng Edward, Glocester usurped his kyngdome."[24]

Nor is Richard's confidence that an intemperate diet, as well as lust, will bring about King Edward's untimely death to be disappointed. His next step is to be named Lord Protector in behalf of the new king, thirteen-year-old Edward V. The elimination of the Queen Dowager's kin, who oppose him, hardly adds up to "breathing time" for Richard. Nor does Richard of Gloucester spare a close friend: even before the Scrivener has had time to copy down the indictments, and hence without trial, Lord Hastings has been beheaded. Richard, no longer the butcher, has emerged as the master of Machiavellian flexibility.

Because a number of critics have pointed out the Providential character of Queen Margaret's curses—although some have seen nemesis and not the Old Testament God as the avenger she invokes—I shall pause only briefly on the import of these curses. Among recent critics identifying Richard of Gloucester as the agent, or scourge, who executes the curses on Rivers, Hastings, and other Yorkists for their crimes against Margaret's house of Lancaster are Moody E. Prior, although with reservations,[25] and Edward I. Berry. Whereas Prior's views (pro and con) are conventional, Berry presents a new focus: "Margaret's presence . . . determines . . . the temporal orientation of the play, for it is through her prophecies that the crimes of the [late] civil wars reach out to destroy the future [of the Yorkist dynasty]."[26] A bit earlier, he remarks: "As each curse [by Margaret] is fulfilled, it becomes increasingly clear that Richard is executing a will greater than his own (and too great to be Margaret's either), the will of Providence."[27] Of the Queen Dowager's kin, mentioned in the preceding paragraph, Richard has dispatched Rivers, Grey, and Vaughan. Margaret's curses, to whose fulfillment she invokes the judgment of God (I.iii.212-14), fall also upon the sons of Edward IV, for they must pay for their father's crimes, including his murder of the Lancastrian heir, Edward. All those that she marks for untimely death (whether in her curses of I.iii or in her later accounting of those curses in IV.iv, or both) are dispatched at Richard's command, for he must not die, she argues, until his "sins be [so] ripe" that "heaven [will] hurl down" upon him, as his desert, its most "grievous plague" (I.iii.217-21). Richard is thus kept free to exercise "the will of Providence" against his fellow Yorkists and, as God's scourge, so to implicate himself in crime that his payment, even within this world, will exceed that of any one of his victims. Such, I believe, are the mechanics of Providence within the play, at least up to the moment that the divine law, through Richard's "accusing conscience," demands its payment of him.

Richard's eighth victim is Queene Anne, a drawback to the holding of his plundered throne. Upon her last stage appearance, at the time she is summoned to her husband's coronation, Anne has made a pathetic but significant observation, which gives a hint of the type of death that awaits her and, more important, a telltale glimpse of what has begun to cast a pall over Richard's mind:

> For never yet one hour in his bed
> Did I enjoy the golden dew of sleep,
> But with his timorous dreams was still awak'd.
>
> [IV.i.83-85]

The reader is surprised to learn that Richard, until now the paragon of brazen confidence, has suffered even a qualm of conscience, much less highly disturbed dreams. As will be evident near the end of the play—and prior to that come other hints—there are, in a sense, two Richards: the man of impetuous craft and the privately haunted man.

Even before Anne is reported dead, Richard, now king, has dealt with two more victims, the deposed Edward V and young Richard, Duke of York, of both of whom he is the guardian. From the moment that their deaths are confirmed, if not shortly before, Richard's agility of mind, and the gusto of his verbal darts and retorts, hang fire. The zest is gone, except fitfully. The scene in which Richard, mindful that he must strengthen his position through a second marriage, asks the Queen Dowager for the hand of the princess Elizabeth is intended, with its stichomythia and ritual balance, as a piece that counterpoises his glib and supremely confident wooing of Anne in the second scene of the play. But the tone is markedly altered, although the situation is every bit as challenging. In the former instance he woos the widow of a prince

whom he has slain; in the later wooing scene, he asks for the hand of
a young lady whose two brothers have been murdered at his command.
In the scene with Anne, Richard of Gloucester has surmounted every
obstacle: Anne speaks of the murdered Henry VI, her father-in-law:
"Thou mayst be damned for that wicked deed! / O! he was gentle,
mild, and virtuous!" (I.ii.103-104). Richard retorts: "The fitter for the
King of Heaven that hath him" (I.ii.105). And when Anne accuses him
of having slain both her father-in-law and her husband: "Thou wast the
cause and most accurs'd effect" (I.ii.120), Richard rises to a transcen-
dent spirit not unlike that of the Marlovian superman:

> Your beauty was the cause of that effect—
> Your beauty that did haunt me in my sleep
> To undertake the death of all the world
> That I might live one hour in your sweet bosom.
>
> [I.ii.121-24]

The enraptured spirit finds a marked contrast in the labored courtship
of the later scene; Richard commands no deft repartee but finds himself
most often on the defensive. Queen Elizabeth speaks of her daughter:
"Nay, then indeed she cannot choose but hate thee / Having bought
love with such a bloody spoil" (IV.iv.289-90). Richard responds, as
elsewhere in the scene, apologetically:

> Look, what is done cannot be now amended.
> Men shall deal unadvisedly sometimes,
> Which after-hours give leisure to repent.
>
> [IV.iv.291-93]

He then withdraws into sophistic quiddities:

> If I have kill'd the issue of your womb,
> To quicken your increase, I will beget
> Mine issue of your blood upon your daughter.
> . . . .
> Your children were vexation to your youth;
> But mine shall be a comfort to your age.
>
> [IV.iv.296-98; 305-306]

In the second courtship scene, Richard is obliged to rely on carefully chosen patterns of logic, more like the schoolmaster than the buoyant adventurer of the scene with Anne. Carefully constructed logic is a poor substitute for spontaneous response if a man is to have a woman's admiration. Richard cannot say, as he does after his courtship of Anne: "Was ever woman in this humour woo'd? / Was ever woman in this humour won?" (I.ii.227-28). He departs from the second courtship scene with a vague promise of marriage which is not to be kept, nor does this outcome surprise the reader. The self-styled "jolly lover" is no longer the master of charming impudence.

Immediately before the second courtship scene, Richard's mother, the Duchess of York, has put a hostile curse upon him as he prepares for war against Henry of Richmond:

> Therefore take with thee my most grievous curse
> Which, in the day of battle, tire thee more
> Than all the complete armour that thou wear'st!
>
> [IV.iv.187-89]

To this and a second denunciation by his mother, Richard is uncharacteristically silent; for the first time in the play he has no retort at hand. In the episode immediately after the labored courtship scene, he reflects an unaccustomed preoccupation of mind: he issues orders to Catesby and Ratcliff almost perfunctorily and then must either be reminded as to why he gave the order or else, as with Ratcliff, forgets what he had in mind. Having arrived at Bosworth and slumped at a table inside his tent, he asks for a bowl of wine and then explains his need for it: "I have not that alacrity of spirit / Nor cheer of mind that I was wont to have" (V.iii.73-74). His oppression is, to say the least, uncharacteristic of his famed galvanic image.

What do all these episodes—the curse to which no retort is made, the sluggish attempt at courtship, the forgetting of orders, and the need of a large portion of wine as a stimulant—add up to? John Palmer has noted the "decline in [Richard's] genius for decisive action" and adds that whatever task remains after the two young princes have been murdered "must necessarily be something of an anti-climax."[28] This observation is sensible, but in view of the critical task that awaits King Richard III—namely, the military confrontation with the Earl of Richmond—it is difficult to accept the idea that all obligations subsequent to the murder of the princes are anticlimax. But Palmer is right in one respect: from the time of the death of the two princes, Richard no longer has the capacity to lift himself to the crisis at hand. His total want of confidence and gusto during the second courtship scene prepares the reader for his failure at Bosworth Field. The reader has become accustomed to Richard's capability of thrusting aside the most difficult obstacles, and without a prior humiliation, his defeat by Richmond would strain credulity.

Queen Anne has mentioned that Richard does not sleep well: he suffers, even before he has become king, from "timorous dreams." In the background, in contrast to the galvanic cutthroat known to us, there appears to be a second Richard far from indifferent to the crimes that the cutthroat has committed. Publicly Richard has the politician's knack of putting on a front: in a moment of crisis he can casually compliment the strawberry patch of a colleague. But are we to judge the entire man by his public image? Are we right in judging a U.S. senator or a British member of Parliament, in entirety, by what he says or does for the public's edification? If we did so, almost certainly we would come to wrong conclusions, in some instances quite flattering ones. In Shakespeare's play, we learn almost nothing about Richard of Gloucester's private life; even his soliloquies, unlike Hamlet's, are obvious glosses and have the purpose of illuminating the image and not the inner man. Therefore, what little his wife, Anne, tells us about him cannot properly be ignored. Her evidence is our only glimpse of the private man, who is characterized as a poor sleeper unnerved by bad dreams.

The dire effect of the two princes' murders upon the historical King Richard, as first recorded by Thomas More and then repeated almost verbatim by Hall and Holinshed, tends to confirm the hypothesis that Richard was not bereft of conscience: "I have harde by credible reporte [John Morton, Bishop of Ely] . . . that after this abhominable deed [was] done, he never was quiet in his mynde. . . . he toke evill reste on nightes . . . , rather slombred then slept, troubled with fearefull dreams. . . . so was his restlesse harte continually tossed and tombled with . . . remembraunce of his abhominable murther and execrable tyrannye."[29] Aware of this passage found in Hall's account, Shakespeare, with his understanding of human nature, has chosen to show that Richard had troublesome dreams even before the time of his most "abhominable murther." How much worse, Shakespeare suggests, was to be the torment once he has committed that most atrocious and next to last of his crimes.

Irving Ribner has contended that "Richard III could not be exhibited on the Tudor stage as other than totally evil."[30] In contrast, the Tudor chroniclers, as I have just noted, provide him with a strong element of conscience, a man's last frontier against unbridled barbarism. In the murder of the two princes, the Richard of Shakespeare's play has crossed this frontier and then has pulled back in a stunned and, as I have suggested, indecisive frame of mind. For the first time a murder has had an observable effect upon him; he has lost, because of shock and fatigue, what has been most fundamental to his political art: his remarkable control of the crisis of the moment. This loss is evident in that comparatively tiny episode of his forgetting either intended or actual orders, as given to Catesby and Ratcliff. It is also apparent in the other episodes that I have just outlined, for in none of them does he exercise the self-possession that has become his mark.

When Richard, upon dreaming of the Ghosts, identifies conscience as a "coward," his evident meaning is that, by force of conscience, a man is shaken with fear and agitation, for among the Elizabethans the conscience was thought to be structured by God and, of itself, could not be cowardly. Speaking of conscience, Timothy Bright contended that a sense of "guiltiness" comes not from the "breach of humane lawes . . . but of the Law divine, & the censure," he proceeds, "[is] executed with the hand of God."[31] Ten years later, in 1596, the theologian William Perkins was to formulate a more detailed analysis of the conscience than had Bright: the "conscience is of a divine nature, and is a thing placed by God in the middest betweene him and man, as an arbitratour . . . to pronounce either with man or against man unto God."[32] To this, he adds: "The binder of [a man's] conscience . . . is the word of God, written in the booke of the old & new Testament," and he concludes: "God is the onely lord of conscience: because he once created it, and he alone governes it."[33] Because it is of an "accusing and condemning" nature, Perkins later informs us, the conscience can "stirre up sundrie passions," in particular "feare," but also "desperation" and "perturbation."[34] The violator of God's law, should he escape other punishment, was therefore held to be subject to the lash of his own "accusing" conscience, for it was constructed of the biblical commandments, most of them in the form of prohibitions. Only after Richard's vision of his victims' ghosts will he become aware—and his reaction can hardly be judged otherwise—of the cause of the oppression that has overlaid his accustomed "cheer of mind."

The Ghosts of the eleven murdered persons, which include that of Buckingham and appear to Richard on the eve of the battle at Bosworth Field, have been variously interpreted. In a recent interpretation Manfred Weidhorn has stressed their function of recapitulation.[35] To Weidhorn they also symbolize "the judgment of God" upon Richard.[36] Their capacity to recapitulate is not insignificant. Any audience is hard put to recall precisely all the persons murdered by Richard, and of course, two of them have attained potential ghosthood at the close of *3 Henry VI*. E.M.W. Tillyard has observed that the Ghosts are "essentially of the Morality pattern." His suggestion that they are prepared for by Henry of Richmond's "solemn prayer" makes more understandable the blessings directed to him while they focus, alternately, their condemnations upon the sleeping Richard. On "the Morality pattern," Tillyard elaborates: "Res Publica or England is the hero. . . . Each Ghost as it were gives his vote for heaven, Lancaster and York being at last unanimous."[37] To Tillyard and Weidhorn the Ghosts are apparently dramatic artifices, since neither critic tries to explain them in terms of natural phenomena. John Palmer identifies the Ghosts as effects of Richard's conscience and explains why this is so: "Conscience has crept upon him in his sleep and afflicted him grievously."[38] This explanation, supported by Richard's outcry upon conscience when he awakens, fits the interpretation which I have so far given: for a long time, historically two years, Richard has been a victim of "timorous dreams." Like Macbeth, he has not the hardness of mind to withstand the psychic consequences of his crimes. Awakening, after the last Ghost has departed, he makes an effort to escape the horror of the dream; with his former gusto he cries out: "Give me another horse. Bind up my wounds." But he cannot escape, horse or no horse. His conscience demands that he pause and reconsider his crimes; he finds himself powerless in the presence of the accuser: "O coward conscience, how dost thou afflict me!" And a few moments later:

> My conscience hath a thousand several tongues,
> And every tongue brings in a several tale,
> And every tale condemns me for a villain.
>
> [V.iii.193-95]

What Palmer has neglected is Henry of Richmond's dream. Can a man of good conscience experience a vision of ghosts, in particular those of persons largely unknown to him?

Most of the dreams in Shakespeare's serious plays are prophetic while at the same time fitted to both present circumstance and character. In this sense they combine an ancient concept with contemporary principles. Among the ancient Hebrews, dreams were customarily thought to come from God, and likewise their interpretations. Of that most famous dream, the twofold dream of Pharaoh, the divinely inspired Joseph explains: "God hathe shewed unto Pharaoh, what He is aboute to do."[39] Likewise, among the Greeks, a god was thought to have a part in the shaping of prophetic dreams: an example is the pregnant Hecuba's dream of giving birth to a firebrand, interpreted as Paris. The nearness of man to his deity in those ancient eras, untroubled by the now tremendous stress on nuclear science and materialism, provides plausibility for a theistic interpretation of dreams. The Elizabethans, by contrast, thought of dreams as deriving from the bodily humors, especially melancholy, as remarked upon by those genial interpreters of abnormality, Timothy Bright and Robert Burton; or they could arise from conscience. The Tudor theories better explain the type of dream that besets King Richard—"The conscience," writes Burton, "is a thousand witnesses to accuse us"[40]—than that experienced by Richmond. If melancholy was thought to be a cause of bad dreams, it follows that the sanguine, or blood, humor might be a cause of pleasant dreams. Falstaff, even when dying, does not dream of hobgoblins or fiends; according to the Hostess, "'a babbl'd of green fields" (*Hen 5*, II.iii.18-19),[41] a vision that attests to his jovial nature. One Homeric superstition had become, in the Elizabethan age, a type of metaphor: the belief that a dream, coming from the underworld, passed through one of two gates, the gate of ivory if it was a false dream and the gate of horn if it was true. In *The Odyssey*, Penelope's dream of the eagle and the twenty geese has come, as she is to learn, through the gate of horn. By contrast, in the Tudor period, the dream commanded by Archimago of Spenser's *Faerie Queene*, since its purpose is to delude the Red Cross knight, comes by way of the ivory gate. Indeed, the doubly oriented dream of the Ghosts that visit Richard and Richmond is not directly illuminated by the metaphor of the two gates, for neither dream is false. But one is dark and ominous, the other ebullient with golden promise, as if each had a separate origin: by this interpretation Richard's dream arises from the dark recesses of a violated conscience and that of Richmond finds its shape in the congenial attunement of heart and mind to the mission at hand—namely, the purging of England of the tyrant Richard.

Early in the seventeenth century, Owen Felltham made a statement that is especially applicable to the double dream of the Ghosts: "In sleep we have the naked and natural thoughts of our souls."[42] In terms of this interpretation, the messages of the Ghosts and, in consequence, the diametrically opposed responses of the two dreamers are readily comprehensible. The quality of the soul of each is laid bare in his dream, as well as its present disposition. Richard of Gloucester, although he at first delighted in the prospect of murder (for example, he has arranged to have "Clarence . . . pack'd with posthorse up to heaven"), later is to find that murder has begun to pall upon him. Not only does he suffer "timorous dreams"; he has also become perfunctory, and no longer gleefully demonic, in arranging the later murders, in particular those of the two young princes; and when they are dead, he has no joke to spare them: his only interest is a serious one—confirmation of their deaths. The "natural thoughts" of his soul are marked no longer by levity but rather by a mistrust of himself and oppression. Richmond, by contrast, knows that his cause is right and, with that knowledge, has positive hope of victory; on the eve of battle he can state:

> O! Thou, whose captain I account myself,
> Look on my forces with a gracious eye;
> . . . .
> Make us Thy ministers of chastisement
> That we may praise Thee in the victory!
>
> [*R3*, V.iii.108-109; 113-14]

He has established in his mind the certitude that he has been chosen by God for the purpose of avenging the house of Lancaster upon Richard

III and bringing England back into Heaven's favor. With this confidence, he retires to his bed in a mood productive of the most sanguine dreams.

"The naked and natural thoughts of [the] soul"—as projected through the medium of the double dream—find an embodiment in the Ghosts and, especially, in their messages. For King Richard, in contrast to Richmond, each Ghost, in its turn, has oppressive news: "Let me sit heavy on thy soul tomorrow. . . . Despair and die." This is the customary but not invariable pattern of their curses and images the guilt and the despair that have weighted both Richard's soul and mind: "I have not that alacrity of spirit / And cheer of mind that I was wont to have." The reader, or spectator, tends to react to the Ghosts in terms of the injustice done by Richard to each of them; and, with some sense of proportion, Shakespeare has given those most wretchedly betrayed the longer speeches. The specters of the two princes, Edward V and little Richard, are certain to command the reader's—and especially the spectator's—most responsive sympathy, and judging from the character of their curse, it is their murders that press most heavily upon Richard's soul, for symbols of heaviness are predominant:

> Dream on thy cousins smothered in the Tower.
> Let us be lead within thy bosom, Richard,
> And weigh thee down to ruin, shame, and death!
>
> [V.iii.151-53]

To this curse, the Ghost of Buckingham adds: "Die in terror of thy guiltiness!" These visions, internally originated, are the responses of King Richard's "naked" soul, no longer comforted by those rationalizations with which he has sought to justify his brutal pilgrimage to the throne. Revealed in full to himself by the terrifying vision of the Ghosts—the inevitable product of his guilt-laden soul—Richard, once awakened, exclaims:

> Perjury, perjury in the high'st degree;
> Murder, stern murder, in the dir'st degree;
> All several sins, all us'd in each degree,
> Throng to the bar, crying all "Guilty! guilty!"
>
> [V.iii.196-99]

"Surely," states Felltham, "how we fall to vice, or rise to virtue, we may by observation find in our dreams."[43]

Stripped ethically naked and deprived in sleep of the comforts that derive from status and high office, Richard has been brought by the Ghosts to a man's most terrifying experience—the stark knowledge of himself. How else, unless King Richard, once the most feared soldier of the Scottish border, is weighted with a final and shocking revelation of himself, can the unskilled Richmond defeat him in hand-to-hand combat? Directors of the play tend to solve this problem, in the episode at Bosworth Field, by portraying King Richard, just at the moment that he is poised to cleave Richmond from chaps to navel, as the victim of an accidental slip. Their logic is not wrong: God, since He was recognized "as the highest Avenger" by the medieval mind, "was confidently expected to chastise the sinner through the agency of the combatant," no matter how inferior in strength and skill was the latter.[44] The device of the slipping foot is simply not Shakespeare's intention, although today it makes good theater. The eleven Ghosts—and it can be argued that they, like Richmond, are instruments of God, since they are the products of His violated commandments—have sapped Richard of almost his last ounce of self-assurance. By preoccupying his thoughts, they have paralyzed his capacity to focus upon the objective at hand.

King Richard's accustomed skill in putting on a mask of carefree deportment is not completely lost as he readies himself for the engagement at Bosworth Field. Having confided to Ratcliff that "shadows tonight / Have struck more terror to the soul of Richard / Than can . . . ten thousand soldiers," the King is able to dismiss the Ghosts as "babbling dreams," at least for the edification of his officers and men. But for himself, his brave words are but a moment's finery. As remarkable as is the outcry "A horse! a horse! my kingdom for a horse!" it is the echo, somewhat elaborated, of the cry "Give me another horse!" with which he sought to escape the presence of the accusing Ghosts. What he cannot escape, even though he offer a kingdom, is the image of himself as revealed to him and to us in his last and most frightful nightmare. "It was the wise Zeno that said, he could collect a man by his dreams. For then the soul, stated in deep repose, bewrayed her true affections, which, in the busie day, she would either not shew or not note."[45] Our customary judgments of Richard III, whom we have observed on many a "busie day," have been, by circumstance, superficial;

not until the eve of Bosworth Field have we, as readers or spectators, had a chance to observe the fundamental and soul-tormented man emptied, as now, of that reservoir of demonic resourcefulness that has carried him, through crisis and maneuver, to the throne.

For Henry of Richmond, the Ghosts have nothing but encouragement: "God and good angels fight on Richmond's side." Upon awakening, he observes: "Methought their souls whose bodies Richard murder'd / Came to my tent and cried on victory" (V.iii.230-31). Most persons undoubtedly look upon the Ghost scene as a dramatic artifice, a vision largely impossible, but nevertheless an absorbing spectacle. The Ghosts, although symbolic of God's judgment, are not factitious contrivances. Both the historic Richard's guilt of conscience and a dream that he experienced on the eve of Bosworth Field have been recorded by the chroniclers. Hall, for example, makes mention of "a terrible dreame" suffered by Richard according to "fame," a dream in which "develles . . . pulled and haled hym." He adds: "But I thynke this was no dreame, but a punccion and pricke of his synful conscience."[46] Shakespeare, although a hint may have come from the anonymous *True Tragedy of Richard III*, has amalgamated these two ideas—"develles" and "synfull conscience"—into the horrifying dream in which the murdered victims, and not "develles," become the embodiments of Richard's accusing conscience. "Our memories are packed away under pressure like steam in a boiler, and the dream is their escape-valve."[47] In short, both Richard's dream and that of Richmond are composed of fragments of an overladen memory. The substance of each dream takes shape from an excess of that substance locked in the mind of the sleeper: Richard's mind is sorely oppressed with the recollection of those whom he has murdered; that of Richmond, as attested by the immediately precedent prayer, is vibrant with the image of himself as God's captain and the desire for affirmation of that image. In each instance, the dream is an inevitable response to what has long been the dreamer's principal preoccupation. That the figures in the double dream are seen and heard by the audience is the only effective means of communicating it in the theater. To that extent only, the dream is a dramatic artifice.

Of Shakespeare's characters, Richard III and the two Macbeths, because each of them is both a murderer and a person of some conscience, best exemplify Timothy Bright's doctrine of "the afflictions of conscience for sin," which are caused, he explains, by "the fierce wrath

of Gods vengeance against the violation of his holy commandements."[48] He later argues that, once the "sinnefull soule" has apprehended "Gods judgement, / . . . the whole frame of our nature" is
driven "into extreame miserie and utter confusion."[49] Robert Burton,
who wrote thirty years later than did Bright and echoed Elizabethan
doctrines in the security of retrospect, states the same matter with characteristic conciseness: he ascribes the afflictions of conscience to "God's
heavy wrath . . . kindled in [men's] souls"[50] and adds, "Many of
them in their extremity think they hear and see visions."[51] This brief
analysis poses an obvious question: Are the eleven Ghosts, since they are
products of Richard's disturbed conscience, the ultimate worldly portion of "Gods judgement" upon him?

Elizabethan doctrine—and in this, William Perkins is our best in-
structor—insisted that the human conscience was structured on God's
laws: "The binder of conscience," as I again cite him, "is the word of
God" as found in the two Testaments. In short, at the core of the
Englishman's moral fabric were the prohibitions of the Old Testament
and the precepts of the New. This being so, "conscience [if violated]
speakes with God against the man in whom it is placed."[52] Bright,
speaking more mundanely than does Perkins, has arrived at a similar
conclusion: commenting upon "the ingraven lawes of nature, which no
man is voide of,"[53] he warns his reader of the harsh tormentings of a
conscience provoked by a violation of these laws, which are clearly those
of the Ten Commandments, or Decalogue, said to have been engraved
on stone. What, then, is a person, not necessarily a religious one, to
think of King Richard, who has broken the Sixth Commandment
("Thou shalt not kill") on at least eleven occasions? Shakespeare's audience almost certainly saw in both King Richard's dream, in which the
Ghosts confront him, and his tormented response to it the punitive lash
of God.

God's punishment of Richard, of course, is not to be confined to the
torments of conscience, of which the Ghosts are the transmitters. The
Elizabethan spectator can hardly have doubted the prompt fulfillment of
the exhortation made by the last of the Ghosts (that of Buckingham):
"God and good angels fight on Richmond's side" (V.iii.175); for it was
God's traditional duty to avenge the unjustly slain. Nor can the same
spectator have looked on Richmond's repeated reminders that he is
God's "captain" as an idle boast, especially since Richmond is about to

chastise King Richard, "One that hath ever been God's enemy" (V.iii.252). Equally valid, in the Elizabethan mind and perhaps in ours, is Henry of Richmond's ultimate claim that his victory over King Richard and, especially, the political resolution that follows it are the fulfillments of "God's fair ordinance" (V.v.31). Of Richmond's replacing Richard III on the throne of England, Edward Hall had written: "This erle Henry [was] so ordeined by God."[54] The young Shakespeare, who has stressed Richmond's function as God's instrument, had no compulsion to question the theological statements of the respected chronicler, who was also his principal source.

My suggestion that Richard's tormented conscience, the tribunal at which the Ghosts have pled against him, is a factor in his defeat at Bosworth Field, as that episode is presented by Shakespeare, finds support in his deportment on the field of battle. As if attempting to rub from his mind the intense preoccupation that has beset it, and hence to refocus his concentration, he exposes himself to reckless encounters and ignores any attempt at good generalship. Although Richard is gallant, in that gallantry there is a strong evidence of gloss and bravado:

> A horse! a horse! my kingdom for a horse!
> . . . .
> I think there be six Richmonds in the field;
> Five have I slain today instead of him.
> A horse! a horse! my kingdom for a horse!
>
> [V.iv.7; 11-13]

The echoes of this remarkable outcry reverberate with a somewhat hollow sound upon the ear; gallant on the surface, the outcry suggests an inward desperation, a vacuum of true courage, the mark of which is the sword and not a fine piece of Black Friday oratory. As Hall and, later, Holinshed inform us, the historic Richard was doomed, regardless of the character of his gallantry, factitious or not: "Kyng Richard . . . was appoynted nowe to finyshe hys last laboure by the very devyne justice and providence of God, which called him to condigne punyshement for his scelerate . . . and myscheveous desertes."[55] To the Earl of Richmond, better qualified to be a priest than a soldier, is granted the doubtful glory of confronting and defeating a Richard already marked for death by God and, at best, put much out of countenance by the accusations of those whom he has murdered. The Ghosts have frightened Richard forty times more grievously than has Richmond. The apparent fact that from the weakness of Richard, oppressed and disconcerted by the Ghosts, who have returned to haunt and destroy him, derives the strength of Henry of Richmond has customarily been overlooked by both critics and directors of the play; for the Ghosts, hinted at by Hall and developed by Shakespeare, are clearly instruments of God's plan, which was held to have been the destruction of King Richard.

In Shakespeare's sources, in particular the chronicles of Hall and Holinshed, the defection of Lord Stanley to the army of Richmond had been a decisive factor in the defeat of Richard III at Bosworth Field. Shakespeare chose to play down this factor in favor of a psychological portrait of Richard.[56] To this portrait the Ghosts are essential. In addition to their unnerving impact upon the King, the spectacle of Ghosts in *Richard III* provides a conspicuous affirmation of the thesis, often proposed by Shakespeare, that no man can escape his past, especially if it holds the awesome power of men unjustly slain. The violent fate of such men was thought to command the special attention of God.

SIX

Prince Hamlet and the Double Mission

Three of Shakespeare's tragedies, although with significant variations in emphasis, are constructed on the formula central to the two historical tetralogies: the crime of homicide, its significant repercussions, and God's judgment upon the criminal. In one of these tragedies, *Julius Caesar* (briefly discussed in chap. 1), the theme of judgment is so explicit and hence overt that I shall give detailed attention only to *Hamlet* and *Macbeth*, in which, by contrast, the theme is complex. An advantage of chapters on *Hamlet* and *Macbeth* is that both plays attest to the greater ingenuity with which Shakespeare was ultimately to handle the topic of retribution. If my reading of the first of these tragedies, *Hamlet*, is correct—that is to say, fully justified in light of the evidence—then the play has as much to say about divine judgment as does any other Shakespearean play. Prince Hamlet, as I shall hope to show, is not only the minister of the punishment inflicted upon Claudius but also, as repeatedly substantiated by the text, the instrument of a second and much more comprehensive mission. The Elizabethan audience, as Fredson Bowers, among others, has recognized, was well aware that a ghost (like any other underworld spirit) was thought to return to earth only when so permitted by God and that God, at the very least, would have foreknown, and hence worked to His purpose, the consequences of that intercession. Bowers casts this relationship into a specific focus: "Since divine permission alone could free [King Hamlet's] Ghost to revisit the earth, the Ghost's demand for the external punishment of Claudius [is] the transmission of a divine command, appointing Hamlet as God's agent to punish the specific criminal Claudius."[1] He does not identify any mission beyond that of the vengeance upon the King. It is my opinion, however, that the second mission, as shown by my analysis of it, has as much the approval of God as does the first.

Before this chapter can focus on the two missions that stem from the Ghost's return to earth and have the sanction of God, it is imperative to examine, in some detail, the problem of the Ghost's identity; for in the minds of many scholars, this specter was deprived of the last of its technical attributes of ghosthood, in 1951, by R.W. Battenhouse's exposure of its pneumatological unsoundness (*Studies in Philology*, vol. 48, pp. 161-92). The basic question is, of course: What did Shakespeare and the Globe audience believe to be the Ghost's identity? My reader, while I pause to address this and related questions, should hold in mind that my assessments of the Ghost and its identity—fundamental to the thesis of this chapter—are indirectly statements on the divine judgment, of which the visitant (no matter what its precise spiritual nature) is the emissary; for even if the Ghost is considered a devil (as some critics believe), its return to earth, as well as what it is allowed to do and say, has of necessity the sanction of God.

Thirty years ago, the problem of coming to an understanding of King Hamlet's Ghost seemed not so entangled, and hence so uncertain of illumination, as it does today. What was, even then, an imposing array of critical theory appeared to be surmountable if the writer were both perceptive and persevering. Unhappily for each successive critic, his fellow critics have boldly persevered, sometimes with bright lanterns that lead us into darkling caves. Yet much of the criticism has been thoughtful and also justified by the integrity of the writer and his theme. The caverns, meanwhile, have become not so much darker as more numerous: the Ghost has been identified as a "post-Christian" pagan visitant and, by others, as a malign devil. If it were not that the nature of my topic makes specific demands, I would almost certainly choose not to undertake the present venture into the problem of which the Ghost is the hub. I come to it, however, armed with two principal tenets (aside from the Ghost's identity) that help to provide an original and, I hope, a constructive view of the Ghost and Hamlet's dual responses to it. The more fundamental of the two tenets arises from a piece of criticism that was published anonymously and with such unpretentiousness, in 1935, that it seems to have been barely noted by students of Shakespeare and then forgotten. Because the identity of King Hamlet's Ghost is fundamental to a clear comprehension of the anonymous piece, I shall turn first to that most noted specter, pen-worn and stageworn but remarkable in its resourcefulness.

A number of critics, including this writer on two minor occasions, have insisted on regarding King Hamlet's Ghost as a Renaissance phenomenon. This interpretation tends to put the critic immediately at horns with the devil, in a very literal sense. The sixteenth-century Protestant church had denied the existence of purgatory and, with it, the reality of ghosts, for the reason that ghosts had been thought, in Roman Catholic ideology, to return only from purgatory and not, with the rarest exceptions, from heaven or hell.[2] The purpose of the purgatorial ghost was to request a remission of sins or, as a minority has suggested, to ask "that a murderer might be brought to due punishment."[3] The Protestant writers of the Renaissance such as the Swiss Protestant Ludwig Lavater, King James of Scotland, and the Anglican minister William Perkins have confirmed the Protestant denial of ghosts: "[Contrary to] the opinion of the Church of Rome," wrote Perkins, "dead men doe neither walke, nor appeare in bodie and soule after death."[4] Meanwhile, following Lavater's example, James VI of Scotland had also, and with equal firmness, denounced the idea of ghosts: "Neither can the spirite of the defunct returne to his friend [there being no purgatory], or yet an Angell use such formes."[5] The gist of the problem is that well-informed critics, confronted with a royal court which, to them, is undeniably Protestant (Hamlet and Horatio, for example, are students at Luther's Wittenberg), have had a difficult time in accepting King Hamlet's Ghost as an authentic specter. They insist that it is a devil (as Hamlet also supposes) or perhaps a figment of a melancholic mind. Or, like Robert H. West, they on occasion contend that the Ghost is a product of an "ambiguity" that was Shakespeare's deliberate intent and, in consequence, the emphasis has been placed upon "its supernaturalness" and not upon "its intelligibility."[6]

The likelihood that King Hamlet's Ghost may have been thought a devil by the Elizabethan audience is certainly not to be rejected. King James of Scotland contends in *Daemonologie* that a devil often assumed a lately "deade bodie" and thus communicated with country persons; the intent was "to make them [being ignorant of formal Protestant dogma] beleeve that it was some good spirite [a ghost] appeared to them . . . to discover unto them the will of the defunct, or what was the way of his slauchter."[7] This mode of deception, an Elizabethan commonplace, is properly accepted by modern students of the play but only so long as they are convinced that the spirit seen by Hamlet is a Renaissance phenomenon within a world that is inflexibly Protestant. In such a context the assumption that the Ghost may be a disguised devil is hardly to be avoided.

Not only has the Ghost, when viewed in a strictly Protestant frame of reference, been difficult to accept; equally difficult to justify is the Ghost's command of vengeance, since the private right of blood revenge contravenes both Elizabethan law and doctrine. Moreover, it is this command that Battenhouse finds so objectionable; its vindictiveness, he argues, is much at odds with a tenet of Roman Catholic pneumatology. The critic can, of course, argue that King Hamlet's Ghost, once he has dismissed—as Hamlet must ultimately do—the probability that it may be a devil, is after all a non-Protestant Christian ghost, which speaks of purgatory ("confin'd to fast in fires" until "purg'd" of its sins) and makes reference to the sacraments (the holy communion, absolution, and extreme unction)[8] but retains the most evident and most ineffaceable characteristic of the stage tradition to which it belongs—namely, the Senecan implant of vengeance. Although this simple adjustment has been advanced by no critic of whom I know, it allows for the not uncommon insistence of a stage device of exceptional and proven theatricality. Those who have dealt with the Ghost's command of vengeance, which troubles them far more than whether it is a Protestant or a Roman Catholic phenomenon, have customarily taken recourse to one of three solutions: the spirit is a "post-Christian" paganesque ghost (Roy W. Battenhouse);[9] Shakespeare has deliberately made the ghost ambiguous, part demon and part specter, to enhance its aura of mystery (Robert H. West and, by strong implication, Eleanor Prosser);[10] or, in one way or another, the revenge problem as it relates to Elizabethan doctrine is to be compromised, whether logically or not (J. Dover Wilson, I.J. Semper, and Fredson T. Bowers).[11] Battenhouse, West, and Prosser are in evident agreement that the Ghost, because of its thirst for vengeance, cannot be a Christian spirit, especially in terms of Thomistic doctrine; in consequence, they come to conclusions that stand apart from a head-on confrontation with the nature defined for it by Shakespeare, West somewhat excepted. Both Wilson and Bowers hint at what I believe to be the appropriate character of the Ghost. Each of these critics contends that it comes from a medieval underworld, but not in the unperturbed belief that the Ghost is a totally medieval phenomenon; on the contrary, they enforce the brand of medievalism upon it as a means of insulating it from the Protestant principles that denied both the reality of ghosts and (in conformity with a New Testament admonition) the private right of blood revenge.

To ascribe to King Hamlet's Ghost any kind of *specific* identity (as I shall do shortly) has been, in the last quarter century, a kind of ultimate in scholarly indiscretion. Battenhouse's revelation, in 1951, of a tenet of pneumatology, first enunciated by Gregory I and elaborated by Thomas Aquinas, has so confined for us the potentialities of the purgatorial ghost, or " saved soul," that it must conduct itself, on stage or off, in the manner of Caspar Milquetoast or, if at all forward, be branded as an impostor, be it a pagan ghost or a demon.[12] The purgatorial soul, so Battenhouse has interpreted the Roman Catholic tenet, is in such a condition of beatitude that, even should it return to earth, it is incapable of vindictiveness and would ask only for a remission of sins.[13] The fundamental problem lies in Battenhouse's insistence upon making this interpretation the cardinal criterion in his evaluation of the character of King Hamlet's Ghost. In short, he imposes a totally theological criterion and shows no apparent regard for the play's inherent assumptions and structural demands, to both of which the criterion is an unsettling force. A revealing effect of this criterion—for it automatically transforms King Hamlet's Ghost, by judging it too vindictive to be a Christian soul, into a pagan "tutelary demon"—is that, years later (1969), in a discussion of the play itself, Battenhouse is brought (with the assistance of several additional theological distinctions) to the conclusion that Prince Hamlet's "soul," like those of Othello and Macbeth, is "lost in damnable error."[14] He has abstracted from church dogma this conclusion; in so doing, he has lifted Hamlet out of the play's context and has distorted Shakespeare's *fundamental* view of him. Battenhouse and those who have followed him, among them Eleanor Prosser, have suggested, in effect, that Horatio's tribute to the dead Hamlet "Good night, sweet Prince, / And flights of angels sing thee to thy rest!" (V.ii.351-52) should properly have been assigned to Lieutenant Pistol; for it becomes, in view of Hamlet's deception by a demon and his almost certain descent into hell, as inflated a piece of bombast as ever was spoken on the British stage. Evidently Battenhouse and his most earnest followers have not paused and asked themselves: "What did Shakespeare conceive to be the nature of the Ghost?" There is, despite the difficulty that the Battenhouse school of criticism has in sustaining

Shakespeare's dramatic assumptions, a basic similarity between his version of the Ghost and mine: in each the Ghost, because of its uncommon vindictiveness, is at times pagan in its deportment. We differ principally on fundamentals. On one point, with which I shall begin, we are barely apart on the rationale behind King Hamlet's Ghost.

Battenhouse, in his 1969 study of *Hamlet*, makes a statement which tends to modify his 1951 portrait of the purgatorial soul as imperturbably benign: "They [holy souls] are engaged in a crushing of the will's obstinate holding to its own judgment."[15] The suggestion—quite a logical one—is that a soul, newly arrived in purgatory, will not for a time attain a condition of beatitude, for it must rid itself of its worldly imperfections. The soul's need to "crush [its] will's obstinate" nature finds support in a belief emphasized by T.F. Thiselton-Dyer, a Victorian authority on ghost lore: to wit, souls of murdered persons "have carried into their new existence an angry longing for revenge."[16] This statement is, of course, speculative, but it supports the likelihood that the disciplines of purgatory do not—and cannot—rid the soul immediately of its mundane preoccupations. Thiselton-Dyer cites two examples illustrative of his hypothesis. Of Amy Robsart, Robert Dudley's first wife, who died in 1560, we are told: "Ever since the fatal event [her sudden death] it was asserted [by the country folk] that 'Madam Dudley's ghost did use to walk in Cumnor Park and that it walked so obstinately that it took . . . nine parsons from Oxford to lay her.'"[17] In view of the ghost's persistent obstinateness, are we not justified in suspecting that it sought, in the minds of the observers, "reparation for the cruel wrong done"?[18] Seventy-one years later, in 1631, in the county of Durham, the ghost of Anne Walker, who had been murdered with a pickax and thrown into "a coal pit," is said to have appeared to a miller, James Graham, and to have shown him five wounds on its head. It gave him the names of the two murderers. When Graham did not take immediate action against the two men, the ghost, determined on vengeance, made a second appearance, "the last time with a threatening aspect." The murderers were apprehended and were later hanged.[19] Each of these two accounts is at odds with the formal Roman Catholic tenet cited in 1951 by Battenhouse, namely, that a purgatorial ghost is incapable of vindictive behavior or even a show of it. Neither account, however, is notably at odds with his 1969 modification, for a soul, if it must first crush "the will's obstinate holding to its own judgment" (as a part of the purgatorial experience), might spend some time in the attainment of its expected state of perfect beatitude. It might, at times, be obstinate or even "threatening." In terms of popular beliefs about the lately departed soul, in contrast to fundamental Thomistic doctrine, the obstinate resolve exhibited by the two ghosts that I have cited provides the vindictiveness of King Hamlet's Ghost, itself mindful of recent foul play, with a modest degree of credibility.

King James, as I have quoted him on popular belief, ascribes to the purgatorial ghost, which he genially terms "some good spirite" and which the devil is at pains to impersonate in the deluding of ignorant folk, two motives for its return to earth: "to discover unto them [the ignorant folk] the will of the defunct or [secondly] what was the way of his slauchter." These motives, it should be kept in mind, are those of the ghost and not of the devil who is said to impersonate it. The revelation of the dead man's murder (the second motive) by a purgatorial soul could have (as illustrated by the ghost of Anne Walker) but one likely purpose: the hope of vengeance being taken. In the deceptively simplistic observation noted above, King James, a highly reliable authority on the occult beliefs of his times, has enunciated (among others) two significant points: (1) despite the official Protestant denial of purgatory, many uninformed Protestants continued to believe in the purgatorial ghost; and (2) many of them, moreover, and perhaps most of them had not as yet rejected the belief that a purpose of the returned soul was to seek retribution or atonement for the crime of murder.

The dichotomy between Anglican church doctrine, which denied both purgatory and, even more adamantly, the reality of ghosts, and popular sentiment, which in many parts of England and Scotland, whether Protestant or Roman Catholic, doubted neither purgatory nor its ghost, is of course manifest. Shakespeare, who shows not the slightest prejudice with respect to either popular sentiment or official doctrine when one or the other better fits the demands of a particular play, had no evident hesitancy in ascribing to King Hamlet's Ghost a purgatorial abode. The vindictiveness of King Hamlet's Ghost, even though it may find justification in popular sentiment, was not basically derived from it. And to this vindictiveness Battenhouse and those who subscribe to his views most emphatically object. Its principal source is, quite simply, the stage play which Shakespeare undertook to "update" and which had long been the property of his company, the Lord Chamberlain's Men. The play is, of course, the *Ur-Hamlet* (now lost) and its ghost, as we learn from Thomas Lodge, was famous for having "cried," in a high-pitched voice, "Hamlet, revenge,"[20] a stage act often repeated. The *Ur-Hamlet* had been acted as early as 1589, and hence, as was the dramatist's practice then, the ghost's underworld was almost assuredly Hades. In 1594, the play is known to have been acted by the Lord Chamberlain's Men and was almost certainly on the company's repertoire as late as 1596 and very possibly until 1600. During these years the *Ur-Hamlet*, in prompt copy form, was immediately available to Shakespeare. The fact that it is the principal and probably only source of his *Hamlet* finds affirmation in the total absence of any ghost in the two earlier versions of the Hamlet story, neither of which, moreover, was at that time in English translation. The four references to the *Ur-Hamlet* that have come down to us—spread over twelve years (1589-1601)—attest to its enduring popularity.[21]

In short, Shakespeare had a commitment to "update" a stage play of highly noted popularity; this being so, he was not inclined to tamper unduly with the "Hamlet, revenge" theme of the prototype ghost, in particular since revenge was the catalyst of both the *Ur-Hamlet* and his *Hamlet*. Nor would a strain of Tartarus—if confined solely to the Ghost and not, unless for coloring, to its abode—have seemed unduly incongruous to an audience which had yet to see a Christian ghost upon the stage (possibly excepting John Marston's in *Antonio's Revenge*, produced about the same time as *Hamlet*) and which, confronted at that time by a flux of competing ideologies about ghosts, was better prepared to respond to a ghost's theatrical values than to specific questions of its orthodoxy. Shakespeare, in brief, was bound by the enduring success of his source play to a ghost that insisted upon revenge; he was, at least equally, committed by Renaissance conceptions—now that the themes of the "academic wits" had been supplanted by a taste for existing values—to a ghost of Christian and not pagan origin. The result was, as to be expected, an amalgamated ghost, although fundamentally purgatorial in its nature.

The fact that King Hamlet's Ghost describes a purgatory which, in Battenhouse's words, "would [best] fit . . . certain descriptions of hell as pagan authors pictured that place"[22] can be explained, as I have suggested, by Shakespeare's professional obligation to his highly regarded source play, itself of a pagan mold. Although he kept but "a strain of

Tartarus" and concentrated most of it into the vindictiveness shown by King Hamlet's Ghost, something of that strain colors the Ghost's references to its underworld, which it rightly holds to be purgatory. Shakespeare's purpose was to contemporize, but not to emasculate, a proven "potboiler." Moreover, my information on conceptions of purgatory—as gathered from several old authors—indicates, persuasively, that a soul was not necessarily as conformable to its punishments as Battenhouse has suggested. The Thomistic "sense of pain," for example, ascribed by Battenhouse to purgatorial souls as the limit of their suffering is rendered by several ancient authorities as a sense of "torment." Dante, having noted in his *Purgatorio* the disparate burdens assigned to the souls—in this instance, those punished for an excess of pride—speaks of the souls as "unequally tormented."[23] Even Aquinas, pointing out that fire is an "instrument of Divine justice," concludes that "the soul, seeing fire as something hurtful to it, is tormented by the fire."[24] Here the torment is spiritual. In the late Renaissance, Pierre Le Loyer, speaking in behalf of the Roman Catholic Church, wrote: "The souls of Purgatory come back to beg of living persons aid and consolation in the pains and torments [tourments] which they endure for their unpurged crimes [my translation]."[25] For a popular view of purgatorial torments—a view to which Shakespeare here subscribes—Romeo's outcry against purgatory and Hell upon his banishment from Verona is worthy of examination: "There is no world without Verona's walls / But Purgatory, torture, Hell itself" (III.iii.17-18). In this tight context, much more than a "sense of pain" is seen as the lot of the purgatorial soul. The outcry identifies "torture," which entails a restive torment, as the dues of purgatory while conceding, through the reflexive pronoun "itself," the somewhat greater torture of Hell. A ghost come back from purgatory—in the minds of those not bound by a rigidly puristic doctrine—need not have had totally horror-free thoughts about its habitat.

Mindful of the Ghost's complaint that the harsh penance appointed it in purgatory is an effect of King Hamlet's deprivation, because of his abrupt death, of certain vital sacraments, Battenhouse has contended: "The sacraments are no more than shells to him, leaving him actually a hollow Ghost."[26] Shortly, he adds: "He is a sixteenth-century post-Christian ghost [meaning a pagan one] in that he mentions the sacraments."[27] In the abstract sense, he is correct: since the Ghost is uncommonly vindictive, it cannot be from purgatory and hence has learned of the sacraments only by indirect means. We are, however, at least equally much obligated to honor the inherent assumptions of the play *Hamlet*. Logic works just as well—and in better service to the tragic stature of Shakespeare's play—if we consider the significance of being deprived of the sacraments first and then decide whether or not they are only "shells." Recalling that King Hamlet died "unhous'led, disappointed, unanel'd," the Ghost immediately cries, with excellent cause, "O, horrible! O, horrible! Most horrible!" for without holy communion (from which comes reaffirmation of grace), without confession (which entails penance for crimes done), and without extreme unction (which conveys a remission of sins), the King indeed died "with all [his] imperfections on [his] head." His soul has come to purgatory laden with the full weight of his earthly "crimes" uneased by the last rites, the most essential in terms of both penance and God's forgiveness. Its punishment, because of the deprivation of these sacraments, is therefore incalculably in excess of what would otherwise have been its purgatorial debt. Of the "pains and torments" that Le Loyer (Shakespeare's contemporary) defines as the common grief of purgatorial souls, it should surprise no one that the penance as yet required of King Hamlet's Ghost is structured almost wholly upon the torments. The Ghost's complaint over the loss of the sacraments—a loss so vital to an understanding of its harsh purgatorial lot—should not, I think, be dismissed as a cheap facade.

The marks of evil that the Ghost bears—the vindictiveness transplanted from the pagan ghost of the *Ur-Hamlet* and the sullenness of aspect imposed, in large part, by the punitive effects of its having come, deprived of highly crucial rites, to purgatory—are, I believe, totally extraneous to its fundamental nature, for both these traits (it being basically a Christian ghost) are adventitious and not inherent. The murder of King Hamlet has cost the Ghost dearly. Not only did the King, in a single dispatch, lose his life, his as yet beloved Queen, and his crown; the sudden dispatch has done equally bad service for the Ghost. Its harsh punishment—justified by its having come to purgatory (through no fault of its own) "unhous'led, disappointed, unanel'd" but excessive in terms of its fundamental character—is only one aspect of its unbending misfortune; the dark implications of a punishment in excess of the purgatorial norm compounded with its overt vindictiveness have invited upon it, being a stage ghost, a second and more mundane type of harassment: repeated probes, from outside the play, which impugn its Christian integrity. If its vindictiveness against its murderer—no matter what debt this element owes to the *Ur-Hamlet*—is much in excess of purgatorial orthodoxy (and it apparently is), it is not, on the other hand, uncommonly at odds with the popular Tudor and Stuart notions about the obstinate deportment of ghosts. King Hamlet's Ghost perhaps belongs more to the lumber camp than to the parlor, and its Christianity shows a few spots of rubbed-in dirt. Nor do I claim that my explanation of it is any more meritorious than is that of Battenhouse, to which it offers a pragmatic alternative. My efforts have focused on the difficulties inherent in Shakespeare's transformation of the pagan ghost of a highly popular revenge play into a Christian ghost at a time of uncommon nonconsensus as to the nature of ghosts. The Christianity of King Hamlet's Ghost is rough-hewn of these difficulties.

Having come thus far, I am mindful of an astute observation made by Herbert Coursen: "Dramatically, it is Hamlet's problem—not the critics'—to determine the nature of the Ghost."[28] So wisely fundamental is the truth of this statement that I would like to have accepted the caveat that it poses. I have not done so, for the reason that Coursen and others, such as Robert G. Hunter, have. Rather than confront the infallibility of Battenhouse's argument, they have wisely evaded both the issue of the Ghost's vindictiveness and the fact that the severity of its penance suggests that its abode is hell, not purgatory. Hunter has made a brief attempt at response. He sees the Ghost as a mixture of "handy bits of Catholicism, Protestantism, and Senecan classicism,"[29] but he adds little beyond stating the dual purpose of this composite, one part of which is "to define the world of [the] play."[30] I share with Coursen and Hunter their apparent self-consciousness, for Battenhouse's 1951 article had the effect of prompting some difficult second thoughts about the play. Nor was the Ghost's exposure in 1951 as an apparent sham necessarily its first such exposure. A hypothesis has been current, over many years, that the "revenge ghosts" which in the early 1600s succeeded King Hamlet's Ghost on the London stage—namely, George Chapman's two ghosts and that depicted by Tourneur in *The Atheist's Tragedy*—were intended, in their unoffending deportments, to be professional responses to the blunt and headstrong and therefore unorthodox portrait presented by Shakespeare. Because Chapman's two ghosts, each of which is the mender of certain unresolved difficulties and not a true suppliant, stand apart from doctrine, the only meaningful response is Tourneur's Ghost of the murdered Montferrers (ca. 1610). The question prompted of us by this ghost is: To what, specifically, does it owe its unoffending conduct? To a purgatorial discipline? Or to a restraining force extraneous to its post-mortem world?

The Ghost of Montferrers, reflecting a philosophy quite opposed to that of King Hamlet's Ghost, cautions Charlemont, its son and would-be avenger, against private blood revenge: "Attend with patience the success of things / But leave revenge unto the king of kings" (II.vi.21-22). And again, more forcibly: "Let him revenge my murder and thy wrongs, / To whom the justice of revenge belongs" (III.ii.36-37). When D'Amville, the murderer, in attempting to behead Charlemont with an ax, has instead struck out his own brains, the latter sees in this "accident" the judgment of God:

> Only to heaven I attribute [this] work.
> . . . .
> Now I see
> That patience is the honest man's revenge.
>
> [V.ii.268; 270-71]

The phrase "the honest man's revenge" is also the alternative title of the play. Hence, the last line of Charlemont's speech, as quoted, takes on a preconceived emphasis. Since it duplicates, in a crucial context, the alternative title, it suggests that Tourneur's principal concern is focused not on the deportment of ghosts (an aspect not without importance) but, rather, on the problem of an individual's right of private blood revenge: it concludes that such a right must be regarded with "patience," that is, with restraint. Tourneur's omission of the vindictiveness of the stage ghost is not, therefore, to be ascribed primarily to the Thomistic principle, as explicated by Battenhouse, that the purgatorial ghost is, by its nature, incapable of vindictiveness. On the contrary, the strong restraint that the ghost (the playwright's spokesman) places on its avenger is occasioned, almost certainly, by Tourneur's unqualified endorsement of the Jacobean law which, like its Elizabethan prototype, made private blood revenge a capital offense and hence a flagrant sin against both man and God. He may have been equally aware of the public sentiment behind the law, as this statement was summed up a decade later by Owen Felltham: "The right of vengeance rests with God alone, and he that takes it out of his hand, he so far dethrones him as to put himself in his place."[31] In short, Protestant London was conscious of the nation's prohibition against private blood revenge. It may have had little knowledge—perhaps none—of the fine points of the Roman Catholic tenet that insisted upon the beatitude of purgatorial souls.

The basic objection in applying the Thomistic tenet identified by Battenhouse in 1951 to King Hamlet's Ghost is twofold: (1) no proof known to me has been offered that either Shakespeare or his largely Protestant audience had an indisputable knowledge of this tenet, namely, that a purgatorial ghost is of such moral refinement that it cannot be vindictive; and (2) Battenhouse's quite logical conclusion (when drawn from his premise) that the spirit that confronts Hamlet in the shape of his father is not from purgatory and hence cannot be a Christian ghost stands in evident conflict with the context of the play, which insists (at least ultimately) that it is a Christian ghost. Consider, for example, Shakespeare's position: he was writing at the midpoint of the short stage history of the Elizabethan revenge ghost; his only dramatic precedents of note were the Greco-Roman ghosts of the earlier revenge plays; he probably had, at best, an uneasy knowledge, and very likely no knowledge at all, of the Thomistic restriction illustrated by Battenhouse, for it was alien to both the worldliness and the Protestantism of London; he shared, however, with most of his fellow Londoners, the general notion of purgatory. Add, also, the fact that he required, for the opening scenes of *Hamlet*, a dynamic ghost (e.g., the *Ur-Hamlet* source ghost) and not one restricted by social or religious dogma. Equally important, Shakespeare's own depictions of the supernatural—such as his sketch of Tybalt's vengeful ghost in *Romeo and Juliet* and his lively vignette of Puck in *A Midsummer Night's Dream*—are rarely drawn exclusively from orthodox doctrine. As I understand Shakespeare (and Robert Ornstein, among others, is of a similar view) he rarely allowed his imagination to be restricted, undramatically, by either historical fact or church doctrine; he shaped his materials for the London stage, and this being so, the poetic license of each element, as it relates to the whole, may be fairly judged only by the artist's criteria, not by whether or not it conforms with an extrinsic fact, however important. A fundamental "understanding of Shakespeare's art," Ornstein has perceptively stated, "precludes the dogmatism of the learned."[32]

Tourneur's ghost, in its forcible warnings against private blood revenge, directs attention to the second breach of doctrine caused by the vindictiveness of King Hamlet's Ghost: because the Ghost commands young Hamlet to avenge his father's murder, it opposes diametrically the strong Elizabethan prohibition against extralegal blood revenge. For this violation, Shakespeare, as will be illustrated in the next three paragraphs, has prepared his audience by artfully excluding the Ghost from contemporary strictures. His handling of the Ghost, as I observe it, eliminates the difficulties with which such critics as Wilson and Bowers have been confronted. Wilson, as is well known, must transform the "King of Lutheran Denmark," upon his death, into a Roman Catholic ghost so that it will not stand in violation of two doctrines: the Protestant denial of ghosts and the Renaissance prohibition against private blood revenge. Such clever manipulations, while avoiding Charybdis, are usually exposed to the clutches of Scylla, a difficulty inherent in most past treatments of the Ghost. Meanwhile, the pneumatological violation called to our attention by Battenhouse—although its damaging effect on the Ghost's nature (if appropriate allowances are made) can be greatly eased—must apparently remain unresolved, short of a papal retraction. West, I believe, has best reconciled the welter of criticism (especially that of Wilson, Battenhouse and, later, Prosser) that has made of King Hamlet's Ghost a kind of five-and-a-half-headed monster; he concludes that an audience (when it sees the genuine *Hamlet*), having put aside the Ghost's pagan, "post-Christian" pagan, demonic, and other extrinsic aspects, and not marking its Lutheran apostasy, is customarily left with the impression that it is a legitimate ghost "returned from Purgatory"; if it were anything else, he implies wisely, it could not be "conformable to its dramatic function."[33] Without ignoring the Ghost's pagan and demonic aspects, we should redirect our attention to its *fundamental* nature. This can be discovered only from a focused examination of both the total text of the play and, collaterally, the author's contemporized view of his materials.

For me, and I hope that the reader may have a similar profitable response, the unpretentiously printed statement of 1935, which appeared in the weekly magazine *The Nation*, has done as much to illuminate the pages of *Hamlet* as has any other piece of criticism. The statement is disarming in the simplicity with which it generalizes Hamlet's problem and indicates the character of the Ghost. Of Hamlet, it says: "He was hesitating between the world which was dead and the world which was powerless to be born."[34] The powerful implication of this metaphor of Hamlet's problem is that two worlds, each having its own ethic, confront one another within Shakespeare's play. If this is so, if a double chronology is sustainable, we need not do what most critics have attempted: that is, to evaluate both the Ghost and Hamlet's response to it in terms of a single political, ethical, and religious community. All such attempts have inevitably brought compromise upon the critic; he (or she) becomes compelled to manipulate the world of the play so that it will accommodate both the Ghost and Hamlet's response to it. Or else the critic manipulates either the Ghost or Hamlet so that each will conform to a world to which only one of them rightly belongs. Both Wilson and, less evidently, Bowers have found it necessary to revamp the environment of the play. Wilson, in an effort to accommodate both a Roman Catholic ghost and a prince of Protestant education, has pushed back late Elizabethan England some sixty years and has called it "post-medieval England." West and, especially, Prosser, since they preserve an Elizabethan world, emphasize the Ghost's demonic habits, the most compelling of which (such as vindictiveness) are equally traceable to the insistence of the Senecan stage tradition. The acceptance of the confrontation of two worlds—medieval and Renaissance, respectively—within Shakespeare's play has the immense advantage of eliminating sometimes awkward compromises, in particular of the Ghost's identity, which is medieval, whereas Hamlet is a Renaissance man.

For those of a pragmatic bent of mind, double chronology is not essential to the confrontation of which I have spoken. King Hamlet's Ghost need not belong to a distant past. The Reformation, which swept Europe in the 1500s, meant that, within a particular generation of that century, a newly Protestant son must necessarily have had a Roman Catholic father. Moreover, the tendency to "Elizabethanize" the play *Hamlet* has made many of us think of its milieu as closely contemporary with the later years of Elizabeth I's reign. This tendency, of course, can have misled us. As a prince of Denmark, Hamlet might well have attended Wittenberg (founded in 1502) some time around 1520, when

Martin Luther's influence on the thought of that university had been well established. At any rate, in contrast to the less sophisticated Marcellus and Bernardo, Hamlet and Horatio have immediate doubts about the authenticity of the Ghost—doubts that are later renewed. In this, of course, they reflect the Protestant doctrine that denied the reality of ghosts. The court at large is, in all probability, Roman Catholic, as was the lately dead king; for not until about 1540—as Shakespeare could well have been aware—did the Danish court, under Christian III, embrace Lutherism.[35] The Roman Catholicism of Claudius's court—aside from its historical conformity—is at best thinly evident. It is identifiable in a few fragments of doctrine that break through Claudius's conscience-smothered prayer and is again suggested in the stress placed upon Ophelia's "maimèd rites." The court, in terms of its secular and not religious focus, appears to be so unaccustomedly Renaissance that its mode of novelty—contrasting sharply with Hamlet's habit of philosophical inquiry—is made up mainly of violations of honored medieval tradition such as the incestuous marriage and the recurrent presumptuousness shown by subordinates, whether Polonius or the Gravedigger, in the presence of their betters. Impertinence, as in Laertes' untempered demand of the king that he account for Polonius's death, and not a sense of high pursuit, is the principal Renaissance mark of the Claudian court.

Fundamental to the present evaluation of Shakespeare's King Hamlet is the report, made by Horatio (I.i.80-95), of the former monarch's hand-to-hand combat, thirty years ago, with King Fortinbras of Norway. This piece of information, above all others, identifies King Hamlet as a medieval figure, for single combats to decide the issues existing between two nations belong largely to a distant past. That the combat, as described, is apparently ancient is suggested by the fact that, in its cause and in the binding effect of its outcome, it closely mirrors the wager by combat fought by Horwendil,[36] the Danish prototype upon whom Shakespeare models his King Hamlet. Although Horwendil, a sea rover, is a chivalric figure and the combat fought by him dates to about A.D. 920, the same combat—although less chivalric in tone—would not have been out of place in fifteenth-century Europe, even as late as the 1490s. Shakespeare, for example, depicts Prince Hal as proposing a wager by combat against Hotspur (1403) and actually stages what is tantamount to such a combat (only the formal ceremony is missing) between Richard III and Henry of Richmond (1485), for the outcome of their duel at Bosworth is totally decisive. Hence he would have seen nothing unlikely in placing King Hamlet's wager by combat in or about 1490. Moreover, as I showed in chapter 2, William Segar and Edward Coke, as late as the early 1600s, argued forcibly for the restoration of the wager by combat, for God (as Coke has pointed out) revealed His sanction of the wager "by the single battail between David and Goliath."[37] Although the wager is customarily associated (as in the legends of Arthur and Roland) with the age of chivalry (1100-1300), a pragmatic use of it was hardly alien to the temper of late medieval times; for the wager by combat was not impossible to accept as long as men believed that God, in His justice, determined the outcome and, equally important, were willing to honor His verdict. In short, the confrontation between the medieval world of the Ghost and the Renaissance world of young Hamlet need not be explained in terms of a double chronology. Because Hamlet was born (as we are told) on the day of his father's combat, I shall establish (for the sake of perspective) the year 1490 as the general date of the two events and 1520 as that of the play's action. The Ghost's "dread command," a part of the medieval ethic, imposes upon Hamlet a task for which, because of his recent Protestant indoctrination and consequent nagging scruples about both the reality of ghosts and blood revenge, he is psychologically ill prepared. Of these scruples, since Hamlet has spent the past few years at Luther's Wittenberg and rarely at Elsinore, his father's ghost can have little prior knowledge.

A ghost, as I have earlier suggested, was thought to reveal itself and its message only by permission of God. Pierre Le Loyer, the sixteenth-century Frenchman who defended the Roman Catholic doctrines about ghosts, has written: Souls "may appear visible by permission [*congé*] of God to those persons whom it pleases Him."[38] A few pages later, Le Loyer indicates that the mission of the ghost was closely bound to God's intent. Purgatorial ghosts "are not able to come back to earth without the specific command [*sans l'exprès commandement*] of God."[39] Noel Taillepied, the French monk, came to the same conclusions in his *Treatise of Ghosts* (1588) as had Le Loyer: "Spirits do not come back at their own will or by their own power . . . but, on extraordinary occasions if God so permits."[40] He makes one point especially pertinent, I think, to any discussion of King Hamlet's Ghost: "God suffers [Spirits] to show themselves in divers shapes . . . in order to do His bidding and fulfil His command."[41] This statement tends to illuminate what Le Loyer has implied when he contended that souls do not come back "sans l'exprês commandement de Dieu," that is, they "do His bidding and fulfil His command." Eleanor Prosser interprets an expanded version of the statement by Taillepied as meaning: "Souls were released from Purgatory only to serve God's will."[42] In brief, as made clear by Taillepied, not only might a ghost have a personal mission; equally likely, it could be an instrument of a second mission imposed by God and hence expected to "fulfill His command." This ethic, as will be shown, is a central function of King Hamlet's Ghost, which may not have a full knowledge of God's specific intent.

Although Eleanor Prosser has made a strong case for regarding King Hamlet's Ghost as a devil, she is pulled up short by her own argument: "If we could unequivocally pronounce the Ghost a demon and its command a damnable temptation, the tragedy would be destroyed."[43] Let us assume that it were not a ghost: it would still have the capability (if it were an angel or a demon) to "fulfil [God's] command" and hence have an objective other than its own. Most of us, however—even if we must consult the stage directions of the second quarto or of Folio 1 to reassure ourselves—know that the Ghost is Shakespeare's stage conception of an honest Christian ghost, however vindictive. "All creation stands ready," according to the medievalist Mary B. Mroz, "to carry out [God's] judgments."[44] Normally, God chose a human instrument, but his options included all creatures: a ghost, itself mindful of "the cruel wrong done," might thus be a suitable instrument of God's purpose or, more likely, an intermediary of that purpose, which need not be the same as its own. At the very least, in the play *Hamlet*, God stands behind the Ghost's mission, for without His approval no spirit (as universally recognized) might intervene in human affairs. God is, therefore, to be accepted as the responsible initiator of the total process of justice that arises from the Ghost's command to Hamlet, and, later, controls the play's major events. A question of this chapter is: To what extent did God either plan or foreknow these events, most of which have to do with retribution? Indications of the restricted authority consigned by God to the Ghost are evident in the Ghost's introductory words to Hamlet; these words reflect, moreover, a well-known biblical prototype, which illustrates the nature of the God-spirit compact.

Just as God was thought to grant permission to the devil to molest a person such as Job, likewise He placed restrictions upon him. Of Job He advised Satan: "Only upon him selfe shalt thou not stretch out thine hand."[45] Any spirit, in particular a purgatorial ghost, was thought to be divinely restricted. King Hamlet's Ghost is extremely cautious lest it speak of a topic forbidden by God:

> But that I am forbid
> To tell the secrets of my prison-house
> I could a tale unfold whose lightest word
> Would harrow up thy soul.
>
> [*Ham*, I.v.13-16]

Restrictions that are not to be compromised have been put upon the Ghost; just as obviously, what it is allowed to reveal to Hamlet is the God-permitted assignment. It speaks only of revenge—"Revenge his foul and most unnatural murder"—and matters that relate to, or justify, the execution of vengeance upon Claudius. On all other matters, it must hold its silence. Meanwhile, lest the Globe audience, almost totally Protestant, be too ready to identify it as a devil, Shakespeare is careful to establish the medieval character of King Hamlet and hence of the Ghost upon its first appearance. Not only does Horatio explain that King Hamlet, "Dar'd to combat," had engaged King Fortinbras in a hand-to-hand duel and had thereby won for Denmark, thirty years ago, a war both heroic and, by all but a few, forgotten; also, the Ghost has been garbed in the armor of that remote occasion. Of perhaps equal significance, Shakespeare has provided it with an aura of authority worthy of an important emissary of God. The Ghost carries, in its hand, the truncheon, symbol of medievalism and, even more so, of kingly power. "King Hamlet comes [back] not so much on a personal mission," M.F. Egan has perceptively observed, "as on a mission for the salvation of Denmark."[46] I do not know precisely what Egan means by "salvation"; nevertheless, at the play's end, a new Danish court has, beyond all expectation, replaced one inextricably enmeshed in crime.

Why, we may pause to ask, is King Hamlet's Ghost—aside from the display of its medieval nature—garbed in armor? Why, moreover, need that armor be "the very armor" worn in the duel with King Fortinbras? The reader/spectator may, of course, answer: it is essential that

Horatio be prompted to inform the audience of the ancient wager "that was and is the question of these wars" (I.i.111), namely, the impending wars threatened by young Fortinbras. Such an answer may neglect much of Shakespeare's intent. It is possible that God, Who was held to be the sole Judge of every wager by combat, is now dissatisfied with his former judgment, for King Hamlet's crown has come, by treachery, into Claudius's hands. In light of the total play's evidence, God (it would seem) has decided to reverse His earlier judgment against the Fortinbras family and to allow young Fortinbras not only to regain the lands lost by his father but also, because of an ancient right, to succeed to the Danish throne. At the play's end, Fortinbras substantiates that right: he has, he explains, "some rights of memory in this kingdom, / Which now to claim my vantage doth invite me" (V.ii.381-82). If what I have said has merit, God must choose between young Fortinbras and Hamlet. A handful of critics will cry: "Yes, exactly right. Hamlet is a reprobate and must be denied promotion." I do not accept their interpretation. We do not, for example, know the particular "rights of memory" which warrant Fortinbras's claim. They may or may not exceed Hamlet's right to the throne. Hamlet, moreover, cannot have both the right of private blood revenge and the right of succession, for the revenge (even if God allows him to expiate the sin of murder) will have soiled his claim to the succession. To Hamlet, in consequence, devolves the unexpected mission of preparing for Fortinbras a court purged of its blight and contamination, the cause of which are Claudius's crime and his court's subsequent deprivation of God's grace; for his principal associates, in abetting him, however unknowingly, in the concealment of his crime, have (like him) aligned themselves against God. The Ghost's armor, then, becomes a symbol, in terms of God's will, of the ancient overthrow of the Fortinbras family at the very moment that He has ordained the family's return to its former high status. This interpretation is supported by the unhesitant acceptance of Fortinbras's right to the throne, by Horatio and others, at the play's end.

The Ghost asks only for the punishment of the murderer Claudius, and in this request, according to established tradition, it has the permission and favor of God, for the crime against King Hamlet has been a crime against God's honor. But of a more comprehensive plan, young Hamlet for obvious reasons cannot be told: fundamentally an ethical instrument, he would, for example, pause on such a plan. The impulsive stabbing of the eavesdropper behind the arras, had he been Claudius, as Hamlet supposes, and not Polonius, would have satisfied in full the personal mission demanded by the Ghost and authorized by God; instead, it becomes the pivotal act that makes all but impossible the fulfillment of the Ghost's expressed command and, at the same moment, puts into operation a larger course of events completely unanticipated. Behind these strange events, none of them premeditated by Hamlet, there evolves, little by little, a rational plan: the methodical destruction of all those who have served Claudius in concealing his crime and, hence, have added to the pall of God's disfavor that hangs over the court. The plan does not entail specific moral principles; still, it has the advantage of removing not only those who bear a personal guilt but also those, like Polonius, who are inclined to an instability of judgment. At the close of the play, when the new and unblemished claimant to the throne arrives at Elsinore, he finds a court voided not only of its evil members but also of those who, because of their wrongheadedness, would have been a grave liability to the new court. In short, among the persons of status, young Fortinbras finds only Horatio, who is neither mentally imbalanced nor tainted by criminal propensity, alive and fit.

The apparent rationality of the plan that I have outlined could, of course, be only fortuitous. This view, very probably, was not shared by the Elizabethans, especially those who had some knowledge of spirit lore. That a ghost could come back to earth only by God's permission, and subject to His binding restrictions, was a medieval belief identical to that relating to the infernal fiend. The lesser-known doctrine, well known in France and not, to my knowledge, in Protestant England, that God was able to work His own chosen objectives by means of a ghost, which could then be said to "fulfil His command" and not its own purpose, may or may not have been known to most Elizabethans. Such a potentiality was, of course, deducible from the belief that God could employ any kind of spirit (whether good or evil) as his instrument in what purpose He chose. No Elizabethan, on the other hand, would have questioned God's foreknowledge of events deriving from the intervention of a spirit, whether demon or ghost, in human affairs. Among Elizabethan theologians, William Perkins reminds his reader: "The foretelling of things to come . . . is a propertie peculiar to God (to whome all things are certenly knowne)." Such foreknowledge includes, in particular, "the alteration . . . of kingdomes" and "the deaths of

Princes."[47] Richard Hooker, the spokesman of Anglican doctrine, accepts God's foreknowledge as a fundamental premise: "God . . . by his knowledge foresee[s] all things,"[48] whether by necessity or contingency.[49] A question of the play Hamlet is: Does God merely foresee and approve the consequences of the Ghost's command, or has He both the power and the intent to bring about precisely the events He chooses? We are confronted with a play which pits a medieval Roman Catholic ghost against a prince of Lutheran background while an audience, predominantly Anglican but not entirely so, looks on. Whatever the faith, the Renaissance conviction was that God does *not* permit the intervention of a spirit, whatever its kind, without His exact foreknowledge of the consequences of that permission. Hooker contends that such permission is tantamount to God's will: "He willeth by permission that which his creatures do."[50]

To the truth of Le Loyer's and Taillepied's statements that God might make use of a ghost to "fulfil His command" (meaning a mission distinct from that purposed by the ghost) the play Hamlet attests, I believe, with a self-sufficing and affirmative voice. We should hold in mind, however, that God, when necessary, has the resource of intervention at any critical moment He chooses. To this, also, Shakespeare gives repeated testimony—four times, in fact.

The briefest account of Hamlet's attempt to carry out the Ghost's command does much to establish the broad judicial reach of the deity who has permitted the Ghost's return to earth, and has imposed certain restrictions, and who is to be accepted (I believe) as the God of the total play. Ordered by the Ghost to avenge his father's murder, young Hamlet, high in self-assurance, promises "to sweep to my revenge," for at the moment he is caught in the spell of the Ghost's medievalism. Shortly, when confronted by the harsh light of his Protestant rationale, he is to modify, rather drastically, the potential of his free will. That he may conceal his intent he must assume "an antic disposition." He then concludes: "The time is out of joint. O cursèd spite, / That ever I was born to set it right!" (I.v.189-90). He has become aware of obstacles, but the most difficult of them, as we later learn, is his Protestant skepticism about the Ghost: "The spirit that I have seen / May be a devil" (II.ii.594-95), who he thinks may purpose his damnation. At the close of act II, the devising of the play scene, in which Hamlet hopes to trap Claudius, restores his confidence in his capability to complete the mission expressly demanded by the Ghost: "The play's the thing / Wherein I'll catch the conscience of the king." This self-confidence is sustained up to the critical episode in which, meaning to kill Claudius, he murders Polonius and shortly concludes that "Heaven hath pleas'd it so," for he has intuited an extraneous prompting. From this point on, the accelerating current of events sweeps him away from, instead of toward, the fulfillment of his known mission until, by apparent chance, he is able to board the pirate ship. On his return to the court at Elsinore, he evidences, undoubtedly because of the unexpectedness of recent events, a philosophy of detachment toward his mission of vengeance, in which he has seemingly failed, for he has killed two more men and not yet Claudius. Aware of an intangible power that has withheld him and his resolve from the fulfillment of that resolve, and mindful of the three murders that he has so recently committed but had not planned, Hamlet comes to terms with the paradox: "There's a divinity that shapes our ends, / Rough-hew them how we will" (V.ii.10-11). Against this "divinity," as he has now discovered, his own will has no power to act.

What, then, are the manifestations of the deity who has permitted the Ghost's return to earth and has, as Taillepied has suggested, a larger purpose, both more significant and more comprehensive, than that of which the Ghost is itself cognizant? At the close of the play's fourth scene, a brief dialogue takes place, immediately after Hamlet, beckoned by the Ghost, has followed it offstage; behind this dialogue is an obvious fear of the import of the Ghost's return to earth:

> *Horatio.* Have after. To what issue will this come?
> *Marcellus.* Something is rotten in the state of Denmark.
> *Horatio.* Heaven will direct it.
>
> [I.iv.89-91]

Marcellus's quotable remark about "the state of Denmark" is apt to cause Horatio's response to pass unnoticed. A moment's focus may remove the reply's prosaic wrapping. To what does the statement "Heaven will direct it"—particularly the pronoun "it"—specifically refer? To "the state of Denmark"? or to what is "rotten" in that state? There is a third possible reference, but in each instance, the statement seems clearly to affirm that Heaven, by intervening, will purge Denmark of the rottenness that threatens its welfare; in this manner Heaven (as Horatio is confident) will "direct' the state through a perilous malaise to restored health. In light of the later neutralization of Hamlet's will, especially his admission of its being powerless to withstand "a divinity that shapes our ends," Horatio's statement ("Heaven will direct it") is, I believe, an early clue to our understanding of Heaven's part in the welfare of Denmark. The term "rotten" (as used in context by Marcellus), with its implication of *internal* corrosion, establishes the impression that the wrong that besets Denmark and is serious enough to have prompted God to permit the intervention of King Hamlet's Ghost must be an inner decay or putrefaction, something festering at the core of the state. And such is precisely the case, as we learn in the next scene: the source of the decay is the present king, who is both an adulterer and a murderer. Horatio, with customary simplicity, has assured Marcellus and ourselves that Heaven will purge, in its own way, Denmark of the blight (for he does not, at the moment, know its nature) that now threatens the nation's health. And although Hamlet, in the next scene, learns from the Ghost what is "rotten in Denmark," even the Ghost seems not to know the full significance of the blight, for so far the Claudian evil has tainted no one except Gertrude.

No more is said about Heaven's, or God's, control over the welfare of Denmark until late in act III. At this critical time, there is the unmistakable suggestion (half-understood by Hamlet) that Heaven's purgative role is not directed solely at Claudius, the source of the infection. While in Gertrude's chamber, Hamlet has impulsively thrust his sword at the "arras" and has then found, in defiance of marital logic, that he has killed Polonius and not Claudius. Standing over the old man's body, he shortly identifies, with unruffled assurance, the cause of the unexpected mishap:

> For this same lord
> I do repent; but Heaven hath pleas'd it so,
> To punish me with this, and this with me,
> That I must be their scourge and minister.
>
> [III.iv.172-78]

To this point in the play Hamlet's role in plotting to kill the fratricide Claudius has been, by definition, that of God's minister, for the Ghost's

"dread command," being permitted by God, has also His overt authority. The external obstacles—two of which are the valid Protestant doubt
as to the Ghost's identity and, apart from that doubt, Hamlet's dread
of being proclaimed a regicide and hence, for all time, dishonored—have
made the task of executing the Ghost's medieval command, as God
would have foreknown, so painfully difficult that it is doomed to unsuc-
cess from the outset.[51] Now, at the critical moment that his revenge is
frustrated, Hamlet sees the apparent accident that has caused Polonius's
death as the will of Heaven. In consequence, Horatio's much earlier
statement that "Heaven will direct" the troubled state of Denmark to
restored health has been provided with a strong piece of affirmative
evidence in terms of Heaven's active intervention. My reader, for the
moment, may question the expendability of Polonius, who is morally
decent. Hamlet, however, is not wrong in having described him, earlier
in the scene, as a "rash, intruding fool." Apart from Polonius's uncivil
practice of eavesdropping, both his senile turns of wit and his forget-
fulness ("What was I about to say?"), together with his incessant habit
of lecturing other persons, pose an almost certain embarrassment for the
new court, over which young Fortinbras is destined to preside. Polonius
has become, in short, a dawdling busybody unfit for his high office, nor
is he likely to be humored out of it. Add to this the fact that, in aiding
Claudius—even though unknowingly—to conceal his crime, he has
obstructed justice and fallen from God's favor.

Hamlet has now, for the first time, found himself in the role of
Heaven's scourge, for in the killing of Polonius he has no claim to
ministerial privilege. He foresees that he may have to continue in this
unvirtuous role, for he expects that Rosencrantz and Guildenstern, as
Claudius's spies, will prompt him to "knavery," and if he is to outwit
them, he must "delve one yard below their mines / And blow them at
the moon" (III.iv.209-10). Exhausted by months of self-doubt capped
by a painful disillusionment and, with it, the shock that he is *now* the
hunted man, Hamlet indicates no opposition to the will which, in
frustrating his lately revived trust in the mission against Claudius, has
made him its scourge and which, after other twists of destiny, he is to
identify as "a divinity that shapes [men's] ends." A central principle insisted upon by Thomas Beard in his *Theatre of Gods Judgments* (1597),
a book almost certainly known to Shakespeare, helps to illuminate and
confirm the unremitting character of the "divinity" identified by Ham-

let: "And unto him [God] belongeth the direction . . . of humane matters. . . . nothing in the world commeth to pass by chance . . . , but
onely and alwaies by the prescription of his wil."[52] If this principle
(not uncommon in Renaissance times) informs the play—and Hamlet,
as I have so far quoted him, has on two occasions attested that it does—
the "accidental judgments" and "casual slaughters" [meaning "unpremeditated killings"][53] reported at the play's end by Horatio become
explainable, almost entirely, in terms of a Providential plan. Hamlet's
talent for premeditated thought and philosophic reflection, once his mission of vengeance has been abruptly frustrated, is to be replaced more
and more by intuitive response in the form of impulses. In short,
although the failure to avenge his dead father will once or twice torment
him, he has not the will and the energy fundamental to the reshaping
of that objective. If "Heaven hath pleas'd it so" that Polonius, and not
Claudius, should be the first to die, it is not illogical to believe that the
others killed by Hamlet, all but one by impulse, are to die at Heaven's
pleasure.

That Hamlet is now resigned to the service of a will immeasurably
more powerful than his own, and that he no longer commands the vigor
of mind to oppose it, are illustrated emphatically in the crucial episode
that highlights his aborted voyage to England. He has been strangely
kept awake, as he later explains to Horatio:

> Sir, in my heart there was a kind of fighting
> That would not let me sleep. Methought I lay
> Worse than the mutines in the bilboes [fetters]. Rashly,
> And prais'd be rashness for it—let us know,
> Our indiscretion sometime serves us well,
> When our deep plots do pall; and that should learn us
> There's a divinity that shapes our ends,
> Rough-hew them how we will.
>
> [V.ii.4-11]

Moved by a sudden fit of "indiscretion," he had (he explains) mounted
a ladder to the cabin of his former schoolfellows, now his betrayers,
found and opened the royal commission that demanded his immediate
death, made the necessary alterations, sealed the new commission, and
sent Rosencrantz and Guildenstern to the execution block—all this as

the effect of a compelling indiscretion. Asked by Horatio how he sealed the revised commission, he quickly responds: "Why, even in that was Heaven ordinant [predeterminative]" and explains that he had with him, although he had not so intended, "my father's signet," the counterpart of the present "Danish seal." This highly crucial and recent action, as Shakespeare holds it before us, is seen in entirety as the working of "a divinity," to which Hamlet is bound as the scourge.

From the time of his first encounter with the Ghost, Hamlet has been motivated by repeated indiscretions—in his badgering of others, in the fatal thrust aimed at the unseen Polonius, and most recently in the compulsion to find and open the royal commission. A person's "indiscretion," Hamlet has discovered, is likely to serve a man better than his "deep plots," for the reason that it may be the sign of a divine being who, in turn, has an absolute control over the outcome of events. To Hamlet's contention that "a divinity . . . shapes our ends," it should be noted that Horatio replies, without hesitation: "That is most certain" (V.ii.12). Hamlet has responded to a strange impulse, in which there is not an iota of forethought, and this impulse is to cost his two former schoolfellows their lives while it spares his own. Both Hamlet and Horatio—and apparently Shakespeare, too—see in this uncommon episode the prompting of a higher intelligence, certainly of a Providential character.

We may properly ask: "Did Shakespeare actually believe that Providence could alert the impulses of a person such as Hamlet? Is the method of communication exclusively recondite, or is the whole business a bit of humbug?" The answer lies, I believe, in several remarks found in Shakespeare's history plays, three of which I noted in my third chapter. Carlisle, for example, must be "stirr'd up by God," for without divine prompting he would not be able to forecast, accurately, the grim events of a distant time. A second remark in *Richard II* is equally pertinent. York ascribes the cruelty of those Londoners who have cast dust on the captive Richard's "sacred head" to divine intervention: "God," he says, "for some strong purpose steel'd the hearts of men" (*R2*, V.ii.33-34) lest those hearts melt into pity. Again, in *2 Henry IV*, the dying king interprets Hal's removal of the crown from his bedside as providentially motivated; he addresses Hal: "God put it in thy mind to take it hence, / That thou [by so wisely defending that act] mightst win the more thy father's love" (*2 Hen 4*, IV.v.179-80). A fourth piece of evidence, not cited earlier, is significant in that it attempts to identify the medium of extramundane communication. In *Richard III*, a citizen, fearful of the repercussions of Edward IV's death, explains: "By a divine instinct men's minds mistrust / Ensuing danger" (*R3*, II.iii.42-43). In the use of the term "divine instinct" Shakespeare attempts to identify that tiny piece of divinity which persists in the individual man, however worldly, and through which God is able, at His chosen times, to communicate with him. When Hamlet interprets his bizarre shipboard experience as the consequence of a propitious "indiscretion," he is prompt to place the habit of "indiscretion" in diametric contrast to "our deep plots," which are products of the human mind. He then concludes that, behind indiscretions of particular note, is a divinity that "shapes" our destinies. The overt implication is that Hamlet's principal indiscretions, whether propitious to him or not, are the effect of the prompting of a "divine instinct" within him as it reacts to an external and inscrutable power, which we term Providence.

Shortly after the unexpected return from the sea, Hamlet again senses the presence of an extrinsic force within him. In his confrontation with Laertes at Ophelia's grave, he must urgently warn: "Yet have I in me something dangerous, / Which let they wiseness fear. Hold off thy hand" (V.ii.256-57). He is aware, it appears, of the same power which compelled his ruthless action against Rosencrantz and Guildenstern and, in respect to Laertes, is fearful of it. For no compulsion of his own—as distinct from that of the extrinsic force—moves him to injure Laertes. That Hamlet is mindful of the "something dangerous" within him, even though his own nature (as he insists) is not "splenitive and rash," attests only to his repeated awareness of an inner compulsion much alien to those promptings that are native to him. An irony helps to explain why, at this time, the prompting of the "something dangerous" is moderate enough to be withstood. Laertes, not only in his own schemes but also in the more universal plan, has yet a function to perform. An ancient dogma held that God, once His scourge has fulfilled the appointed mission, must destroy him and, for this purpose, often makes use of a second human scourge.[54] This role, of course, is to be assumed by Laertes.

Of the people marked for death other than Laertes, why is it that Hamlet browbeats each, in turn, so unmercifully? In most unconscionable fashion he has badgered Polonius, Rosencrantz, Guildenstern,

Ophelia, Claudius, and even Gertrude. The insulting and bold character of these outbursts is not easily explainable in terms of the antic disposition that he has planned, for they are marked by an indiscreet aggressiveness that, in attracting undue attention to Hamlet, tends to destroy the purpose of the assumed disposition, which was to conceal, and not to publicize, his mission of vengeance. The thrust at the arras in Gertrude's chamber is not Hamlet's first major indiscretion. While badgering Ophelia in the "nunnery" episode and rightly suspecting that Claudius and Polonius are eavesdropping, he casts highly provocative barbs at each of them, but in particular at Claudius: "I say we will have no moe marriage: those that are married already—all but one—shall live" (III.i.147-49). For this indiscretion Claudius instantly decides to have Hamlet shipped to England. The King's countermove against Hamlet has thus found its first important impetus from a most undisciplined indiscretion. Has Hamlet either much overplayed his "antic disposition," or equally possible, has something alien to his customary nature, which has made him "the glass of fashion" capable of "most sovereign reason," been implanted within it, if only temporarily? The fact that Hamlet has spoken with a ghost indebted for its return to the approval of God provides his sensory capabilities with a potential keenness of sensitivity not shared by his fellow characters. This potential, of course, finds substantiation in the play's second half in his extrasensory recognition and ultimate acceptance of a controlling Providence. Might not his early and often crude indiscretions—in Ophelia's "closet" and in the browbeating episodes—be caused by rudimentary promptings of Providence? After all, it has an evident motive to enforce a fission between him and his associates. The task of scourge, of course, presupposes an absolute detachment from sympathy.

Whatever the reasons for Hamlet's verbal humiliation of those marked for death, he becomes, in the eyes of the audience and the reader, the judge of who is fit or not fit to execute the sober duties of the next royal court: by means of enunciating glaring defects of ethics or mentality he identifies the unfit, of whose deaths he can have no foreknowledge. In terms of ethics, both Claudius and Laertes, each a murderer, are deserving of death, as is Gertrude, for adultery, under God's law (Exod. 20.14 and Lev. 20.10). Although Rosencrantz and Guildenstern, as far as we know, do not violate a commandment which dictates capital punishment, they serve a treacherous king against a boyhood friend,

whom they mercenarily and callously betray.[55] Amoral, they honor duplicity and self-advantage at the expense of the last scrap of ethics and
would pose an utmost danger to the welfare of any beneficent social
order, in particular since their natural inclination is to serve evil. By contrast, Polonius (as I have suggested), being accustomed to high station
but much declined in wit, has no hope of improving his own fortunes
and, largely because of his incessant wrongheadedness, shows considerable promise of harming those of Fortinbras. Omitting Ophelia's short-
comings for the present, I have attempted to justify the motive behind
what appears to be, largely in terms of the play's internal evidence, a
foresighted and rational plan on the part of God. Simply stated, the "accidental" deaths, since they expunge not only the wicked and the
criminal but also the mentally unqualified, bespeak a rationality not explained by the motives within the play, for only two of the eight deaths
(Claudius's, indirectly, and Hamlet's) are an effect of a premeditated
human purpose. The external power to which Hamlet is compelled to
surrender his will, while he assumes the role of its scourge, is rational,
Shakespeare seems to have told us; for he is at pains to show that in
destroying not only the criminal and the wicked but also the mentally
unstable, that power establishes a systematic pattern: the subordination
of the claims and the rights of the individual to the founding of a new
royal court devoid of both the highly corrupt self-interest and the nagging preoccupations that have entangled its predecessor. In retrospect,
when we are finally aware that the new king, Fortinbras, has no one
of the Claudian court more objectionable than the trustworthy and
stoical Horatio with whom he must deal in matters of state, we are able
to recognize the logic, however ruthless, of the Providence that controls
the play.

Shakespeare's portrait of the destruction of a royal court perverted,
essentially, because of one man's crime is founded on the stern justice
of the Old Testament God. In this respect, it is a modest variation on
the theme of the two historical tetralogies, including the Lancastrian
purge. For not only was Jehovah an avenger on the individual criminal;
equally often, He was a destroyer of both wicked cities and selected
groups of maleficents,[56] but only when the Law that He had given
to mankind was unenforced or neglected. Shakespeare had, thus, an
ample biblical precedent for the judgment of God upon the closely knit

Claudian inner circle, for at the very least its members, in serving the King (however ignorantly) against the exposure of his crime, bear the infection of his evil.

Ironically, of the two missions in which Hamlet participates, his private goal of revenge is to be successful only when, at the play's end, it finds alignment with the extrinsic force which has made of him its scourge. In the meantime, even though Hamlet has solved (for himself anyway) the problem of the Ghost, he has failed to solve the problems posed by Claudius, whom he has a divine sanction to punish. G.W. Knight, nearly a half century ago, recognized the effectiveness of King Claudius: "Claudius is not drawn as wholly evil—far from it. We see the government of Denmark working smoothly. Claudius shows every sign of being an excellent diplomatist and king."[57] How right he is— "every sign"! Together with Claudius's suave and sugared talk, his very effectiveness is a part of the film—"the glittering surface of Claudius' court," as Maynard Mack has phrased it—that conceals from the King's associates, and even from the reader and the audience, the enormity of his evil. On the surface the court of Denmark shines fairly; beneath that surface, formerly honest people are being prostituted, not once but over and over again, to the habits of conspiracy, eavesdropping, and duplicity in order to conceal an abominable crime of which none of them has knowledge. Advantaged by his facile outward graces, Claudius has extended his control much beyond his immediate associates, for he has been elected king by the courtiers at large, who also, in willful acquiescence to his persuasive charm, have approved the incestuous marriage, itself an affront against God.

Some critics have marveled why, once Hamlet has eliminated his doubt of the Ghost's integrity, he does not turn for support against Claudius to the commoners of Elsinore, whom under similar conditions Laertes is able to arouse against the King. That Hamlet has entertained a notion to enlist the commoners' help is, of course, speculation. Whether he has such a plan, or is capable of devising it, is obscured by his undisciplined response to Claudius's self-revelation of guilt ("Give me some light. Away!"), for instead of focusing on his next move against the King (his first move having been the play scene, carefully thought out) he is caught up in a whirlwind of overexcited moods, tempered momentarily (in the prayer scene) by cautionary restraint,

renewed again as he bursts into his mother's chamber, and brought to
a climax (without a moment's reflection) by his stab at the arras. Oscar
J. Campbell has attempted to explain this kind of behavior by Hamlet:
"Adverse fate so times the rhythm of Hamlet's malady that at a given
moment he is in the grip of the emotions that fit him least to deal with
the situation confronting him."[58] It is much easier, of course, to strike
at a curtain in one's excitement than at the image of the living man.
When he finds Polonius dead and not Claudius, Hamlet not only
discovers himself the instrument of a will much superior to his own.
Equally significant (as later events make clear), he can no longer turn
to the commoners of Elsinore for support against the King; Hamlet has
the blood of Polonius on his hands, and the old man had friends.

Hamlet's task of revenge, especially after he has cut himself off from
the opportunity to muster the populace against Claudius, entails much
greater difficulties than those experienced by the avengers of the history
plays. In these earlier plays, the agent of God, whether the pragmatic
Bolingbroke or the sanctimonious Henry Tudor, recognizes the mission
to which he is summoned and performs it because it has been destined
and because it fits his own will. Each of these two men, however, has
bided his time, waiting for the right turn of destiny. Hamlet, for trying
to manipulate events (both before and during the play scene and in Gertrude's "closet"), is less fortunate. The impatient man, he has come too
late to recognize, is promptly locked within a destiny and "rough-hew"
his own ends "how [he] will," he must perform its purpose and not
his own. In Hamlet's haste to stab at the arras under only a moderate
provocation, he has none of the prudently disciplined judgment illustrated by Bolingbroke and fundamental, in Shakespeare's perspective
of life, to both the control of a person's fate and survival. Hamlet, if
he is to confront his private mission once again, must find it in events
beyond his own power to manipulate.

Having told Horatio of the action against Rosencrantz and Guildenstern, Hamlet is warned that Claudius will soon hear from England of
their executions. To this warning he gives no indication of alarm: "It
will be short; the interim is mine, / And a man's life's no more than
to say 'one'" (V.ii.73-74). Our expectation is that he will present to
Horatio a fit plan of action against Claudius, as he has earlier done in
explaining the purpose of the play-within-the-play. Instead, his

thoughts turn, in the very next line, to the bad manners he showed to Laertes at Ophelia's grave, and this affront continues to preoccupy him. What then are we to think of the immediately preceding line: "And a man's life's no more than to say 'one'"? Is it not also—and less consciously—a reflex of the recent graveyard experience? He has most certainly learned from the graveyard, the book of death, some things about the limitations of life. He has been struck by the fact that the sum of a man's achievements is to have "his fine pate full of fine dirt," a condition that may persist for millions of years. Hence, when he tells Horatio that "the interim is mine, / And a man's life's no more than to say 'one,'" is he not implying in effect: "Why should a man lay plots for great achievement and insist upon long life? His sought-after achievements, even the greatest, are not worth two handfuls of dirt and his life span, at best, is one second as measured on the cosmic clock." Having learned that a man's true value is something less than one iota above zero, and having found a sense of purpose in responding to "indiscretions," whereas his "deep plots" have brought him nothing but defeat and unfulfillment, is Hamlet to be thought neglectful in laying no further plots in response to the Ghost's "dread command"? Hardly, I think. He now knows that, if he is to kill Claudius, he must reject human logic in favor of an unsought opportunity; for it is in judgment, not in opportunity, that Hamlet has met with self-betrayal.

Even after the opportunity arrives, unasked for—a gentleman's fencing match with Laertes, at which Claudius will be present—Hamlet shows much more interest in badgering the messenger, unknown to him but typical of the neophyte courtier, than in his message. He has no plan except to wait on the opportunity. As for the duel itself, he will "follow the King's pleasure: if his fitness speaks, mine is ready" (V.ii.193-94). Fitness *only* for the fencing match with Laertes? Somewhat more, I think, is implied. He knows now that, behind his recent shipboard "indiscretion" (which has spared his life, significantly perhaps) and acting through it, has been the will of a higher power which he no longer has the impulse to question and which holds the destinies of both Claudius and himself.[59] If otherwise, if he is thinking only in terms of a gentleman's fencing match with the odds "laid on twelve [touches] to nine," the swords being tipped, how are we to account for the sudden and pronounced premonition of death which now seizes him (V.ii.203-208)?

Nor is the qualm (as a few have said) a punishment; it is prompted by
Hamlet's realization that he, like Claudius, must now stand under
God's judgment.

Buoyed, shortly, by his sense of rightness—for his own will and that
of the "divinity that shapes [men's] ends" have now an evident common purpose—he concludes that the death required by a man's "special providence" is neither tragic nor, in terms of his new vision, untimely: "what is't to leave betimes?" It is better to achieve one high
deed of justice in the service of God (he appears to reason) than to live
one hundred years, which by cosmic standards is nothing; of death, he
has learned the one fundamental premise: "The readiness is all." Strong
as Claudius may feel with the odds of human ingenuity (in this instance,
the murder plot) on his side, his faith is woven of complacence. To
Hamlet, strengthened by a new and expanded vision of relative values
and hence unfearful of death, have shifted the better odds. He has
learned, moreover, as Claudius has not yet entirely, that "deep plots"
often turn upon the plotter. As he prepares to fence with Laertes, he
has not even the stark outline of a plan, for he has acquired, in terms
of the Providential presence in the play, the humility and the trust that
reject the faulty values of the human mind in favor of intuitive response.
If this were not so, he would even now be lying in a grave in England.

Whereas his long-deferred vengeance upon Claudius is shortly and
strangely fulfilled, in front of Hamlet lies the final testimony of the more
comprehensive mission which he neither sought nor pursued of his own
will—the dead bodies of Laertes and Gertrude, the last two (except
Claudius) of the Claudian inner circle. Whatever his regrets, his next
to final words, prompted by the arrival of Fortinbras, open a curtain
upon the future and, in so doing, attest to the beneficent objective of
the divinely structured plan:

> . . . I do prophesy the election lights
> On Fortinbras; he has my dying voice.
> So tell him.
>
> [V.ii.347-49]

The next king of Denmark, we are assured, has Hamlet's unqualified
approval, a commendation—among the characters of the play—shared
only with Horatio. Meanwhile, in the play's final task, Hamlet has

again become the minister, and not the scourge, of Heaven. He has fulfilled an authentic trust which, sanctioned by God and verified by the Sixth Commandment, demands the death of the murderer Claudius. In this task, as next of kin, Hamlet has acted as the uniquely orthodox agent of God's judgment.

The portrait of Hamlet, because he resolves to do one thing and accomplishes something quite apart from it, is permeated with irony. His promise to "sweep to my revenge" is not to find fulfillment until, directly or indirectly, he is the instrument of six deaths that he has not premeditated. The difficulty of Hamlet's carrying out the Ghost's command has made the overthrow of the corrupted Danish court inevitable. For without the external problems—such as the honest Protestant doubt as to the Ghost, the Swiss bodyguard that protects the King, and the loyalty of the courtiers to Claudius, who is king by their election[60]— the command might have been so readily (and perhaps unwisely) executed by Hamlet as to demand no more than a dagger and the presence of Claudius. A major deterrent, as Coleridge and (later) Bradley stressed a long time ago, is Hamlet's ethical attitude toward an objective for which, as a well-educated Renaissance prince, he is not psychologically conditioned. "The whole concept of the duty of private vengeance [was] a medieval idea."[61] As a consequence, reflecting the tension between the manifold scruples of Renaissance Protestantism and the stolid self reliance of the medieval world, the best-intentioned resolves of Hamlet tend to fragment, because of his tendency to inquire and not to act, before the hard insistence of the Ghost's command. It is the uncommon complexity of Hamlet's dilemma, foreseen by God, that qualifies him to be the scourge of a larger purpose unknown to him; for he brings to this second mission the pent-up emotional reserve, and with it an aptness for unpremeditated response, that are the recoil of the agonizing frustration of his private mission. He brings to it, also, a bit of the latent knave.

That Horatio remains alive is telltale evidence. His survival attests that, although the will of God may destroy the impertinent and those who slavishly serve the trespasser—and, of course, the trespasser himself—it has no inclination to harm the man who, in normalcy of detachment, neither expects other persons to wait upon his self-interest nor allows himself to be a puppet of theirs. The ultimate effect of the Ghost's command of vengeance—a part of the medieval ethic—has been to cleanse the halls of Elsinore; it has rid them, in particular, of those elements that are products of minds and passions not yet ready to cope with the Renaissance relaxing of both the medieval societal structure and, in consequence, its built-in moral restraints: witness the hasty and incestuous marriage and its brazenness; the nightly drunken revels; the network of spies; the forwardness of Polonius in imposing his assumptions on the King, customarily in the form of presumptuous platitudes; Ophelia's porcelainlike fragility, unfit for the strategems of the court; and the hot-headed impudence of Laertes, who also plots and commits a murder. Even more unfit for the new court of Denmark are Rosencrantz and Guildenstern, each of whom, being of a servile and amoral nature, is ready—in fact, even anxious—to present his soul to the highest bidder, however evil. Horatio, by contrast, is the paragon of propriety. What Shakespeare has shown us is that Horatio has in him enough of the medieval solidity of temperament and mind not to lose his habit of self-containment when confronted by the complexity of a world that is both Renaissance and, in the Elsinore of the play, Machiavellian. We tend to hope that, as an unlooked-for effect of the Ghost's "dread command," the impassive Horatio is destined to become a trusted adviser of Fortinbras's court. To him belongs the opportunity, as well as the proven cast of temperament, to reorient a society that, in the area of ennobling and substantive values, has as yet been "powerless to be born."

SEVEN

Macbeth, the Devil, and God

The play *Macbeth*, in terms of its source materials, is a conspicuous link between Shakespeare's English history plays and the Christian tragedies. Like the histories, it is a medieval British play and, like them, it draws its principal historical materials from Holinshed's *Chronicles*. What sets it in almost diametrical contrast to the history plays is the tone that derives from Shakespeare's concentration on Scottish demonology and, most important, on the effects of that multifaceted demonology as it shapes Macbeth's responses to it; for this tone, often intuitive and hence implicit, places an unabridgeable distance between the reportorial style basic to the English histories and the enigmatic intensities of language that are the essential substance of the tone itself. The play, as a consequence, in its psychological probes into the dark recesses of a man's mind and in its attendant study of the waste of a high human potential, is Shakespeare's most tragic; for what is written of the aspiring Macbeth is implied of other men as well. Shakespeare found only a small portion of the supernatural substructure in Holinshed's *Chronicles*. For most of it he was indebted to contemporary pamphlets on the occult, in particular (as is fitting) to King James's then famous book on Scottish witchcraft. In my chapters on Shakespeare's history plays, I have isolated one important factor and at least two minor ones behind the sometimes puzzling delay of God's ultimate judgment, a topic that had once been of peculiar interest to Plutarch. In the present play, the delay of God's judgment finds, apparently, yet another explanation: the stubborn ascendancy of demonic forces.

Macbeth, unlike Richard III, at the time that the play named after him opens, has no evident reason to fear God's retribution. Aside from enemy soldiers slain in battle he has killed nobody. But the forces that are to compel him to the murders of Duncan and, later, Banquo are already in motion and, better to comprehend his predicament before and after each murder, as well as the delay of the divine punishment, it is necessary to have a look at the motives that organize the highly compelling forces. Without these forces—which are largely supernatural—Macbeth's murders would have remained uncommitted; there would, ultimately, be no powers of retribution in behalf of the dead and, in all probability, no Shakespearean play of note entitled *Macbeth*.

It is tempting to accept the theory of Henry N. Paul that the Witches are avenging the death of the rebel Macdonwald upon Macbeth; [1] the present chapter, like those upon *Richard II* and *Hamlet*, might then have a direct focus upon the theme of vengeance from inception to end even though Satan, in much of the play, preempts God as the presiding Judge. Paul contends that in Shakespeare's play the atmosphere of Scotland is "filthy" (I.i.11) and "infected" (IV.i.138) because witches and demons "swarm everywhere in the air."[2] He adds confidently: "With this picture of Scotland in mind, consider what the bleeding sergeant means when he says that the merciless Macdonwald was worthy to be a rebel because 'the multiplying Villanies of Nature doe swarme upon him' . . . They [the "Villanies of Nature"] are witches transported by their devils, swarming about Macdonwald and inciting him to rebel against his king."[3] Hence, Paul concludes, the Witches "are quick to avenge [Macdonwald's] death" upon Macbeth, who has slain him. If we choose to accept Paul's thesis, *Macbeth* becomes a play in which the avenging of the dead upon the living is the central theme that structures the plot from the opening scene to the climactic slaying of Macbeth. Such a reading, however, is based upon a statement—namely, "the multiplying Villanies of Nature doe swarme upon him"—which is obstinate in its ambiguity and is made about a man never again mentioned in the play. Paul's interpretation of *Macbeth* provides the play with a novel and perhaps adequate reading; but I do not believe that such a thesis was Shakespeare's conscious purpose.

As the play opens, the immediate intent of the Witches is "to meet with Macbeth" and to inform him of the prophecies. As Paul has recognized, they are not merely amusing themselves: they have both a fundamental purpose and a compelling interest in the intended meeting. Behind the scenes is a conspiracy, almost certainly of demonic character, and its intent, if we may judge by the darkling prospect that awaits Macbeth, is undeniably sinister. In some way Macbeth has offended against the harmonized structure of nature and, losing the protection of God, has exposed himself to demonic intervention. By almost every Renaissance demonologist, including King James, George Giffard, and William Perkins, we are told that a demon can work his mischief only by permission of God and, second, that a witch has no power to harm (or to prophesy) outside her partnership with the devil. For the slaying of Macdonwald, a notorious rebel, Macbeth cannot be thought to have lost the protection of God. His guiltiness apparently lies in another, albeit related, area.

Two statements by King James, Shakespeare's principal source on witchcraft in Scotland, help to explain why Macbeth has become vulnerable to demonic intervention: the devil, he stresses, seeks to destroy "either the soule or the body, or both of them, that he is so permitted [by God] to deale with: God by the contrarie, drawes ever, out of that evill, glorie to himselfe . . . by the wracke of the wicked in his justice."[4] The second statement is especially pertinent: "That olde and craftie Serpent, being a spirite, hee easilie spyes our affections, and so conformes himself thereto, to deceave us to our wracke."[5] Since there is unquestionably a malefic motive, permitted by God, behind the Witches' intervention—and they, in turn, have the power of prophecy only from a devil, for of themselves they have none—the sin lies in an "affection" that has taken hold of Macbeth and has thrust him outside the pale of God's established order and hence of His protection. The Witches may indeed be motivated by the slaying of Macdonwald; God uses such motives, however, to His own ends.

Critics have called attention to the fact that the prophecies made by the three Witches are responsive to thoughts already in Macbeth's mind, in particular his ambition to be king. Matthew N. Proser states the matter succinctly: "The weird sisters do not even plant the seed of desire in Macbeth, but rather, their 'All hail's,' incantatory and enigmatic, act as an objectification of a desire already resident within Macbeth."[6] A bit more inclusive is a statement by Cumberland Clark: "The Sisters appear to Macbeth in his weakest moment. . . . The hour of success is always the most dangerous for those who are madly ambitious. In their prophecies they echo Macbeth's secret hopes and desires."[7] The victories over both the rebel army and the Norwegian invaders, together with Macbeth's ruthless but much admired exploits, have provided an obvious stimulus to his pride. He has achieved what is beyond the capacity of his cousin King Duncan, overly mild and temperate. In his mind—and undoubtedly he is right—he has attributes of kingship which are grievously lacking in Duncan. As hero of the hour, as one who has wrought "strange images of death" upon the battlefield, he has entertained for himself thoughts unfit for a subject, namely, that he and not Duncan is, by right of manhood, the appropriate king of Scotland. Such an aspiration is shortly to be substantiated by Lady Macbeth, when she soliloquizes upon her husband: "Thou wouldst be great; / Art not without ambition" (I.v.15-16). Of his "vaulting ambition" Macbeth is equally aware. It is this "affection"—one of prideful ambition—which, inflated by an almost unparalleled success, has put Macbeth outside the boundaries of the established order as recognized by God. Nor will the devil allow the "affection" to languish: "As an old practisian, he [the devil] knowes well inough what humour domines most in anie of us, and . . . can subtillie walken [waken] up the same, making it peccant, or to abounde . . . when God will so permit him."[8] At the moment of his most significant success, Macbeth has had thoughts of a traitorous mold and, in consequence, has become vulnerable to the devil, to whom, as James affirms, "witches are servantes onelie and slaves."[9]

When Macbeth is told that the prophecy of the Second Witch has come true—namely, that he has been appointed Thane of Cawdor—the response of Banquo, who overhears, accords precisely with both Scottish and English demonology: "What, can the devil speak true?" (I.iii.107). "The Devill," King James informs his reader, "may prophesie to them [witches] . . . when he plainely speakes unto them . . . for their prophesying."[10] George Giffard, an Anglican minister, describes the devil-witch relationship more gracefully and, in this instance, with an added point: "[The devil], especially where he hath power given him [by God] to work and to bring a matter about, he can and will tell it beforehand."[11] By these interpretations, the Witches are merely the Pythic agents of one or more devils who, having found Macbeth at a moment when he is high in treasonous pride and hence out of God's favor, are intent on enticing him into a sin whereby they may work his damnation. The three imps of the play—Harpier, Graymalkin, and Paddock—never obtrude for the reason that (unless in the shape of the Apparitions) they are kept offstage; but they have a dreaded power: Macbeth, at the end of the play, is compelled to look back and curse the "juggling fiends. . . . / That palter with us in a double sense" (V.viii.19-20). Devils, and not the Witches, are the main plotters of the "valiant" Macbeth's ultimate transmogrification into a man-beast, so opposite to his former nature. Of witches and their craft, the Elizabethan demonologist Perkins has aptly stated: "All [evil] that is done commeth by the worke of the devill."[12]

Macbeth's hope of becoming king by means of the normal channels of succession is not illogical: "If chance will have me King, why, chance will crown me" (I.iii.143). The medieval doctrine of kin-right, rather than that of primogeniture, was in the eleventh century still prevalent in most European countries: as maternal cousin to Duncan, Macbeth stands, partially because of his renowned valor, an apparently good chance to be elected as Duncan's successor. Malcolm, however, is appointed Prince of Cumberland, a title that Macbeth has undoubtedly hoped to possess because, as explained by George Buchanan in his *History of Scotland* (1582), "the command of Cumberland was always considered the next step to the crown."[13] The consequence is that, through the Witches' prophecies and the carefully calculated goadings of his wife, Macbeth is brought to consider the murder of Duncan, a deed for which he has no native capacity. He can be ruthless upon the battlefield, but not in his domestic relationships.

It may be argued that the Third Witch, in prophesying to Macbeth that he "shalt be King hereafter," does not foresee his need to murder Duncan and hence is not conscious of her wicked purposes. Of a greater certainty, if we are to believe the Elizabethan demonologists, as well as King James, she has her "prophesying" from a devil (very possibly, her imp Harpier), whose only purpose in revealing a truth shortly to be fulfilled is to gain, thereby, a convert for hell. Banquo, after observing (with his customary objectivity) the sinister intelligence behind the immediate fulfillment of the Second Witch's prophecy ("What, can the devil speak true?"), proceeds to warn Macbeth of the danger inherent in such an occult actualization:

> That, trusted home,
> Might yet enkindle you unto the crown,
> Besides the Thane of Cawdor. But 'tis strange;

> And oftentimes to win us to our harm,
> The instruments of darkness tell us truths,
> Win us with honest trifles, to betray 's
> In deepest consequence.
>
> [I.iii.120-26]

In warning Macbeth that he may be "enkindle[d] . . . unto the crown"—that is, tempted to seize it—if he trusts unduly in the fulfillment of an "honest trifle" (the thaneship of Cawdor), Banquo sees the Witches as merely "instruments" in the service of a dark and foreboding intelligence. Importantly, the context of Banquo's warning is taken directly out of King James's *Daemonologie*: the devil "oblices [obliges] himself in some trifles to them [intended victims], that he may [by winning favor] obtein the fruition of their body & soule, which is the onlie thing he huntes for."[14] In short, Banquo has seen in the prophecies, and in the prompt fulfillment of one of them, an attempt by demons to seduce Macbeth into a crime having, for him, ".deepest consequence." In summary, then, it is not the Witches but their acknowledged "masters"—the mysterious demons that are the backdrop of the play— who hold the important and critical foreknowledge that Macbeth, once his ambition has betrayed him, is destined to have recourse to a crime essentially damnable. The Witches' prophecies, devised by their masters, are a goad to this ambition. To Shakespeare's audience, heedful of biblical example, Satanic devices were fashioned not of caprice but of occult foresight. The only task overtly incumbent on the demonic conspiracy is to bring Macbeth's ambition into a "peccant" and hence vulnerable state.

Proser has contended that Macbeth, confronted by a deed much beyond his grasp, "acts in order to free himself of the agonizing and guilt ridden compulsion to act."[15] Macbeth's feelings of guilt have been noted not only by Proser but by a large majority of critics from A. C. Bradley's time to ours. Rolf Soellner, with a debt to Richard G. Moulton's *Shakespeare as a Dramatic Artist* (3rd ed., 1893), sharply dissents from the traditional view. He argues that Macbeth's fear is not the fear which derives from human conscience—a psychic phenomenon (as shown in chapter 5) established by the Elizabethan authorities Timothy Bright and, especially, William Perkins—but, rather, the

embedded fear that man shares with beasts.[16] It seems to me that both
fears are a customary part of the human experience: a person is fearful
of committing an act because he has been taught that the act is explicitly
forbidden by God; he is also fearful when someone or something
threatens his well-being. Soellner points out, rightly, that Macbeth
repeatedly uses the word "fear" but never mentions the word "conscience." It might be noted, however, that Lady Macbeth, a person of
less moral substance (I believe) than is her husband, does speak of conscience, although not identifying it by name; she invokes evil spirits and
then commands them:

> Make thick my blood,
> Stop up th'access and passage to remorse
> That no compunctious visitings of nature
> Shake my fell purpose [the murder of Duncan].
>
> [I.v.40-43]

A compunction, we are advised by Webster's *New Collegiate Dictionary*,
is an "anxiety arising from guilt" and, by the *Oxford Universal Dictionary*, "a sting of conscience": hence the "compunctious visitings of
nature" feared by the Lady are an effect of guilt or conscience. Once sustained by her demonic spirits, she is bold and unswerving in crime,
whereas Macbeth, who does not invoke them, remains hesitant and
shaken with fear. But are we to say that Macbeth's fear is prompted entirely by the fear that man shares with beasts? Are we to say, in short,
that Macbeth has no fear-provoking conscience because he never mentions the word "conscience" by name? Are we to say that Timothy
Bright is in utter error when he tells us that "a molestation . . . riseth
from conscience, condemning the guiltie soule of those ingraven lawes
of nature [the Ten Commandments], which *no man* [my italics] is voide
of"?[17] Did the Globe audience have reason to believe that Macbeth was
an apostate to human experience and hence "voide" of the slightest
respect of God and His commandments, which Perkins has identified as
"the binder of [a man's] conscience"?

And if Shakespeare observed no close interplay between conscience
and fear, how do we explain Richard III's outcry "O coward conscience, how dost thou afflict me!"—for the vocative (as shown in

chapter 5) clearly means "conscience that induces cowardice"? A sizable majority of critics has agreed that the Lady, no longer sustained by her demons, is destroyed by a violated conscience; yet, however much she fears "the compunctious visitings of nature," she shares with Macbeth the fact that she never once utters the word "conscience." Soellner, by contrast, once he has denied Macbeth the normal pangs of conscience, must, for the sake of his argument, repeatedly refer to Macbeth's "moral sense," an impropriety only because he has thus implied an organic separation between moral sense and conscience. Finally, wherein is the powerful fascination of the play *Macbeth* if we take from the central character his conscience and conclude that his fear is, from the outset, that of a beast and has nothing whatsoever to do with his violating of the divine law? Can the fall of such a man—if man at all—induce a tragic response? The Macbeth of this chapter—in contrast to Soellner's view— is a person of moral substance and, largely for that reason, unfit for the first of the crimes he commits.

That the crime of his first murder is all but unendurable to Macbeth's moral perspective is illustrated by his repeated hallucinations which, being unreal in themselves, are symbols of the incredulity with which Macbeth views his own participation in the murder. The hallucination of the airborne dagger is followed by a series of strange imaginings, which are to culminate in the vision of the gory-locked Banquo. At the moment of Duncan's murder comes the second hallucination, and this time it is one of hearing, not of sight; the hallucinated voice, probably in the intonation of Duncan, foretells the agony that Macbeth intuits and that he shall not escape: "Sleep no more; Macbeth does murder sleep" (II.ii.35-36). The nightmarish unreality in which Macbeth holds his present crime, since it lies outside the pale of his norm of ethics, comes to a forcible climax: he startles at the sight of his blood-spattered hands and cannot, for the moment, comprehend them as his own:

> What hands are here? Ha! They pluck out mine eyes.
> Will all great Neptune's ocean wash this blood
> Clean from my hand?
>
> [II.ii.59-61]

He thereupon expresses a thought indicative of incredulous wonder at what that hand has done:

No; this hand will rather
The multitudinous seas incarnadine,
Making the green one red.

[II.ii.61-63]

The hyperbolic exaggeration of the hand and the blood upon it is a measure of the distance between the enormity of murder, as Macbeth views it, and his as yet undeveloped capacity to plot and to perform, of his own initiative, such a deed. To him the deed, although performed, remains beyond his capability to identify with it.

That Macbeth has a "guilt-ridden compulsion to act" implies, of course, that the compulsion to act is much at odds with his ethical sense. Why, then, we may ask, has he murdered Duncan? He has given strong moral reasons *not* to act: as kinsman and host to Duncan, he recognizes a "double trust" to protect, and not to murder, the man who is also his king. Both Macbeth and the Lady, as circumstances are to make clear, are people of embedded morality, although that of the Lady, as fits Elizabethan doctrine, is of a much more fragile substance than is Macbeth's. Whereas the Lady, with the help of demonic spirits, capitulates willfully to an overriding temptation, Macbeth's moral nature has the strength and toughness to withstand the demands of both his ambition and the powerful external persuasions that are its allies. Bright, whose *Treatise of Melancholie* (1586) was probably known to Shakespeare, makes a statement that illuminates the problems of both Lady Macbeth and Macbeth. Satan, being aware of man's "universall corruption," so Bright contends, has power "to discover the vanity of our mindes, and the secrete thoughtes of our heart: which after he hath found, he suggesteth . . . instigation of sinne & disobedience against God & his holy commandements."[18] The devil (whether Satan or a subordinate) has spied out, as already touched upon, "the secrete thoughtes of [Macbeth's] heart"; in appraising Lady Macbeth, a person of relative shallowness, he need not look so deeply: he need but "discover the vanity of [her] minde," that is to say, her hope of royal status, which will relieve the drabness of a life confined, year in and year out, to her husband's isolated castle. The news (I.v.1-12) that has made her husband pensive has made her giddy with high expectation. She gives no sustained thought to the wrongness of murder or to its consequences. Within three minutes of receipt of the letter that promises

greatness to Macbeth, she has planned Duncan's murder and has summoned deadly spirits, who are to "unsex" her; and that these "mur-
d'ring ministers" may make her "topfull / Of direst cruelty," she has
vowed to exchange the milk of her breasts for the gall of their natures
(I.v.37-47). In the context of Scottish witchcraft as described by King
James in *Daemonologie* and as delineated within the present play, the
Lady's transformation into an invoker and a confederate of demons
must, I think, be taken very literally. Having shown more will to venture the temptation than will to oppose it, she has allayed the rebukes
of conscience by means of a manifest demonic compact.

Apart from the hallucinations that beset Macbeth before and after his
murder of Duncan, an even more telltale incident points up his unfitness
for the crime. Upon his return from Duncan's chamber, his immediate
preoccupation has to do with the words of the two grooms, one of
whom has cried, "God bless us," and the other, "Amen." He explains
to the Lady:

> I could not say "Amen"
> When they did say "God bless us!"
> ....
> But wherefore could not I pronounce "Amen"?
> I had most need of blessing, and "Amen"
> Stuck in my throat.
>
> [II.ii.28-33]

"Indirectly," writes G. R. Elliot, "[Macbeth] confesses that by his deed
he has rejected that of which he had 'most need,' the divine 'Bless-
ing.'"[19] Macbeth has clearly found the crime of murder, in every
aspect, abhorrent to his nature. He had been but tempted by the prophecy of the Third Witch. When his "vaulting ambition" has demanded
of him the murder of Duncan, his moral nature (in which God is
thought to have a part) has remained stalwart and uncompromised:
"We will proceed no further in this business," he pronounces to the
Lady. Macbeth's downfall, like that of Othello, is made the more terrifying for the reason that a powerful moral nature—perhaps not quite so
indestructible as Othello's, however—must be exposed not once but
over and over again to increasingly stronger persuasions before it breaks.
When Macbeth, on the morning after the murder, goes back to Dun-

can's chamber and slays the grooms, whose only words but one in the play are "God bless us" and "Amen," he confirms what has already happened: in the murder of Duncan, he had unknowingly excluded himself from God's grace and therefore could not say "Amen." In slaying the grooms, he has symbolically murdered the very words through which men petition God. He has taken a kind of vengeance on God for having betrayed him, at the moment of his greatest need of divine comfort, to a display of quavering fear and unmanliness. It is not possible for me to say whether Macbeth's intuitive purpose is to reestablish his image of manliness (which is important to him, as Matthew Proser has shown) by a bold act in which he renounces God as God has renounced him or whether his purpose is to cut his final ties with God so as to be free from His commandments and hence from a further torment of conscience. In either case, he has not taken into account the latent strength of his moral nature.

Of persons tormented by conscience, Bright has concluded: "The whole nature, soule and body, [is] cut off from the life of God."[20] In most instances, the alienation from God is but temporary. An offender has, apparently, two choices: he may accept the punishment for his crime and hope henceforth to live at peace with his conscience; or, if the crime is a major one and the will for evil is abnormally strong, he must and will, unless he is apprehended, somehow destroy his conscience. An intermediate state, in which the crime is unpunished and the conscience remains strong, is not acceptable. Robert Burton has defined the perils of this intermediate state: men, being troubled by "the enormity of their offences,"[21] and "God's heavy wrath [being] kindled in their souls . . . , they have . . . a most intolerable torment and insufferable anguish of conscience."[22] This is precisely Macbeth's condition immediately after Duncan's murder. His trembling dread that he shall not sleep again and his incredulous horror at the sight of the blood upon his hand are evidence of his defenselessness against the recoil of his conscience; for without the grace of God (which he has been denied) he has no comfort to sustain him. By contrast, the Lady—sustained apparently by the demons that she has invoked for the occasion—is a paragon of cold efficiency. It is, of course, to the credit of Macbeth's moral nature that he is unable to complete the details attendant on Duncan's murder. At the end of this scene he assures us that his moral nature still looks toward God; for he shudders at what he has done:

176 THE DEVIL, AND GOD

> To know my deed, 'twere best not know myself.
>   [*Knock*, at castle door]
> Wake Duncan with thy knocking₁ I would thou couldst!
>   [II.ii.73-74]

"To know [his] deed," he dare not; for to do so would entail a knowledge of a self (already hinted at by his blood-soaked hand) so horrifying that he is, at present, too shaken to confront it.

In the next scene, which comes at dawn and during which the murder of Duncan is revealed to the thanes, Macbeth shows an unexpected and, for him, a remarkable capacity to discipline himself, as he later does in his confrontation with Banquo at the beginning of act III. His cool manipulation of the hired murderers, whom he has convinced of Banquo's enmity against them, is to provide a further evidence of his masterful self-possession (III.i.74ff.). Paul A. Jorgensen has made a significant statement upon which he does not, perhaps wisely, unduly elaborate: "Thus abandoned by God, [Macbeth] is befriended by the Devil, to whose service he has consecrated his body."[23] The statement is positive and bold. If we hold in mind that Lady Macbeth has dealt directly with demons, and not merely witches, and that her exceptional capacity for "direst cruelty," which is essential to the ruthless execution of Duncan's murder, is derived by her own testimony from more than human powers, it is not impossible that Macbeth's unexpected show of absolute self-control, before which his pangs of conscience are summarily dismissed, has a demonic source, for otherwise it is hardly credible. His discreet handling of Macduff and Lennox, the early callers, while he diverts suspicion from himself, comes only minutes after he has washed from his hands that "ocean" of blood before which his moral sense has made him quail in torment. Again, in contrast to the horrors that beset him in the murder of Duncan, he is to show a remarkable shrewdness and cool-headedness, even an unruffled capacity to tell at least one monstrous lie, in devising the murders of Banquo and Fleance. These shows of machinelike effectiveness, first in the cover-up of the murder of Duncan and, later, in the skillful devising of the Banquo-Fleance murder, stand in marked opposition to the introspective and conscience-haunted man of the early scenes. Has the crime of Duncan's murder been sufficient to desensitize completely, almost immediately, and of itself, Macbeth's fine moral nature? Or have demons, who could foresee at least the damaging of that nature, taken advantage of Macbeth, upon his loss of God's grace, and so possessed or manipulated him that he has the hardness—no longer, for public reasons, suitable for the Lady—to be an instrument of their purposes? Macbeth's suddenly acquired precision in the working of evil—note, for example, how cleverly he drops the question to Banquo, "Goes Fleance with you?" (III.i.35)—shows a mentality at work much the opposite of that of the doubt-ridden man who was prodded to Duncan's murder by the outward forces of rhetoric and metaphysics. The demonic influence, although not necessarily a particular demon, has become internalized.

An interpretation of an Elizabethan or Jacobean play—especially one that focuses upon the occult sciences—must have a basic concern for the dogmas of Tudor and early Stuart England. Even though Macbeth has been victimized by a demonic conspiracy and even though devil-possession was a common Tudor-Stuart diagnosis, we cannot be fully certain that he is, at any time, actually possessed. Jorgensen, for example, has suggested that Macbeth is possessed by a fiend on one very important occasion: "And during the murder [of Duncan] his fears are muted by a trancelike state that is probably possession."[24] The evidence of the play makes apparent that, just before each of the two carefully plotted murders and not just the first, Macbeth is cast, for about one minute, into a trance, but the cause of it, at best, is implied. Having shuddered in fear and doubt before the hallucinated dagger, which points the way to Duncan's chamber, Macbeth becomes, at the critical moment, suddenly and strangely unperturbed, while focusing on rites of witchcraft:

> . . . Now o'er the one half-world
> Nature seems dead, and wicked dreams abuse
> The curtain'd sleep; now witchcraft celebrates
> Pale Hecate's offerings; and wither'd murder,
> . . . .
> With Tarquin's ravishing strides, towards his design
> Moves like a ghost.
>
> [II.i.49-56]

The tone is one of subdued rapture, of escape from the torment of anxiety, of even a mesmerized indifference to the dreaded task at hand. Again, only moments before Banquo's murder, Macbeth speaks, after a scene of highly perturbed emotion, with an unlooked-for detachment, while again mindful of Hecate, this time of her preparation for magical rites: "O, full of scorpions is my mind, dear wife! / Thou know'st that Banquo, and his Fleance, lives." Unexpectedly, as a calm shrouds his mind, we note a raptured speech rhythm:

> There's comfort yet; they are assailable.
> Then be thou jocund. Ere the bat hath flown
> His cloister'd flight; ere to black Hecate's summons
> The shard-borne beetle with his drowsy hums
> Hath rung night's yawning peal, there shall be done
> A deed of dreadful note.
>
> [III.ii.36-44]

Shortly, he asks "seeling night" to "cancel and tear to pieces that great bond / Which keeps me pale" and then suggests his own close kinship with night by remarking that "night's black agents to their preys do rouse," for he too has in service "black agents," who are, at this very moment, poised to ambush Banquo and Fleance.

There are, I believe, two elements of note in the passages just quoted. First of all, the speaker's instant change from agitation of mind and evident fearfulness to a hypnotic sense of at-oneness with time, event, and place, even though the event [murder] is a highly unnerving one, is so remarkable as to argue that forces alien to Macbeth are now an influence upon him. Whether he is possessed or not is uncertain. Equally important is the indication of the quoted passages that Macbeth has a knowledge of the confidences of the black arts. In the second passage (III.ii), he makes clear that the "deed of dreadful note" will be consummated only moments before "black Hecate" is to summon her worshipers to an infernal assembly, probably the sabbat. Macbeth has apparently sought an added benefit from the murder of Banquo and Fleance by viewing it as a propitiatory offering to the powers of darkness, now in the ascendant. In this general context, his petition to "seeling night" (a Renaissance symbol of evil) to destroy "that great bond that keeps me pale" acquires a meaningful comprehensibility. He must, at all costs, destroy the bond—whatever it is—that, above all other things, has rent his peace of mind ever since Duncan's murder.

On the purely physical level, the petition calls for the destruction of Banquo, for Banquo, in Macbeth's presence, has made a bond with God by stating, "In the great hand of God I stand," and then by vowing to find and to punish Duncan's murderer (II.iii.129-31). But Banquo is, more importantly, the symbol of a purely abstract "great bond" that torments Macbeth. Irving Ribner has argued that he embodies "ordinary humanity" and has concluded: "This is why Macbeth must murder Banquo."[25] In killing Banquo, as Ribner explains, Macbeth hopes to destroy the Banquo substance in himself "before he can give his soul entirely to the forces of darkness."[26] But if Banquo subdues his personal desires to the orderly plan of God, as Ribner also suggests, is not the "Banquo substance," both in Banquo and Macbeth, a "bond with God," which means placing an accustomed allegiance to God above every personal consideration? This bond is, of course, the motive that has prompted Banquo to undertake the task of God's agent in the punishment of Duncan's murderer. According to this argument, what Ribner terms, somewhat ambiguously, "ordinary humanity" is in more specific terms a man's "bond with God." This bond, from the play's testimony, is particularly strong, in terms of moral nature, in both Banquo and Macbeth. Elliott has provided a commendable analysis of the "great bond" which, instead of sustaining, now torments Macbeth: "This 'great Bond' consists of all the invisible ties and understandings by which his conscience keeps him 'bound' to restless agony."[27] Although Macbeth is cut off from God, it is only God's grace from which he is "cut off," not those dictates of God upon which a man's moral nature is said to be largely constructed. His slaying of the two grooms, whom I shall term God Bless Us and Amen, may have prompted a hope of cutting himself off totally from God. It has, together with Duncan's murder, cut off his access to God and His grace. It has not, however, cut off God's access to him, for a man's moral nature which binds him to God's laws, and them to him, cannot be dispelled instantaneously by an act of desecration. If Macbeth is to escape the repeated torments of conscience, he must, indeed, "give his soul entirely to the forces of darkness," but for a man of strong moral nature, although that nature already be damaged, the task entails an enormous resolve.

The two trancelike experiences of Macbeth strongly argue, and do not confirm, a demonic origin. Nor does Macbeth's appeal that "seeling night . . . / Cancel . . . that great bond / Which keeps me pale" prove anything more, despite its larger implications, than that he wants Banquo dead, even though he has strong motives, if he is to escape the torment of conscience, to terminate his own bond with God. After the murder of Duncan, Macbeth has found himself with but two choices: to be castigated and destroyed by the force of conscience or to give himself so totally to evil that his moral nature (of which conscience is but the spokesman) will become brutalized and, as such, insensitive to issues of Christian morality. Cut off from God's grace by the most flagrant of all possible sins (the killing of a man who is his guest, his kinsman, and his king), he can look for no reprieve. The dark mysteries of evil, which have come more and more to envelop both him and the play, offer an alluring haven to a man who has experienced, and will experience again, although in a different form, the intolerable torture of conscience.

From the play's opening scene, as we know, evil has been in the ascendant, and on the night of Duncan's murder, it has attained an apparent crest, nor will it be firmly opposed until late in act IV, when the forces of divine law begin to assert themselves. The evil that will eventually claim Macbeth (but only when he has made the choice) and will then leave him to destruction becomes particularly manifest in the omens that attend Duncan's death. Lennox introduces the theme of Satanic visitation:

> Where we lay,
> Our chimneys were blown down; and, as they say,
> Lamentings heard i' th' air, strange screams of death,
> And prophesying, with accents terrible,
> Of dire combustion and confus'd events
> New-hatch'd to th' woeful time; the obsure bird
> Clamour'd the livelong night. Some say the earth
> Was feverish and did shake.
>
> [II.iii.52-59]

The darkness is opaque; the omens are not seen but only heard or felt. The omens portending Caesar's death, in *Julius Caesar*, are illuminated by lightning and are clearly the work of Rome's gods. But in *Macbeth*, the total darkness, the traditional haunt of wicked spirits, is rent with "strange screams of death" and "accents terrible": nothing is seen, everything is alien, unnatural, and terrifying. Elliott sums up the uncanny sounds as "supernatural voices."[28] And they probably are. For example, was there ever a species of owl that "clamour'd"? On this strange and terrifying night of unrelieved darkness, the supernatural is unmistakably demonic, as fits the play's context.

More unnatural are the omens reported in the next scene, which takes place later the same morning. The Old Man sets the tone: "I have seen / Hours dreadful and things strange; but this sore night / Hath trifled former knowings" (II.iv.2-4). Ross then makes a statement that substantiates the abnormal darkness reported of the preceding night: "By th' clock 'tis day / And yet dark night strangles the travelling lamp" (II.iv.6-7). The omens next to be related by the Old Man and Ross confirm an inversion of nature, which has been only implied in the omens reported by Lennox. In fact, a reader may rightly suspect that, somewhere in the neighborhood, a perverted mass held in the name of Satan or, better fitting the play's context, that of Hecate has blighted nature and has inverted its functions. "A falcon," we are told, "tow'ring in her pride of place" has been attacked and killed by an earthbound "mousing owl." Even more alarming, Duncan's horses, incomparable in their breeding, have rebelled "'gainst obedience," have broken their stalls and, subverting their vegetarian natures, have devoured "each other." Equally "'gainst nature," Malcolm and Donalbain are thought to have slain their father, Duncan. As the characters do not know, although the murder of Duncan has, indeed, been against nature, the guilt is not that of Duncan's sons. The implication of this scene, with its emphasis upon the unprecedented darkness and the inversion of natural order, is (I think) unmistakable: demonic forces have wrested control over Scotland from its natural guardian, Providence.

In the same scene, an apparent misjudgment by Ross provides the reader or the spectator with a dash of reassurance as to the ultimate rehabilitation of Scotland. Amazed by the overlay of darkness that has made the day "dark night," and unaware of the demonic intervention explicit in the play, he ascribes the cause of the darkness to Heaven: "Thou seest, the heavens, as troubled with man's act [the murder], / Threatens his bloody stage" (II.iv.5-6). Although Ross's assumption about the cause of the darkness is apparently wrong, we are reminded that Heaven, or God, has the capacity and the will to punish the murderer. Throughout the play are found scattered references to the watchfulness of Heaven, for God is, in the eyes of the principal characters, the custodian of man and the punisher of wrongdoing. Macbeth and the Lady, the two characters most responsible for stirring up demons into meddling in Scottish affairs, are both fearful of Heaven's watchfulness. Upon citing substantial reasons not to murder Duncan, Macbeth concludes by expressing his fear of "heaven's cherubim" lest they "blow the horrid deed in every eye" and expose his guilt (I.vii.22,24). The Lady's statement on her fear of a solicitous Heaven has a double importance; this fear, it is implied, is also the cause of the opaque darkness that is to permeate the night of Duncan's murder and, blanketlike, to overspread the next forenoon:

> Come, thick night,
> And pall thee in the dunnest smoke of hell,
> That my keen knife see not the wound it makes,
> Nor heaven peep through the blanket of the dark
> To cry, "Hold, hold."
>
> > [I.v.47-51]

Shakespeare, I believe, has meant us to accept the Lady, who has already invoked "spirits / That tend on mortal thoughts," as the conjurer of the abnormal overlay of darkness that invites the comments of both Lennox and Ross. The fact that both she and Macbeth are fearful that Heaven will witness the murder of Duncan, coupled with Ross's later assumption (see above) that Heaven is about to punish the murderer, is sufficient testimony that God, however discomfited at present by the dark and prideful forces of evil, is still powerful to avenge the unjustly slain. His vengeance will be delayed, and perhaps fittingly: for, as will be shown, the auspices of England's king, "holy" Edward, are fundamental in providing the frightened and scattered Scots (IV.iii) with a renewed faith in the reality of Heaven's omnipotence. God's judgment, in Shakespeare's view, is customarily inseparable from man's trust and overt consent.

Macbeth's obsessive fear of Banquo, and not simply the murder of Duncan, is the decisive experience which, by compounding the very anxieties of which Macbeth would be rid, is to force upon him the ultimate choice of self-dehumanization. Jorgensen believes that demons help to nourish this fear: "And the evil spirit will vex him, as it did Saul, with 'strange feares.'"[29] If true, the tormenting fear is a part of the divine punishment, for demons can vex a man only by God's consent. Considered in this way, Macbeth's self-degradation into a man-beast—his rejection of every Godly element within him—becomes a highly overt part of God's plan. I cannot, however, agree with Jorgensen that Macbeth's fears of Banquo are prompted by "unexpressed or wrong reasons" and have no rational basis: "Macbeth's restless ecstasy simply needs something specific to fear."[30] It is true that Macbeth's mind, tormented as it is, requires the constraint of a single object upon which to focus, and may seek it intuitively, but Banquo is hardly a random choice. Macbeth cannot have forgotten Banquo's warning not to let the Witches' prophecies "enkindle you unto the crown" (I.iii.121). Second, after he has been "enkindle[d] . . . unto the crown," he has overheard Banquo's resolve in behalf of the murdered Duncan:

> In the great hand of God I stand, and thence
> Against the undivulg'd pretence [intent] I fight
> Of treasonous malice.
>
> [II.iii.129-31]

Banquo has identified himself as God's agent in the punishment of Duncan's murderer, and the resolve of this highly honored man, as Macbeth knows, is to be feared. At the beginning of act III Banquo, in soliloquy, says of Macbeth: "I fear / Thou play'dst most foully for 't [the crown]." Later in the same scene, Macbeth has his turn in soliloquy, a kind of counterpoint to Banquo's, to which it responds:

> Our fears in Banquo [who knows too much]
> Stick deep; and in his royalty of nature
> Reigns that which should be fear'd.
>
> [III.i.48-50]

Macbeth's fear of Banquo, as I read the play, is not at all a product of random selection. There is, moreover, a second strong motive: in Macbeth's presence, the Witches have "hailed [Banquo] father to a line of kings." Macbeth has a genuine fear that he holds "a barren sceptre in [his] gripe, / Thence to be wrench'd by an unlineal hand"—perhaps by Fleance. Macbeth's understandable fear of Banquo is augmented by his fear of the son.

Although the fear of Banquo, like the later fear of Macduff, is justified, the fear itself is borne to excess. It disrupts Macbeth's sleep, shaking him nightly with "terrible dreams"; it hampers his will to eat; it preoccupies him to the exclusion of more salubrious thoughts. The remedy of such privation, Macbeth is convinced, is to murder Banquo and Fleance. But why such an excess of fear? In the soliloquy of act III, scene i, in which Macbeth has focused upon his fears of Banquo and his heirs, he provides two clues: speaking of "Banquo's issue," he berates himself:

> For them the gracious Duncan have I murder'd;
> Put rancors in the vessel of my peace
> Only for them, and mine eternal jewel
> Given to the common enemy of man
> To make them kings—the seed of Banquo kings!
>
> [III.i.65-69]

The terrible irony leers upon him. What, however, is the real irritant of this problem—merely the fact that "the seed of Banquo" will be kings? The fundamental irritation is, I think, that Macbeth has killed a "gracious" man and, in so doing, has made a double sacrifice of horrendous proportion in order that a parade of unborn seedlings—in his mind, probably pink-cheeked choir boys—can sit on Scotland's throne. More important to the theme of excess, the passage identifies the murder of Duncan—who is remembered, above all, as "gracious"—and not Macbeth's fears of Banquo, as the sole source of the "rancors" that have denied him peace of mind. Only by an intense focus of mind upon a new object, as Macbeth has learned, is he able to exclude from it the overbearing memory of the past. To escape the torment of conscience over Duncan's murder, Macbeth must transfer not only the object of torment, but also the great pain of that torment, from Duncan, about whom he can now do nothing, to Banquo. Although Macbeth has good reasons for his fears of Banquo and the Banquo heirs, the excessive character of these fears is justified, for he must so preoccupy his mind with them as not to allow his thoughts to turn back (as they have just done) to the greater torment, which is the murdered Duncan. All in all, Macbeth's transfer of the object of torment to Banquo is salutary: however disturbed he is in private, he can, in the actual plotting of Banquo's murder, focus his mind with clarity and dispatch. To escape the intolerable anxieties brought on by conscience, he has given his total being to an alternate pain which offers, although deceptively, a promise of mental rehabilitation and, with that promise, an easing of his immediate anguish. Unhappily, so painstaking has Macbeth been in the plotting of the double murder, he is to find himself totally unprepared to treat with its failure.

Banquo's Ghost (III.iv) has evoked a welter of comment and, although the majority opinion holds that it is a subjective ghost, there are dissenters, such as Willard Farnham and Matthew Proser, both of whom contend that it is, to use Proser's phrase, an "objective reality."[31] Jorgensen, agreeing with W.C. Curry except in details, has concluded that Banquo's Ghost is "the Devil" in the shape of the dead man; he adds that, in frightening Macbeth, it acts "as God's punitive agent."[32] Opposite to the opinions that argue in support of the specter's "objective reality" are those of A.C. Bradley, Cumberland Clark, G.W. Knight, and Henry N. Paul, each of whom insists on the subjective character of the Ghost. "[Macbeth's] half-murdered conscience," according to Bradley, "rises; his deed confronts him in the apparition of Banquo's Ghost."[33] Clark's statement is more specific than is Bradley's: "Banquo's shade is a subjective ghost. . . . It is an illusion of [Macbeth's] perturbed thought."[34] Paul, in turn, provides the most observant evaluation: "In the banquet scene the ghost of Banquo is as purely imaginary as the bloody dagger, coming and going according to Macbeth's fitful hallucinations." He adds: "By De Loier's test, it is a 'phantosme' and not a 'specter,' for 'it hath not any will of its own.'"[35]

In the English translation, in 1605, of Pierre Le Loyer's *Discours des Spectres*, the translator, L. Jones (other critics identify him as Z. Jones), has altered Le Loyer's name to Peter De Loier. Monsieur Le Loyer (or Master De Loier) has made a clear-cut distinction between a "phantosme" and a "specter," only the latter of these two phenomena having a will and purpose of its own. The former is but a product of the mind. Of men who have "usurped a tyrannicall authority over their own native countries," Le Loyer has written: "How often have we seene, that these men have bin troubled and tormented with most horrible phantosmes & imaginations, which do com into their heads both sleeping and waking."[36] That Shakespeare had read, at the time he wrote *Macbeth*, Le Loyer's treatise is almost certain: Henry Paul has noted that, in the year 1605, it was sold "on the book stalls in London."[37] That Banquo's Ghost "hath not any will of its own" and is therefore a "phantosme" and not a real "specter" becomes especially evident in Macbeth's observation of it: "Thou hast no speculation in those eyes," meaning no focus and hence no will or, as Alfred Harbage has suggested, no "power of rational observation."[38] The image of the gory-locked Banquo has a place in the series of hallucinations to which Macbeth has already shown an abnormal inclination and is both the last and the most unnerving: it is, in short, a sign that his anxieties are to remain unresolved and implacable; nor are they to be remedied by mere political craft.

To informed Elizabethans, a theory advanced by the theologian William Perkins was undoubtedly well known: an inevitable effect of conscience was fear, "in causing whereof conscience is verie forcible."[39] A symptom of such fear, as Perkins illustrates, is "monstrous visions," of which the blood-splattered figure of Banquo is a conspicuous example. Why this appalling shape and not another? Macbeth's unconscious mind, at the moment of shock—at the moment that he learns that Fleance has escaped, unhurt—has apparently been unduly sensitized by the First Murderer's depiction of the slain Banquo "with twenty trenchèd gashes on his head," for this hasty sketch fits exactly the "gory-locked" image that Macbeth immediately hallucinates. (Later in the scene, he will unconsciously parody the Murderer's graphic line when he says of the dead: "They rise again / With twenty mortal murders on their crowns.") Nor does the escape of Fleance fail to find its appropriate rationale: Banquo's Ghost sits at the head of the table, and that is the place, as Macbeth *now* knows, in which the Banquo heirs are destined to sit.

The defensiveness of Macbeth's words, upon his first sight of Banquo's Ghost seated on the royal stool, emphatically reaffirms the element of conscience: "Thou canst not say I did it; never shake / Thy gory locks at me" (III.iv.50-51). By hiring two murderers, as Matthew Proser has pointed out, Macbeth had hoped to disassociate himself from the murder: "Thus," says Proser, "is conscience . . . satisfied."[40] But the graphic depiction of the murdered Banquo "with twenty trenchèd gashes on his head," by exciting heretofore controlled guilt responses, has brought the dead man right before Macbeth's eyes and he must deny his responsibility lest he be tormented a second time upon the rack of his conscience. Fear, which has become, for Macbeth, a habitual replacement for his sense of guilt, is to dominate, at least in his conscious mind, his behavioral responses during the second part of the Ghost's visit: "Take any shape but that, and my firm nerves / Shall never tremble." When the Lady, having observed Macbeth's "flaws and starts," terms them "impostors to true fear," she unwittingly defines the kind of fears that Perkins, in 1596, had identified as one of the symptoms of the conscience syndrome: "Yea the guiltie conscience will make a man afraid, if he see but a worme peepe out of the ground."[41] To him, the worm will seem to be a "dragon." And so it is with Macbeth: the mere report of a dead man, whom he now has no logical reason to fear, has taken the shape of an awesome hallucination.

If we accept Perkins's doctrine that an abnormal habit of fear is a symptom of the disturbed conscience, Macbeth's sensitivity toward an excess of fear, in the past and now and in the immediate future, becomes quite readily understood—perhaps too readily. Perkins, furthermore, in his *Discourse of Conscience*, has listed five symptoms of conscience— shame, sorrow, fear, desperation, and perturbation[42]—and Macbeth, until now, has experienced all of them except, I believe, the full measure of desperation. The Ghost withdraws only after Macbeth has identified it for what it is—a hallucination. "Hence, horrible shadow! Unreal mock'ry, hence!" So shaken has Macbeth been by the hallucinated image of the blood-spattered Banquo that it is proper, I think, to call back to mind his ghastly horror of the murdered Duncan's corpse:

> I'll go no more:
> I am afraid to think what I have done;
> Look on 't again I dare not.

> [II.ii.50-52]

After Duncan's murder, Macbeth had feared to come to the knowledge of himself: "'twere best not know myself." Banquo's blood-spattered Ghost is a pivotal experience because, being a projection of Macbeth's psyche, it has forcibly imaged for him the brute part of his own nature, of which he had earlier evaded the full recognition. Because of this revelation, he is henceforth to see his anxieties, frankly and not misguidedly, in an appropriate perspective.

Macbeth has destroyed the man who stands "in the great hand of God" and, in so doing, has put a restraint upon the already discomfited forces of Providence, for Banquo, because of the minority of Duncan's sons, was the rightful agent of God against the murderer. But Macbeth has also learned that his principal danger is not as he had rationalized and cannot be resolved by the murder of any single man: it derives, as it had at the time of Duncan's murder, from an "accusing conscience," which as Perkins has recognized, "speakes with God against the man in whom it is placed."[43] Although Macbeth has rationalized that the murder of both Banquo and Fleance will provide an escape from the syndrome of guilt and fear, his "restless ecstasy" speech (III.ii.13-26), on the very eve of that carefully plotted murder, indicates that, intuitively, he anticipates no such easy remedy; for neither the slaying of God's agent nor the freedom to have the throne for himself and his heirs can resolve the basic problem, which lies in his moral nature. After the murder of Banquo, as the reader is aware, no single enemy, whether Fleance or Macduff, suffices to hold Macbeth's attention except sporadically. He appears to have come to an important realization: if he is to relieve himself of the torment that derives from guilt and fear, the killing of selected enemies can be of no solace and can, indeed, add to the torment of mind that it seeks to relieve by creating further occasions of guilt and fear.

The crux of Macbeth's problem is found, I believe, in his appeal, at the time of Banquo's murder, to "seeling night": the language of the appeal, "Cancel and tear to pieces that great bond / Which keeps me pale" (III.ii.49-50), is unusually connotative and even suggests a multi-faceted mental origin. On the rational and unmistakable level Macbeth is asking that Banquo, as well as Banquo's bond with God, be destroyed. But as G.R. Elliott and Irving Ribner have argued, he is also asking for the destruction of something inside himself. Elliott has suggested that he is probably, at the moment, thinking of the pain of conscience and is hopeful that (somehow) the success of the double murder will eliminate it. The connotative wording of the appeal, however, suggests a more comprehensive meaning of which Macbeth may not, at the time, be fully conscious. In the "restless ecstasy" speech, which precedes the appeal to "seeling night" by only thirty lines, Macbeth has shown such "torture of the mind" (without even a solacing thought of the benefits expected from the double murder) that I find in the proposed remedy of this speech the working of intuition, which sees the truth and probably is unaware of Macbeth's rationalizations and unwarranted hope. Before he can once again eat without fear or sleep without nightmare, he tells us, "the frame of things [must] disjoint [and] both the worlds suffer" (III.ii.16-19):[44] his remedy (if any) lies in deeds of a violent and comprehensive scope. In short, the appeal that night (emblematic of evil powers) destroy "that great bond / Which keeps me pale" has, I believe, two levels of meaning: one is rational and the other intuitive. Although, rationally, Macbeth has invoked "seeling night" against Banquo, his appeal on the nontemporal and intuitive level is to the primordial prototype of evil, of which night (being incomparably ancient) is as symbolic as it is of present evil. Macbeth's intuition (in the "restless ecstasy" speech) has foreseen a solution which his rational mind reaches only *after* his torturous response to Banquo's murder: instead of plotting a few strategic murders, in which he has, for personal reasons, an emotional involvement, he must commit himself totally, and impersonally, to evil for the sheer purpose of destroying the painful reflexes of his conscience. He must, as it were, bathe in innocent blood, for only by totally brutalizing and desensitizing his moral nature can he destroy his bond with God (and God's laws) and thereby stultify his conscience; for the destruction of Banquo (as he has now learned) has not eased but compounded its anguish:

> For mine own good
> All causes must give way. I am in blood
> Stepp'd in so far that, should I wade no more,
> Returning were as tedious as go o'er.
> Strange things I have in head that will to hand,
> Which must be acted ere they can be scann'd.
>
> [III.iv.135-40]

Most important to his long-term plan is to act with such dispatch, as he moves from murder to murder, that there can be neither forethought nor time for remorse. He must put behind him any and all personal involvement.

In Macbeth's resolve to destroy every shred of his humanity, Shakespeare has given to his source material a psychological focus which, in Holinshed's account, is only suggested. Holinshed sees in the historical Macbeth "the pricke of conscience . . . [which] caused him ever to feare, leaste he should be served the same cup, as he had ministred to his predecessor."[45] Shakespeare's Macbeth considers this point (the "poison'd chalice" principle, I.vii.10-12) but before, and not after, Duncan's murder. Holinshed, shortly, elaborates on the general fear among Macbeth's subjects and his reaction to it: "Even as there were manie that stood in feare of him, so likewise stoode he in feare of manie . . . [and] began to make those awaie . . . whome he thought most able to worke him anie displeasure. . . . At length he found suche sweetnesse by putting his nobles thus to death, that his earnest thirst after bloud . . . might in no wise be satisfied."[46] To explain "such sweetnesse" in killing people, Holinshed promptly adds, "For ye must consider he wan [won] double profit": not only was Macbeth rid of enemies, but also "his coffers were inriched by their goods."[47] Shakespeare wisely rejects the motive of wealth given by Holinshed. His Macbeth must resolve a highly critical problem psychologically, for otherwise his conscience and its unrelenting censure will pin him, to his dying day, on the cross of anxiety and torment. Such, of course, is the harsh fate of the Lady, for she is denied, because of medieval strictures upon her sex, a rehabilitative course of action: more than Macbeth, she is "cabin'd, cribb'd, confin'd."

Aware that his "initiate fear . . . wants hard use" and mindful that "we are but young in deed," Macbeth chooses to meet with the Witches a second time that he may learn "by the worst means the worst." He must know from them, before he gives a full loose to the reins, the consequences of a total commitment to evil. King James, in *Daemonologie*, has included perceptions that anticipate precisely Macbeth's ill-placed confidence in the Witches: the devil "will make his schollers [witches and sorcerers] to creepe in credite with Princes, by fore-telling them manie greate thinges; parte true, parte false."[48] Under the belief that the Witches, on the first meeting, had told him certain truths intended for his betterment, Macbeth has confidence that they can resolve his present crisis. For his pains he will be granted half truths that purpose his destruction. To his demand "Answer me / To what I ask," the Witches, divulging the source of their present and past knowledgeableness, reply: "Say, if thou'dst rather hear it from our mouths, / Or from our masters?" (IV.i.62-63). Macbeth, a practiced status-seeker, will be answered only by the "masters." According to James's principles of demonology, the apparitions that are now to confront Macbeth may be either demons, for the devil was thought to "transforme himself" into "divers shapes,"[49] or "impressiones in the aire, easelie gathered by a spirite."[50] In either case, the voice is that of a devil who, knowing "the meanes by which men doe speake," can frame a voice "answerable to mans understanding."[51] Upon sight of the Armed Head, Macbeth is promptly told by the First Witch: "He knows thy thought. Hear his speech, but say thou naught" (IV.i.69f). Again, as at the beginning of the play, the demons are to show their power to read a man's inmost thoughts. Their answers provide the clue to Macbeth's unspoken questions.

Although Macduff is on his mind, Macbeth's principal interest is the safety with which he may indulge his wicked intents, for he sees in their fulfillment the only means of frustrating his moral nature and the dangers posed by it. Of the Devil, James has written: "His Oracles [are] alwaies doubtsome."[52] The demonic answers, specifically the second and the third, are of course disquietingly ambiguous. To this ambiguity Macbeth's mind is totally unresponsive. An outcast of God and His grace, Macbeth has been repeatedly and painfully reminded by his conscience of the persisting presence of God within him, especially of God's Sixth Commandment, and to question the demons' promises of indestructibility would be to turn back to the torment of mind from which he seeks desperately to escape. He must escape "the maddening horrors of meditation," as John C. Bucknill stated long ago, and he can do so only by resolving upon "a course of decisive resolute action."[53] It must be of a kind, however, that will desensitize, beyond possible restitution, his moral nature. He is thus disposed to look on the demons as infallible counselors.

Assured by the demonic oracles that if he be "bloody, bold, and resolute," as well as "lion-hearted" and "proud," he need fear no man "of woman born" and no army unless "great Birnam Wood" move upon Dunsinane Castle, Macbeth is prepared to march upon Macduff. The news that "Macduff is fled to England" prompts him to reaffirm his earlier resolve:

> The flighty purpose never is o'ertook
> Unless the deed goes with it. From this moment
> The very firstlings of my heart shall be
> The firstlings of my hand.
>
>   [IV.i.145-48]

His every murder, henceforth, is to be impersonally decided upon and impersonally consummated for the sheer relish of evil, which is to displace fear (such as that of Banquo) as the overriding motive. He has learned to act with a detachment totally devoid of forethought and subsequent anguish. Ross, an expatriate, reports on his "poor country":

>   It cannot
> Be call'd our mother, but our grave; . . .
> . . . .
> Where sighs, and groans, and shrieks, that rent the air,
> Are made, not mark'd; . . .
>   . . . the dead man's knell
> Is there scarce ask'd for who; and good men's lives
> Expire before the flowers in their caps.
>
>   [IV.iii.165-72]

The metamorphosis of Macbeth into a "demon," for so he is appraised by the thanes now in England, is repeatedly illustrated in their epithets: "black Macbeth"; "Devilish Macbeth"; and, climactically, "this fiend of Scotland." The image is that of a man who, finding a demonic delight in evil, can kill without a trace of remorse. The transmogrification, happily, is to come short of complete fulfillment.

In enforcing Scotland to bear the agony that he can no longer tolerate, Macbeth has structured, out of his countless murders, the forces destined by Providence to destroy him. Even before Duncan's murder, Macbeth foresaw the possibility of Heaven's avenging it:

>   Heaven's cherubim hors'd
> Upon the sightless couriers of the air,
> Shall blow the horrid deed in every eye,
> That tears shall drown the wind.
>
>   [I.vii.22-25]

This foresight has ultimately proven justified. For, despite the pride of the demonic presence in Scotland, the scouts of Heaven (such is the implication of what we are now to be told) have witnessed the slaughters of Macbeth and, in an interchange of tears, have renewed a bond between Scotland and Heaven. Macduff, newly arrived in England, is the speaker:

> Each new morn
> New widows howl, new orphans cry; new sorrows
> Strike heaven on the face, that it resounds
> As if it felt with Scotland and yell'd out
> Like syllable of dolour.
>
> [IV.iii.4-8]

The sympathies of Heaven are aroused but, as Macduff is later to confirm, Heaven (at least in Scotland) has not as yet been able to act. Of the slaughter of his wife and children, he observes: "Did heaven look on / And would not take their part?" (IV.iii.223-24). A principal reason that Heaven has not intervened in Scotland, and even lacked the power to do so, has already been suggested, again by Macduff:

> Not in the legions
> Of horrid hell can come a devil more damn'd
> In evils to top Macbeth.
>
> [IV.iii.55-57]

Macbeth, the archfiend of Scotland, has forged of his country a hell over which, in keeping with his great ambition, he can command, unchallenged in his supremacy. If he must be damned, so his fantasy seems to have deluded him, he will create a hell on his own terms, and he has done so rather admirably. As a result, those who would spearhead the cause of Heaven against Macbeth have been compelled to turn to England.

Shortly before Macduff's arrival in England, his purpose for the trip has been explained by a Lord of Scotland, plainly and factually:

> Thither Macduff
> Is gone to pray the holy King upon his aid
> To wake Northumberland and warlike Siward

That by the help of these—with Him above
To ratify the work—we may again
Give to our tables meat, sleep to our nights.

[III.vi.29-34]

The "holy King," Edward the Confessor, is in the truest sense the deputy of God. Among his many "blessings" derived from God, as Malcolm is to inform us, is the power to cure his grateful subjects of the king's evil, or scrofula. His court, noted for its power to heal and bind together, stands at a pole diametrically opposed to that of the present Scottish court, whose purpose is to destroy and to sunder. A basic correspondence is found between Edward and "the gracious Duncan." Just as Duncan and his two grooms (God Bless Us and Amen), symbols of grace in Scotland, have perished in a chamber offstage, likewise Edward, the fountainhead of grace in England, is never permitted onstage. In this manner Shakespeare has honored the mystery of God's grace. Because Edward, described as "full of grace," has provided the services of "good Siward" and his ten thousand soldiers for the purpose of liberating Scotland, we become aware that his God-granted power to heal relates to stricken nations, such as Scotland, as well as to his subjects. The favor of Edward, who holds the "healing benediction" from God, implies also God's blessings. This interpretation has the full support of the Scottish historian George Buchanan; in 1582, he wrote of the expedition outfitted by "holy" Edward and led by Malcolm against Macbeth: "Nor would the favour of the Deity, to aid a just cause against the wicked, be withheld."[54] In light of this statement, just before the expeditionary force of the play moves north, the integrity of Malcolm's words is unquestionable:

. . . Macbeth
Is ripe for shaking, and the pow'rs above
Put on their instruments.

[IV.iii.237-39]

In effect, he has said: "Prepare to march as the agents of God."

Jorgensen, despite some emphasis on Christian doctrines, has seen Macduff as "a prosaic instrument of Nemesis for Macbeth."[55] Other critics have shared this view, including Proser. *Macbeth*, despite its compactness and its power, is not a Greek play or a pagan play of any sort. It speaks repeatedly of Christian dogma, of both Satanism and a watchful Providence. It is, I think, a sophisticated morality play, in which the justice of God, although long discomfited, is fulfilled. Two men have a right to succeed Banquo as the agent of God's vengeance, Macduff and Malcolm, now an adult. Malcolm, however, even though he is Scotland's heir apparent, has chosen to delegate authority to the experienced Macduff: "What I am truly / Is thine and my poor country's to command" (IV.iii.131-32). Add to this the fact that Malcolm's kinship is to a long-dead father, whereas that of Macduff is to a wife and several children, only recently slain. His, moreover, is the more resolute temper. Macduff takes over, with unquestioned right, the office of God's agent and, in addressing Heaven, acknowledges God as his partner and guide:

> But, gentle heavens,
> Cut short all intermission; front to front,
> Bring thou this fiend of Scotland and myself;
> Within my sword's length set him.
>
> [IV.iii.231-34]

Macduff's punitive purpose has been granted, because of his martial temperament and the recent murder of his family, an unchallengeable divine sanction. He will share with others, however, and "with Him above to ratify the work," the general restoration of the homeland.

Macbeth, on the battlements of Dunsinane, exemplifies in graphic terms the immeasurable cost of a man's evil. The very evil that has sustained him has also emptied him of humane emotions. His preoccupation with evil has attained for him much of his principal objective: he has "almost forgot the taste of fears," and he adds that horror, "familiar to my slaughterous thoughts, / Cannot once start me" (V.v.14-15). If the loss of fear were without other losses, he might have made of evil a beguiling haven of escape. Dolora Cunningham has spoken of Macbeth's "pursuit of indifference" and adds that it "has smothered but not removed his moral sensitivity."[56] The irony is, I believe, that Macbeth had not intended, in his pursuit of evil, to become indifferent to all things but only to what has tormented him—guilt and fear. The pursuit of evil, while desensitizing his moral nature, has deadened, if not actually destroyed, his capacity to relish ordinary pleasures. "I have lived long enough," he concludes, and then pays, to use his own phrase, "mouth-honour" to "honour, love, obedience, troops of friends" (V.iii.25), for he indicates no positive desire to have these pleasures again. Upon report of the Lady's death, he mechanically observes, "She should have died hereafter," suggesting that her death is, at present, an annoyance, not a cause for sorrow. The idea of death, thereupon, tends to jell with some negative thoughts at the back of his mind, and he sees life in the figure of a puppet-like clown, "That struts and frets his hour upon the stage / And then is heard no more" (V.v.25-26). Not only murder, blood, and torment of mind but also all that is noble, expectant, and beautiful have come, in Macbeth's ultimate view of life, to "signify nothing."

Although emotionally both hardened and unresponsive and, admittedly, "aweary of the sun," Macbeth, in the last minutes of his life, provides a little-noted indication that he still harbors within him a scrap or two of God. Confronted by Macduff, he refuses at first to fight, even though he remains (as he is shortly to say) fully confident that "none of woman born" can hurt him: "Get thee back," he warns Macduff; "My soul is too much charg'd / With blood of thine already" (V.vii.5-6). In this response, we are apt to sense a deep-set reluctance in Macbeth lest he add a further pain to the pain of a crime, already felt. He remembers the most nearly personal of his many impersonalized murders and, to this memory, something penitent and a bit Godlike within him has still the power to respond and the touch of painful urgency in his voice reminds us, at the critical moment, of his once respectable moral nature. He may have an "insufficient abhorrence for his sins"[57] to repent his evil deeds at large, but he dies, I believe, with a few rags of his former humanity upon him.

We cannot be certain of the precise purpose of the demonic conspiracy, of which the Witches are but instruments. Its only purpose may be to damn the soul of Macbeth, whose treasonous thoughts arising from his high ambition have put him outside God's protection. Even more likely, it seems to me, the conspiracy has a double objective, for it takes shape immediately after the defeat of the rebels led by Macdonwald, whose evident purpose has been the overthrow of the Scottish ruling class. The demonic conspiracy, having ensnared Macbeth and, later, having admonished him to be "bloody, bold, and resolute," while providing him with seemingly inflexible guarantees of safety, has assured itself that much of Scotland's aristocracy will be destroyed and, to this extent, fulfills the slain Macdonwald's purpose. Macbeth, once he has unwittingly executed an objective of the rebel captain whom he had boldly opposed, is in turn (but only then) betrayed to destruction. Not only have the functions of lower nature, such as those of birds and animals, been inverted; the inversion of nature, indicative of demonic intervention, is evident on a higher plane throughout Macbeth's methodical slaughter of his subjects, for the natural duty of a king is to protect his subjects, not to slay them.[58] When the vengeance endorsed by "the pow'rs above" and armed by the authority of England's "holy King" does come, it strikes with unimpeded swiftness, for it is timed to fit the moment when Macbeth "is ripe for shaking," and such ripeness implies a weakening of the demonic presence, possibly because its primary mission is fulfilled. Macbeth's moment of revelation is the instant that he sees for himself that Birnam Wood "comes toward Dunsinane." Having already, in his initiate doubt, cursed "the fiend / That lies like truth," he is now assured that he has been made the scapegoat of Satanic purposes other than his own.

It is probable that God has, at first, permitted no more than the tempting of Macbeth by evil powers. But Macbeth, unlike Job, is to yield to the persuasions of his wife. In short, Macbeth, already demonically tempted, has failed a critical test illustrated, probably as a warning, in three noted episodes of the Bible. The true victory in the play *Macbeth*, as in *Richard III*, is properly God's, for Richmond and, later, Macduff are but His agents. King James, speaking of the devil and those who consort with him, has already confirmed God's part for us: "God . . . drawes ever out of that evill, glorie to himselfe . . . by the wracke of the wicked in his justice."[59] And wherein, in the play *Macbeth*, is found this "glorie"? If God find "glorie" in His judgment upon Macbeth, who by his own mistaken choice has been deprived of moral and emotional fiber and is ultimately but the shell of the former man, the glory does not lie in the act itself; the act is too meager. It lies, more rightly (I think), in God's having relieved Scotland of the oppression that has stultified its humanity and, above all, in the promise of its return to the vitalizing light of His grace. The bringing by God of a merely wicked man to judgment is worthy perhaps of a perfunctory glory. If, however, He brings to judgment a wicked man who has usurped, against God's law, the throne of a kingdom and who, for his own ends, has delivered that kingdom over to Satanic powers, over which he maintains a nominal command, has God not translated His otherwise perfunctory glory into a kind of magnificent resurrection, in which is seen His real glory? Such, at least, is the suggestion of the denouement of this play.

When Malcolm vows to perform his duties as Scotland's new king "by the grace of Grace," he has assumed, manifestly, a position diametrically opposed to that taken by Macbeth: he has vowed to accept God, and only God, as his principal guide and counselor. In this commitment, which promises the revitalization of the wasted kingdom, lies (I believe) the actuality of God's greater glory. The judgments of God, it would seem, as we find them in Shakespeare's plays, are properly to be evaluated in terms of their beneficent consequences (which are left, at the play's end, partially to conjecture) and not principally in terms of the act of judgment itself. The act finds most of its value—and this is especially noted in *Macbeth*—in the societal reorientation which it has made possible.

CONCLUSION

The play *Macbeth*, in its recurrent reminders of the punitive justice of Heaven, together with its stress on a demonic presence in Scotland, provides a broad insight into the values contributed by the outer world, as treated by Shakespeare, to the comprehensiveness of vision that typifies his mature art. Nor can we ignore, in seeking a judgment on this contribution, the two historical tetralogies, in which Heaven's power of vengeance, as illustrated in both the words of the actors and the events that give credibility to these words, provides a highly essential unifying theme. Nor do I except *Julius Caesar*, in which the dead Caesar, because of the dreaded powers ascribed to him, usurps the function of vengeance customarily ascribed to the Roman gods. And the play *Hamlet* is especially important to the topic at hand, for in it Providential justice is expressed not only in the insights of Hamlet and Horatio but equally in the traditional doctrines about ghosts. In fact, *King Lear*, a play that I have discussed only briefly, for it is a pagan play and has, moreover, no central focus on a particular revenge theme, attests time and again to the values of an outer-world dimension. A good play, like a good story, is held to be three-dimensional, the third dimension deriving from the depth established by what the characters do, say, or think. In an exceptional play or story, such as a Homeric epic or a Sophoclean tragedy, is found a fourth, or outer, dimension. This dimension provides an added comprehensiveness, which comes from superimposing one world upon another and, at times, from integrating them; the effect, however, is merely factitious if the outer world is mechanized in the mode of the deus ex machina. Shakespeare, happily, in treating this outer-world dimension, had the talent of Sophocles and not the expedient intent of Euripides. I shall now attempt—somewhat briefly—to evaluate Shakespeare's talent in the treatment of Providential intervention. He was first to exploit, with full awareness, the artistic and the functional advantages of such intervention, both designedly (as I have shown) and experimentally, in *Richard II*.

In the writing of the *Henry VI* plays and *Richard III*, although there are sporadic references to divine justice, Shakespeare shows only a modest awareness of Providential intervention as a unifying device. For this oversight he made a full atonement when he came, a year or two later, to the writing of *Richard II*, which in its prophecies is the linchpin that unites the two historical tetralogies into a patterned whole: in it are forecast the disasters of the *Henry VI* plays. There are, of course, two sets of prophecies in *Richard II*, both of which recognize God's power to punish the wrongdoer. Those made by Gaunt focus on the criminality of Richard's murder of Thomas, Duke of Gloucester, and are, of course, fulfilled within the play. The two long-range prophecies, by Richard and Carlisle, respectively, as well as York's warning to Bolingbroke, are focused on Bolingbroke's intention of deposing King Richard and, for this sin and that of the usurpation, God's punishment is to fall on "children yet unborn and unbegot" and even on "child's children"; hence the two prophecies establish a significant link with the *Henry VI* plays. They also have the effect of putting Bolingbroke in the position of a scourge, rather than a minister, for in serving God in the punishment of Richard he is branded in them as a wrongdoer, who will bring a curse upon the house of Lancaster, of which he is the head. The two sets of prophecies, with their stress on God's vengeance, do not, however, establish a strong sense of an outer-world dimension within the immediate play. The prophecies of God's vengeance upon the house of Lancaster, although valid, are not to be realized until the third generation. Gaunt's short-range prophecies, by contrast, promise some relatively immediate fireworks: "Heaven . . . will rain hot vengeance on offenders' heads" (I.ii.6,8). At Richard's deposition—disappointingly perhaps—no swords are struck, no fiery appeals to Heaven are made. In short, we sense the presence of Heaven, or God, chiefly in the play's prophecies. There is one clear exception: we are assured, in an afterthought by York, of God's part in Richard's dethronement: "Heaven hath a hand in these events, / To whose high will we bound our calm contents" (V.ii.37-38). This is our only significant assurance; for, aside from Gaunt's prophecies and Bolingbroke's two oaths of vengeance, politics (and not divine intervention) has been allowed to become the focus of the scenes depicting King Richard's overthrow. As a consequence, the very evident outer-world dimension, with its promises of God's justice, tends to be suspended over the world of the play and is, only on one occasion, well integrated into it.

The detached character of the outer-world dimension of *Richard II* is easily confirmed by considering only one statement of the play *Julius Caesar* and its later fulfillment. The statement is made by Marc Antony as he stands over the assassinated Caesar's body:

And Caesar's spirit, ranging for revenge,
With Até by his side, come hot from hell,
Shall in these confines with a monarch's voice
Cry "Havoc" and let slip the dogs of war.
[III.i.271-74]

This prophecy, in contrast to the short-range prophecies in *Richard II*, is fulfilled with vigor and preciseness. From the moment, in the following scene, when Antony lets loose the mob of frenzied commoners, to the close of the play, the spirit of Caesar indeed "ranges for revenge." While Caesar's body still lies in state, we are told that "Brutus and Cassius / Are rid like madmen through the gates of Rome" (III.ii.269-70). They are to be pursued by Caesar's spirit until, at Philippi, each acknowledges the fulfillment of the dictator's vengeance: "Caesar," states the self-wounded and dying Cassius, "thou art reveng'd" (V.iii.45), and Brutus, looking on Cassius's body, adds, "O Julius Caesar, thou art mighty yet!" (V.iii.94); for he knows now that only his imminent death can appease the wrath of Caesar. The outer-world dimension, because of the repeated reminders of a spirit's immediacy, has become an integrated part of the play world. Meanwhile, the appearance of Caesar's ghost at Sardis has contributed, although somewhat factitiously, to the integration of this dimension.

When we turn to *Hamlet*, we find a bolder and much more experienced Shakespeare, for here the outer-world dimension is so skillfully integrated into the play world that, except when we actually observe the Ghost, we are but subconsciously aware of such an integration. From the opening scene the supernatural, exhibited first in the Ghost itself and, later, in its "dread command," informs almost the total action of the play and, in particular, shapes both the deportment and the insights of Hamlet: as we are rightly told, neither "th' exterior nor the inward man / Resembles that it was" (II.ii.6-7). Upon Hamlet are focused the demands of the outer world as well as those of Elsinore and its royal court; thus, in him, the outer world touches, and joins with, the play world at its central focal point. Behind Hamlet stand the Ghost and the authority of God, by Whose permission the Ghost has returned to earth. Opposed to Hamlet are Claudius and those deluded devotees who share, although somewhat awkwardly, their master's remarkable worldliness. Hamlet's blunder in the impulsive and totally unintended killing of Polonius becomes his moment of self-identification. Aware of the defect of his own will, and observing that Polonius has died because "Heaven hath pleas'd it so," he has arrived at an important truth about himself: he is Heaven's "scourge" as well as its "minister." Once he has understood this fact, he makes no hard effort to refocus his will, and pausing only once to upbraid himself for having failed to avenge his murdered father, he places himself and his intuitive responses totally in the service of that higher will which has moved him to kill the wrong man and in which he must have trust if only because he is powerless to withstand it. Having been prompted by an "indiscretion" to the committing of two additional murders, which have the effect of saving his life, and having identified that "indiscretion" as an impulse implanted by "a divinity that shapes our ends," he shortly accomplishes what he had not the ability to accomplish of his own will—the killing of the fratricide Claudius, with whom Laertes and Gertrude must also die, but not by Hamlet's choice. It is in this unobtrusive manner that Providence, making Hamlet its scourge and imbuing him with strange impulses that customarily take the form of an "indiscretion," reveals itself as the controlling destiny of the play.

The presence of an outer world in the play *Macbeth*, noted particularly in the intervention of demonic spirits in the plot, is so evident that, although only the three Witches are seen, we are aware of an integrating supernatural dimension that becomes, at times, more real—in terms of our awareness—than are the characters themselves. Extending, customarily, from the edges of the play world into the outer darkness, this dimension gives the impression of being so cluttered with the demonic presence, as well as the unidentified worshipers of Hecate, that we have not an iota of the sense of spaciousness that we find, for example, in *King Lear*. When Macbeth speaks of being "cabin'd, cribb'd, confin'd," he is speaking not only of himself but, inadvertently, of the play world itself, for encompassing it, and feeding upon its energy, is an oppressive and dark imminence, the awesome danger of which is dispelled only with Malcolm's victory. Nor is Macbeth wrong (although his apparent detachment is deceptive) when, in confirming the "gracious" Duncan's death, he pauses on the consequences: "Renown and grace is dead; The wine of life is drawn, and the mere lees / Is left this vault to brag of" (II.iii.91-93). The vault, of course, is Scotland deprived, and to be deprived, by the demonic presence of all but the remnants of its accustomed cheer and humanity, but not solely because of Duncan's death.

My principal remarks, therefore, shall be confined to the topic of God's grace, which is more needful and, happily, more substantive in *Macbeth* than in any other Shakespearean play, including even *The Winter's Tale*. The doctrine that recognizes God as both the Judge and the Avenger and yet ascribes to a human agent the execution of God's judgment finds in the play *Macbeth*, and specifically in the God-agent relationship, one of the most plausible testimonies of the doctrine's functional integrity, apart from our acceptance of the principle itself. In *Macbeth*, as Jorgensen has shown,[1] are implanted several highly significant uses of the word "grace" in its religious meaning, whereas such a use of this word is rare in both the English history plays and *Hamlet*. In the oaths taken before the trial by combat in *Richard II*, we find the phrase "by the grace of God," as well as "by God's grace," but it is unclear that "grace," as used by the combatants, means anything more specific than "favor" sought for the occasion. Indeed, even in medieval and Renaissance texts that discuss God's punitive justice as recorded especially in the trial by combat, there is no hard evidence that God-granted grace provides the righteous man with victory or, for that matter, that he is unfailingly the victor. The topic of grace is especially important in *Macbeth* for the reason that, of all Shakespearean characters, Edward the Confessor, to whom the term "grace" (or its derivatives) is ascribed four times, is the most completely blessed by God, as attested by his readily shared saintly powers. He, in turn, has bestowed upon the expeditionary force, by means of both his ample goodwill and the loan of ten thousand soldiers, his fullest blessings. God's grace has thus passed, through "holy" Edward, to the army of liberation. Macduff, in confronting Macbeth, may be thought to have a full share of this grace; for such a gift does much to explain his complete confidence of victory over the once indomitable soldier of the Scottish North.

Macduff's blunt and aggressive temperament is not customarily thought to show a profound awareness of grace and its advantages. Of the play's important characters, only Duncan, Edward of England, and

Malcolm impress the reader as persons fully, or largely, gifted with grace. The term "grace," or its derivative "gracious," is applied repeatedly to Duncan and Edward (four times each). Malcolm, a neophyte to the mysteries of grace, shows an increasing awareness of them and uses the term "grace" (or "gracious") seven times, three in reference to Edward. Each of these three characters, being of a gentle nature, is the opposite in temper to the relatively blunt Macduff, who is deserving of grace—his cause being God's—but not, if judged by his nature, richly imbued with it. In short, an efficient soldier, being of a somewhat gruff nature and ever mindful of "kill or be killed," is on occasion of battle the most in need of the divine gift of grace and, in the vulgar opinion, the least likely to be a recipient of it.

Macduff, almost certainly unaware of the grace bestowed upon him by God, is probably equally unaware of Macbeth's mental and physical exhaustion caused, in part at least, by his loss of divine favor. The climactic defeats of Richard III and Edmund of *King Lear* may, much like Macbeth's, be attributed to the deprivation of God's grace. But can the same be said of Hotspur when defeated in single combat? Or is Hal's right to grace simply better than Hotspur's? Would it be correct to say that Bolingbroke and Hamlet, because each has murdered, are totally bereft of grace? Shakespeare rarely saw problems of morality in a black-and-white format, and when he did, as his portrayal of Henry of Richmond exemplifies for us, the white and newly chosen knight, having become too conscious of the gift of God's grace, is certain to be a highly proficient bore. Macduff, by contrast, being unconscious of the grace bestowed upon him and performing his task of vengeance (in God's behalf) like a soldier, offends nobody's sense of fitness. If Shakespeare has made Malcolm—like Richmond—too conscious of the grace he bears, he is at some pains to show us in Macduff the salutary manliness of grace when unconsciously and unoffendingly borne.

NOTES

INTRODUCTION

1. David L. Frey, *The First Tetralogy: Shakespeare's Scrutiny of the Tudor Myth* (The Hague and Paris, 1976), p. 10.

2. All quotations from Shakespeare's plays in my introduction (and throughout) are from Peter Alexander, ed., *Shakespeare: The Complete Works* (New York, 1952).

3. Michael Quinn, "Providence in Shakespeare's Yorkist Plays," *Shakespeare Quarterly*, 10 (1959), p. 50.

4. Ibid.

5. Wilbur Sanders, *The Dramatist and the Received Idea* (Cambridge, 1968), p. 94.

6. Moody E. Prior, *The Drama of Power: Studies in Shakespeare's History Plays* (Evanston, Ill., 1973), p. 49.

7. See Lloyd Berry, "Introduction," *The Geneva Bible* (1560), facs. (Madison, Wisc., 1969), for an estimate of the number of editions printed between 1560 (first edition) and 1603. Until 1575, editions were printed in Geneva and were shipped to England. From 1575 to 1618, the Bodley Press in England issued "at least one new edition of the Geneva Bible . . . each year" (p. 14).

8. Several Elizabethan writers stress the principle that the magistrate (whether the king, the local or itinerant judge, or the hangman) was responsible principally to God. Among them, John Norden wrote: "God himselfe . . . will revenge it [a violation against authority], and the magistrate hath power from him to punish it" (*The Mirror of Honor* [London, 1597], p. 39). Edward Coke, attorney general of England during the last decade of Elizabeth's reign, was to state categorically in his *Institutes*: "Revenge belongeth [only] to the magistrate, who is Gods lieutenant" (*The Third Part of the Institutes of the Laws of England*, written ca. 1620-1630 [London, 1797], p. 157). Mary B. Mroz, whose study of late medieval and Renaissance principles of God's judgment upon human transgression is unusual in its thoroughness, sums up the Elizabethan view of the God/magistrate relationship: "Public magistrates . . . are recognized as the foremost human agents of divine vengeance" (*Divine Vengeance* [Washington, D.C., 1941], p. 48).

9. Regarding God's right and willingness to abrogate the divine right of an intractable king and to sanction his removal from office, see R.R. Reed, Jr., *Richard II: From Mask to Prophet* (University Park, Pa., 1968), pp. 22-31, especially pp. 26-30.

10. A.L. French, "The World of Richard III," *Shakespeare Studies*, 4 (1968), p. 36.

11. Sanders, p. 107.

12. French, p. 37.

13. Fictitious.

14. Sanders, p. 93.

15. William Perkins, *A Discourse of Conscience* (1596), ed. Thomas F. Merrill (Nieuwkoop, Netherlands, 1966), p. 10.

16. Timothy Bright, *A Treatise of Melancholie* (1586), reprint ed. (New York, 1940), p. 185.

ONE: Shakespeare's Eight-Part Epic

1. Henry A. Kelly, *Divine Providence in the England of Shakespeare's Histories* (Cambridge, Mass., 1970), p. 39.

2. Kelly, p. 40, quoted from *The Chronicles of John Hardyng* (ca. 1465), ed. Sir Henry Ellis (London, 1812), p. 18. Kelly modernizes the spelling of all old texts. In a passage referring specifically to the Lancastrian curse of inherited guilt and its origin, Hardyng has written:

> For when Henry the fourth first was cround,
> Many a wyseman sayd full commenly,
> The third heyre shuld not ioyse, but be uncround,
> And deposed of all regalitie.
>
> [Hardyng, p. 18]

3. Kelly, pp. 40-41. Quoted from John de Waurin, *Recueil des chroniques/ . . . de la Grant Bretaigne* (ca. 1447), ed. Sir William Hardy and Edward Hardy, 5 vols. (1-4: London, 1884; 5:London, 1891), 2:393-94.

4. Kelly, p. 50. Quoted from *A Political Retrospect*, ed. Thomas Wright in *Political Poems* (London, 1861), pp. 267-69. The ancient author of this piece on the third heir is anonymous.

5. All biblical quotations are from the Geneva Bible (1560), the most widely circulated version in Elizabethan England. Between 1560 and 1611, it appeared in more than one hundred editions.

6. Kelly, p. 96. Quoted and translated from Polydore Vergil, *Anglica historia* (Basel, 1534), pp. 514-15.

7. Kelly, p. 126.

8. Edward Hall, *The Union of The Two Noble and Illustre Fameilies of Lancastre & Yorke* (1548), reprint (London, 1809), p. 35. Quoted, the spelling having been modernized, by Kelly, p. 115.

9. Kelly, p. 117.

10. Ibid., p. 137.

11. Hall, pp. 245-48; see, in particular, pp. 246-47. For a shorter version, with spelling modernized, see Kelly, pp. 121-24.

12. Raphael Holinshed, *Chronicles of England, Scotland, and Ireland*, 2nd ed. (London, 1587), reprint ed., 6 vols. (London, 1808), 3:325. Quoted and spelling modernized by Kelly, p. 152.

13. Holinshed, 2:869.

14. Ibid., 3:24.

15. Kelly, p. 143.

16. John Donne, *The Sermons of John Donne*, ed. George R. Potter and Evelyn M. Simpson, 9 vols. (Berkeley, 1957), 3:284.

17. Hall, p. 292.

18. Holinshed, 3:448 (misnumbered 478).

19. Robert B. Pierce, *Shakespeare's History Plays: The Family and the State* (Columbus, Ohio, 1971), p. 8.

20. Robert Ornstein, *A Kingdom for a Stage* (Cambridge, Mass., 1972), p. 20.

21. Hall, p. 286.

22. Ornstein, p. 39.

23. Pierce, p. 77.

24. Ibid., p. 51.

25. Michael Manheim, *The Weak King Dilemma in the Shakespearean History Play* (Syracuse, N.Y., 1973), p. 93.

26. Kelly, pp. 208-209.

27. All quotations from Shakespeare's works throughout this book are from Peter Alexander, ed., *Shakespeare: The Complete Works* (New York, 1952). Act, scene, and line numbers cited in the text refer to this edition.

28. Kelly, p. 208.

29. Ibid., p. 210.

30. Carlisle, in his role of prophet, is a composite of Genius and Carlisle of Samuel Daniel's *Civil Wars* (1595). Daniel's Carlisle makes a speech denouncing those persons who are about to dethrone Richard II. His statement on vengeance, however, is confined to the last line of the speech and says nothing about the punishment of a later generation: What traitor to his king, he asks, "can hold out [off] the hand of vengeance long"? (bk. III, st. 24, l. 8.) The basic materials for the two long-range prophecies of Shakespeare's play, Richard's and Carlisle's, may have derived from foreboding remarks made by Daniel's Genius of England, who warns Bolingbroke of the consequences of his rebellion and cites, in particular, "turmoyles [lasting] for many wofull ages hence." She then adds: "The babes, unborne, shall (o) be borne to bleed / In this thy quarrell, if thou do proceede" (bk. I, st. 89, ll. 7-8).

31. Robert Fabyan, *New Chronicles* (1516), ed. Henry Ellis (London, 1811), p. 589.

32. Hall, p. 379.

33. Ibid., p. 413.

34. The closing couplet of the Epilogue, preceded directly by a summary of the *Henry VI* plays, solicits approval from the audience: "Which oft our stage hath shown; and, for their sake, / In your fair minds let this [*Henry V*] acceptance take."

35. Robert H. West, *Shakespeare and the Outer Mystery* (Lexington, Ky., 1968), p. 22.

36. Robert G. Hunter, *Shakespeare and the Mystery of God's Judgments* (Athens, Ga., 1976), p. 70.

37. Ibid., p. 70.

38. Ibid., p. 72.

39. West, p. 168.

40. J.W. Jeudwine, *Tort, Crime, and Police in Mediaeval Britain* (London, 1917), p. 271.

41. Ibid., p. 27.

42. Cumberland Clark, *Shakespeare and the Supernatural* (London, 1931), p. 127.

43. John Palmer, for example, speaking of misjudgments made by Brutus and Cassius at Philippi, writes: "Distraction in the field presents vividly the distraction in the minds of the conspirators." See *Political Characters of Shakespeare* (London, 1948), p. 60.

44. Fredson Bowers, in modeling his interpretation of the structure of *King Lear*, a "fifth-act tragedy," upon Greek dramatic precedents, concludes that the play's climax is not a crucial decision (for that comes in act I) but, rather, Lear's "ethical reversal,"

which Bowers places in the second storm scene (III.iv.28-36). He is right, I believe, because at this point we can be sure that the reversal will stick. The first clear sign of the reversal, as I see it, is Lear's lecture to the storm gods on the nature of justice (III.ii.49-59). The reversal is confirmed in III.iv. See Bowers, "The Structure of *King Lear*," *Shakespeare Quarterly*, 31 (spring 1980), pp. 7-20.

TWO: The Justice of God

1. J.W. Jeudwine, *Tort, Crime, and Police in Medieval Britain* (London, 1917), p. 46.

2. Carl Stephenson and F.G. Marcham, eds., *Sources of English Constitutional History* (New York, 1937), p. 3.

3. Stephenson and Marcham, p. 17.

4. Jeudwine, p. 50.

5. Ibid., p. 69.

6. Ibid., p. 68.

7. Mary B. Mroz, *Divine Vengeance: A Study in the Philosophical Background of the Revenge Motif as It Appears in Shakespeare's Chronicle History Plays* (Washington, D.C., 1941), p. 68.

8. Stephenson and Marcham, p. 16 (section B).

9. Ibid., p. 35.

10. Mroz, p. 70. (The phrase quoted comes from *Select Bills in Eyre A.D. 1292-1333*, ed. W.C. Bolland, p. 125.)

11. Stephenson and Marcham, p. 57.

12. Ibid., p. 178n.

13. Ibid., p. 178.

14. Ibid., p. 179.

15. R. Trevor Davies, ed., *Documents Illustrating the History of Civilization in Medieval England (1066-1500)* (New York, 1926), p. 49n.

16. *The Columbia Encyclopedia*, 1st ed., "ordeal."

17. Ibid.

18. Whereas boiling water was a common ordeal in the trial of alleged criminals, cold water was also an ordeal, although it was used much more commonly to test alleged witches than felons. If a person suspended on a rope sank "an ell and a half," he (or she) was thought to have been "accepted" by the water, symbolic of the baptismal font, and hence was declared innocent of any guilt. Innocence was more difficult to prove by the ordeals of hot water and hot iron, even though the accused was permitted three days for the extremity (usually the hand) to heal. Contrary to common belief, the ordeal of hot iron did not, as a rule, require the accused to walk over red-hot plowshares. He carried the iron, one or three pounds in weight, in his hand over a measured distance of not more than ten feet.

19. Ramón Lull, *The Book of the Ordre de Chyvalry*, trans. Wm. Caxton (ca. 1483), ed. Alfred T.P. Byles, EETS, o.s. 168 (London, 1926), p. 38.

20. Raphael Holinshed, *Chronicles of England, Scotland, and Ireland* (1587), reprint ed., 6 vols. (London, 1807), 2:728.

21. *The Chronicle of Jocelin of Brakelond* (ca. 1202), trans. and ed. L.C. Jane (London, 1925), p. 110.

22. Christine de Pisan, *The Book of Fayttes of Armes and of Chyvalrye*, trans. William Caxton (London, 1489), ed. Alfred T.P. Byles, EETS, 189 (London, 1932), p. 259.

23. Ibid.

24. Ibid.

25. Ibid., p. 260.

26. Ibid., p. 267.

27. Ibid., p. 279.

28. Ibid., p. 278.

29. "Introduction," William Segar, *Of Honor, Military and Civill* (London, 1602), ed. Diane Bornstein, Scholars' Facsimiles & Reprints (New York, 1975), p. i.

30. Segar, pp. 117-18.

31. Segar (?), *The Booke of Honor and Armes* (London, 1590), ed. Diane Bornstein, Scholars' Facsimiles & Reprints (New York, 1975), p. 88. For a trial by combat later than 1441, see John Selden, *The Duello or Single Combat* (London, 1610), p. 35.

32. Segar (?), *Booke of Honor*, p. 86.

33. Edward Coke, *The Third Part of the Institutes of the Laws of England* (ca. 1630) (London, 1797), p. 158.

34. Ibid.

35. Segar (?), *Booke of Honor*, pp. 70ff. (see, in particular, pp. 73-80). The authoritative character of the author's treatment of protocol argues for Segar's authorship.

36. The Horner-Peter duel is based on an actual trial by combat at Smithfield in the year 1446 (25 Henry VI). An armorer named William Catur was "appealed" of treason "by his most offending servant" and, having made too "merry with his friends" just before the combat, was "over-come and slaine" by him. See John Selden, *The Duello or Single Combat* (London, 1610), p. 35.

37. Thomas Beard, *The Theatre of Gods Judgements* (London, 1597), sig. A5.

38. Edward Hall, *The Union of the Two Noble and Illustre Famelies of Lancastre & Yorke* (1548), reprint ed. (London, 1809), p. 210.

39. Richard Hooker, *Of The Laws of Ecclesiastical Polity* (1592-1600), ed. Ronald Bayne, 2 vols. (London, 1907), reprint ed. (1:45-53, 1925; 2:236-37, 1922).

40. John Donne, *The Sermons of John Donne*, ed. George R. Potter and Evelyn M. Simpson (Berkeley, Calif., 1955), 2:313.

41. Donne, 2:316.

42. Mroz, p. 32.

43. Beard, p. 239.

44. Ibid., pp. 255-56.

45. Ibid., p. 316.

46. Ibid.

47. Coke, p. 157.

48. *The Statesman's Book of John of Salisbury*, trans. and ed. John Dickinson (New York, 1928), pp. 385-86.

49. Beard, p. 226.

50. See ibid., p. 251, for a graphic vignette of this scourge.

51. *The Statesman's Book*, p. 375. See also Plutarch, *The Delay of the Deity* (2nd cent.), in *Between Heathenism and Christianity*, ed. Charles W. Super (New York, 1899), p. 174.

52. There is one exception to this statement: Marston's disillusioned and plot-ridden Antonio retires to a monastery. In other instances, an avenger (for example, Macduff) kills the villain on the field of battle and is spared, for such a killing breaks no law. Finally, as Fredson T. Bowers long ago observed, "heavenly vengeance," as in Tourneur's *Atheist's Tragedy*, may intercede directly, and the avenger, in consequence, may remain innocent of blood. See Bowers, *Elizabethan Revenge Tragedy* (Princeton, N.J., 1940), reprint ed. (Gloucester, Mass., 1959), pp. 64, 141.

53. Mroz, p. 48.

54. *Statesman's Book*, pp. 377-78.

55. Hall, p. 423.

56. Timothy Bright, *A Treatise of Melancholie* (1586), (New York, 1940), p. 193. The "ingraven lawes" are the laws of the Decalogue engraved on stone.

57. Bright, p. 185.

58. Peter de La Primaudaye, *The French Academie* (London, 1618), 2:327, quoted in Mroz, *Divine Vengeance*, p. 28. (An earlier English edition appeared in 1594.)

59. *Mirror for Magistrates*, 4 eds. (1559-1587), ed. Lily B. Campbell (Cambridge, 1938), p. 326.

60. Mroz, p. 125.

61. Ibid., p. 14. (Her quotation is from Holinshed, 2:751.)

62. Holinshed, 2:868-69.

63. 2 Chron. 24.20-25.

64. Hall, p. 30.

65. Ibid., p. 31.

66. *Certaine Sermons or Homilies* (folio, 1623), ed. Mary E. Rickey and Thomas B. Stroup (Gainesville, Fla., 1968), p. 292. See also p. 307. For other statements condemning rebellion, see Thomas Lever, *Sermons* (1550), ed. Edward Arber, *English Reprints* (London, 1870), p. 35; John Cheeke, *The Hurt of Sedition*, in Holinshed, 3:987-1011, especially p. 991; and John Norden, *The Mirror of Honor* (London, 1597), pp. 38-39.

67. Beard, p. 226 (paraphrase of 2 Kings 21.20-24).

68. Ibid., p. 279.

69. See *Encyclopaedia Britannica*, 15th ed., s.v. "Helenus" (for Pyrrhus, s.v. "Neoptolemus"). Shakespeare, in particular, emphasizes that Pyrrhus was an avenger. Reflecting Vergil's *Aeneid*, bk. II, the Player in *Hamlet* states: "Roasted in wrath and fire . . . the hellish Pyrrhus / Old grandsire Priam seeks" (II.ii.455-58); he then elaborates on Pyrrhus' "rousèd vengeance" (ll. 482-86). Homer has not included the sack of Troy in the *Iliad*. But Odysseus, in avenging his wife Penelope against the suitors, who have feared neither "the gods who possess broad heaven" nor the "vengeance of men," expresses Homer's view, especially since he is directed by the goddess Athena.

70. Euripides, *Hecuba*, printed in *Greek Drama*, ed. W. J. Oates and Eugene O'Neill, Jr., 2 vols. (New York, ca. 1938), 1:819.

71. Saxo Grammaticus, *The First Nine Books of the Danish History* (ca. 1200), trans. and ed. Oliver Elton (London, 1894), pp. 106-17.

72. Also known as Ella.

73. Saxo, pp. 380-82.

74. Plutarch, *Delay of Deity*, pp. 170-71.

THREE: Thomas of Gloucester

1. A.P. Rossiter, ed., *Woodstock* (London, 1946), p. 47.

2. F.S. Boas, "A Pre-Shakespearean *Richard II*," *Fortnightly Review*, 72 (1902), p. 404.

3. Ibid., p. 403.

4. See Rossiter, p. 16, and, especially, pp. 47-53.

5. In *both* plays, for example, Richard's flatterers are termed "upstarts" and "caterpillars," and Richard, in turn, is called a "landlord" and his kingdom "a pelting farm."

6. Raphael Holinshed, *Chronicles of England, Scotland, and Ireland* (1587), 6 vols. (London, 1807), 2:794.

7. Holinshed, 2:834-35.

8. Ibid., 2:836.

9. Ibid., 2:837.

10. Ibid., 2:868.

11. Ibid., 2:835.

12. Ibid., 2:838.

13. The present quotation and the subsequent quotation from the play *Woodstock* refer to the Rossiter edition.

14. The play *Woodstock* covers the historical period 1381-98. Hence Tresilian, who was executed in 1388, becomes an anachronism after that year.

15. Holinshed, 2:838.

16. Ibid., 2:844.

17. Ibid., 2:869.

18. Lily B. Campbell, *Shakespeare's Histories: Mirrors of Elizabethan Policy* (San Marino, Calif., 1947), p. 196.

19. Mary B. Mroz, *Divine Vengeance* (Washington, D.C.), p. 3.

20. Holinshed, 2:848.

21. *The Chronicle of Froissart*, trans. Sir John Bourchier, Lord Berners (1523-25), ed. W.E. Henley, 6 vols. (London, 1903), 6:338-39.

22. Holinshed, 2:849.

23. Ibid., 2:852. This passage is paraphrased from Edward Hall.

24. Ibid. At this point Holinshed drops Hall, who writes that Bolingbroke went first to London and later to Bristol and Flint Castle.

25. Robert Ornstein, *A Kingdom for a Stage* (Cambridge, Mass., 1972), p. 114.

26. Because of the long pause in the action following line 223 of act II, scene i, at which point a "flourish" is sounded while the king and his favorites leave the stage, the subsequent episode in which Northumberland informs his two comrades that Bolingbroke and his eight warships are "making hither with all due expedience" takes the shape of a detached experience: indeed, a kind of ironic counterpoint to the smug confidence of King Richard's departing line, "Be merry, for our time of stay is short." On the bare Elizabethan stage the episode could be made to appear a separate and hence later scene, but it would lose much of the effect of a counterpoint.

27. Ornstein, p. 114.

28. E.M.W. Tillyard, *Shakespeare's History Plays* (New York, 1946), p. 260.

29. John Palmer, *Political Characters of Shakespeare* (London, 1945), p. 155.

30. Derek Traversi, *Shakespeare: From Richard II to Henry V* (Stanford, Calif., 1957), p. 25.

31. Ibid., p. 27.

32. M. Bradbrook, *Shakespeare and Elizabethan Poetry* (London, 1951), p. 138.

33. Ornstein, *A Kingdom*, p. 114.

34. C. Oman, *Political History of England* (London, 1906), 4:148.

35. Palmer, *Political Characters*, p. 136.

36. The error derives from Holinshed, 3:20-23.

37. Palmer, p. 137.

38. *Chronicle of Froissart* (trans. Lord Berners), 6:146.

39. Holinshed, 2:869.

40. Ibid.

41. Jean Créton, *Histoire du Roi d'Angleterre Richard II* (1399), trans. John Webb, *Archaeologia*, 20 (London, 1824), p. 105.

42. Edward Hall, *The Union of the Two Noble and Illustre Famelies of Lancastre & Yorke* (1548), reprint (London, 1809), p. 210.

43. Holinshed, 2:869.

44. Ibid.

FOUR: Richard II

1. Edward II was the first king of England to assume the throne by means of primogeniture unqualified by the process of election. His son Edward III's primogeniture, at the time he came to the throne, was not legally absolute for the reason that his deposed father was still alive. Hence an election was required.

2. Gloucester is sometimes thought to be the youngest, and hence seventh, son of Edward III. The seventh son was William of Windsor, who died in childhood.

3. M.M. Reese, *The Cease of Majesty* (London, 1961), pp. 53-54. This conclusion is explicit in the chronicles of both Edward Hall and Raphael Holinshed, as I shall stress later in this and the next chapter.

4. J.D. Wilson, ed., Shakespeare's *Richard II* (Cambridge, 1939), p. xvi.

5. Karl Thompson, "Richard II, Martyr," *Shakespeare Quarterly*, 8 (1957), p. 162.

6. R.R. Reed, Jr., *Richard II: From Mask to Prophet* (University Park, Pa., 1968), p. 44.

7. Edward Hall, *The Union of the Two Noble and Illustre Famelies of Lancastre & Yorke* (1548), reprint (London, 1809), p. 8.

8. Raphael Holinshed, *Chronicles of England, Scotland, and Ireland* (1587), reprint ed., 6 vols. (London, 1807), 2:868.

9. Reese, p. 227.

10. Hall, p. 26.

11. Ibid., p. 27.

12. Ibid., p. 36.

13. Ibid.

14. R.J. Dorius, "Prudence and Excess in *Richard II* and the Histories," in *Discussions of Shakespeare's Histories*, ed. Dorius (Boston, 1964), p. 35.

15. Robert Fabyan, *The New Chronicles of England and France* (1516), ed. Henry Ellis (London, 1811), p. 589.

16. Ibid.

17. Hall, p. 47.

18. Ibid., p. 21.

19. Ibid., p. 423.

20. Reese, pp. 52-54; Irving Ribner, *The English History Play* (New York, 1965), pp. 95-96.

21. See Reed, pp. 18-32; in particular, pp. 23-31.

FIVE: The Later Gloucesters

1. Edward Hall, *Union of the Two Noble and Illustre Famelies of Lancastre & Yorke* (1548), reprint ed. (London, 1809), p. 209.

2. Raphael Holinshed, *Chronicles of England, Scotland, and Ireland* (1587), reprint ed., 6 vols. (London, 1808), 3:362.

3. C. Oman, *The Political History of England, 1377-1485* (London, 1906), 4:502.

4. Oman, pp. 287-88.

5. Ibid., p. 297.

6. Hall, p. 209.

7. Oman, p. 339.

8. Hall, p. 210.

9. E.M.W. Tillyard, *Shakespeare's History Plays* (New York, 1946), p. 186.

10. Hall, p. 210.

11. Holinshed, 3:211.

12. Hall, p. 210.

13. Timothy Bright, *A Treatise of Melancholie* (1586) (New York, 1940), p. 193.

14. Mary B. Mroz, *Divine Vengeance: A Study in the Philosophical Backgrounds of the Revenge Motif* (Washington, D.C., 1941), p. 125.

15. Holinshed, 3:220.

16. Mroz, p. 48.

17. H.A. Kelly, *Divine Providence in the England of Shakespeare's Histories* (Cambridge, Mass., 1970), p. 258.

18. Tillyard, p. 183.

19. Ezekiel 25.17. From the Geneva Bible (1560), facsimile (Madison, 1969).

20. Mroz, p. 107.

21. Bright, pp. 111-12.

22. Hall, p. 301.

23. Ibid., p. 303.

24. Ibid., p. 326.

25. Moody E. Prior, *The Drama of Power: Studies in Shakespeare's History Plays* (Evanston, Ill., 1973); see, in particular, pp. 48-58. On the Providential character of Margaret's curses, Prior has taken a basically negative stance. He questions their prophetic validity because they are not "spoken in reason" but in "hatred . . . and lust for vengeance." My only comment, here, is that human reason, although able to predict, is not usually associated with prophecy. Intuition, by contrast, may (however rarely) be divinely inspired, and Prior does not deny Margaret this faculty. Prior, moreover, sees Richard III as "awesome and even somewhat mysterious" (p. 56) in executing

Margaret's curses. In summary, although Prior focuses mostly on "naturalistic" motives, he is not at all convinced of the absence of Providential ones.

26. Edward I. Berry, *Patterns of Decay: Shakespeare's Early Histories* (Charlottesville, Va., 1975), p. 88.

27. Ibid., p. 83.

28. John Palmer, *Political Characters of Shakespeare* (London, 1948), p. 104.

29. Hall, p. 379.

30. Irving Ribner, *Patterns in Shakespearian Tragedy*, reprint ed. (London, 1962), p. 24.

31. Bright, p. 185.

32. William Perkins, *A Discourse of Conscience* (1596), 2nd ed. (Cambridge, 1608), ed. Thomas F. Merrill (Netherlands, 1966), p. 6.

33. Ibid., p. 10.

34. Ibid., pp. 39-40.

35. Manfred Weidhorn, *Dreams in Seventeenth-Century English Literature* (The Hague, 1970), p. 115.

36. Weidhorn, p. 116.

37. Tillyard, p. 208.

38. Palmer, p. 113.

39. Genesis 41.28. From the Geneva Bible (1560).

40. Robert Burton, *Anatomy of Melancholy* (1621), 6th ed. (1651), ed. Floyd Dell and Paul Jordan-Smith (New York, 1951), p. 943.

41. The verb "babbl'd" is Theobold's emendation of "Table" (Folio 1), which makes no sense. An alternative emendation is "talk'd." In any case, a verb is necessary to the sense. Mercutio's discourse on dreams (*Rom*, I.iv.53-85) likewise emphasizes the sanguine humor, which he transposes to his dreamers.

42. Owen Felltham, "Of Dreams," *Resolves: Divine, Moral, and Political* (London, 1677), p. 82.

43. Ibid.

44. Mroz, p. 41.

45. Felltham, p. 82.

46. Hall, p. 414.

47. A.J.J. Ratcliff, *A History of Dreams* (Boston, 1923), p. 99. Quotation from Henry Bergson. (no book title or page is given). In *Dreams* (New York, 1914), Bergson writes: "They [memory images] are like steam in a boiler, under more or less tension," p. 41.

48. Bright, p. 185.

49. Ibid., p. 190.

50. Burton, p. 947.

51. Ibid., p. 948.

52. Perkins, p. 6.

53. Bright, p. 193.

54. Hall, p. 287.

55. Ibid., p. 413.

56. For an argument that Shakespeare's Richard III is not a victim of conscience or of "the aggressive malevolence of ghosts" but rather of "an act of choice exercised by one of his subjects [Lord Stanley]," see Andrew Gurr, "Richard III and the Democratic Process," *Essays in Criticism*, 24:1 (1974), pp. 39-47.

SIX: Prince Hamlet

1. F.T. Bowers, "Hamlet as Minister and Scourge," *PMLA*, 70 (September 1955), pp. 744-45.

2. On unusual occasions, a "spirit of the blessed" [a saint] might come back from Heaven in order to counsel or console a grief-stricken person. For a general survey of the Roman Catholic position on ghosts, see May Yardley, "The Catholic Position in the Ghost Controversy of the Sixteenth Century," in L. Lavater, *Of Ghostes and Spirits Walking by Nyght* (originally entitled *De Spectris*), trans. R.H. (1572), ed. J.D. Wilson and M. Yardley (Oxford, 1929), pp. 221-51. For exceptions permitting a ghost's return from Heaven, see Noel Taillepied, *A Treatise of Ghosts* (Paris, 1588), trans. Montague Summers (London, 1933), p. 117; and Pierre Le Loyer, *Discours des Spectres*, 2nd ed. (Paris, 1608), p. 619. Taillepied, stating the Roman Catholic position, argued that most persons believed that for those souls "who are in Heaven or in hell . . . there is no return." p. 123.

3. Francis Douce, *Illustrations of Shakespeare* (London, 1807), 2:221. Douce's statement is also quoted by T.F. Thistleton-Dyer, *Folk-Lore of Shakespeare* (1883), reprint ed. (New York, 1966), p. 44.

4. William Perkins, *A Discourse of the Damned Art of Witchcraft* (Cambridge, 1610), p. 115 (published posthumously).

5. King James, *Daemonologie* (1597), ed. G. B. Harrison (London, 1924), p. 61.

6. Robert H. West, "King Hamlet's Ambiguous Ghost," *PMLA*, 70 (1955), p. 1115.

7. James, pp. 60-61.

8. King Hamlet has died "unhous'led, disappointed, unanel'd" (*Ham*, I.v.77). These words uttered by the Ghost have the following meanings, respectively: without the Eucharist; without confession; without extreme unction.

9. Roy W. Battenhouse, "The Ghost in 'Hamlet': A Catholic 'Linchpin'?" *Studies in Philology*, 48 (1951), pp. 161-92.

10. West, "King Hamlet's Ambiguous Ghost," pp. 1107-17; Eleanor Prosser, *Hamlet and Revenge*, 2nd ed. (Stanford, Calif., 1971), see chaps. 4 and 5, pp. 97-143.

11. J.D. Wilson, *What Happens in "Hamlet"* (New York, 1935), see chap. 3, pp. 55-86; I.J. Semper, "The Ghost in Hamlet: Pagan or Christian," *Month*, 195 (1953), pp. 222-34; Bowers, "Hamlet as Minister and Scourge," *PMLA*, 70 (1955), pp. 740-49.

12. Battenhouse, "The Ghost in 'Hamlet'"; see, in particular, pp. 190-92 for pagan ghost. In Prosser, see chaps. 4 and 5, pp. 97-143, for a strong argument that King Hamlet's Ghost is actually a devil. Prosser does, perhaps wisely, have some doubts about her interpretation.

13. Battenhouse, pp. 163-65, 167.

14. Battenhouse, *Shakespearean Tragedy* (Bloomington, Ind., 1969), p. 154. (For commentary on Hamlet's qualifications for damnation, see pp. 154-56.)

15. Battenhouse, *Shakespearean Tragedy*, p. 239.

16. T.F. Thiselton-Dyer, *The Ghost World* (London, 1893), p. 64.

17. Ibid., p. 77.

18. Ibid., p. 65.

19. Ibid., pp. 82-83. This account is taken from Surtee's "History of Durham."

20. Thomas Lodge, *Wits Miserie* (London, 1596), p. 62; reprinted in *The Complete*

Works of Thomas Lodge (New York, 1963), vol. 4. (At *top*, the page is numbered "56" and the printed subtitle "Incarnate Devils" appears. Only 400 sets were issued.)

21. For the contemporary references to the *Ur-Hamlet* and a short commentary, see F.E. Halliday, comp., *A Shakespeare Companion, 1564-1964*, rev. ed. (Baltimore, 1964), pp. 510-11.

22. Battenhouse, "The Ghost in 'Hamlet,'" pp. 162-63.

23. Dante Alighieri, *The Divine Comedy*, trans. L. G. White (New York, 1948), p. 83.

24. Thomas Aquinas, *The Summa Theologica*, trans. Fathers of the English Dominican Province, rev. D.J. Sullivan, Great Books ed. R.M. Hutchins, no. 20 (Chicago, 1941), 2:900.

25. Le Loyer, p. 619.

26. Battenhouse, "The Ghost in 'Hamlet,'" p. 190.

27. Ibid., p. 192.

28. Herbert R. Coursen, Jr., *Christian Ritual and the World of Shakespeare's Tragedies* (Lewisburg, Pa., 1976), p. 90.

29. Robert G. Hunter, *Shakespeare and the Mystery of God's Judgments* (Athens, Ga., 1976), p. 104.

30. Hunter, p. 105.

31. Owen Felltham, *Resolves: Divine, Moral, and Political* (London, 1677), p. 294.

32. Robert Ornstein, "Historical Criticism and the Interpretation of Shakespeare," *Shakespeare Quarterly*, 10 (1959), p. 9.

33. West, "King Hamlet's Ambiguous Ghost," p. 1117.

34. "Sweet Prince," *Nation*, 140 (1935), p. 730. (Although the article is unsigned, the author is almost certainly Joseph Wood Krutch, then editor of the *Nation*.)

35. *The New Columbia Encyclopedia*, 4th ed., s.v. "Denmark."

36. Saxo Grammaticus, *Historia Danica*, trans. Oliver Elton, The Folk-Lore Society (London, 1894), pp. 104-105.

37. Edward Coke, *The Third Part of the Institutes of the Laws of England*, 4 vols. (London, 1797), 3:158. Written about 1625-30.

38. Le Loyer, p. 590. The French reads, in the context of ghosts: "Ils apparoissent visibles par le congé de Dieu à ceux des hommes qu'il lui plaist."

39. Ibid., p. 619. The French reads, in the context of returning to earth: "Celles qui sont en Purgatoire ne le peuvent faire sans l'exprès commandement de Dieu."

40. Taillepied, p. 137.

41. Ibid., p. 119.

42. Prosser, p. 115.

43. Ibid., p. 143.

44. M.B. Mroz, *Divine Vengeance* (Washington, D.C., 1941), p. 32.

45. Job, 1.12. Geneva Bible (1560), facsimile (Madison, 1969).

46. Maurice F. Egan, *The Ghost in "Hamlet" and Other Essays* (1906), reprint (Freeport, N.Y., 1971), p. 30.

47. Perkins, p. 75.

48. Richard Hooker, *Of the Laws of Ecclesiastical Polity*, bk. V (ca. 1597), reprint ed., Everyman's Library (London, 1922), 2:517.

49. For Hooker's definition, as well as illustrations, of "necessity" and "contingency," see *Laws* (London, 1922), 2:509-12. As God foreknows by necessity (which He

directly wills), He likewise foreknows by contingency for the reason that, knowing each particular man's nature and comprehending his mind, He knows the man's intent and, except in rare instances, permits its fulfillment. Hence, He foresees by contingency, that is, by his knowledge of what a particular man intends.

50. Ibid., p. 514.

51. Had the Ghost suggested a trial by combat, some critics have argued, Hamlet's honor could have been preserved. In a Renaissance community, however, the broaching of a medieval ordeal (as Hamlet would be forced to have done) would have been countered by disbelief and even by derision.

52. "Preface," Thomas Beard, *The Theatre of Gods Judgment* (London, 1597), fol. A5.

53. The editors of the Pelican and the Signet editions of *Hamlet* interpret "casual slaughters" as meaning that they are "not humanly planned." The Riverside edition sees them as "happening by chance." It is proper, I believe, to view them as "humanly unpremeditated" but not, in a strict sense, as accidental.

54. God always destroyed His scourge. Plutarch writes: "There is no doubt that the Deity sometimes employs certain men after the manner of public executioners, to be the avengers of other villains, then destroys them" (*The Delay of the Deity* [*De sera numinis vindicta*], in *Between Heathenism and Christianity*, ed. Charles W. Super [New York, 1899], chap. 7, p. 174). John of Salisbury has written a statement often quoted in medieval and Tudor times: "For there is prepared a great fire wherewith to consume the scourge after the Father has employed it for the correction of his children." To this he adds: "Sometimes it is His own, and at others it is a human hand, which he employs as a weapon wherewith to administer punishment to the unrighteous" (John Dickinson, ed., *The Statesman's Book of John of Salisbury* [selections from John's *Policraticus*] [New York, 1928], p. 375). The scourge, in turn, becomes "unrighteous" and hence was to be slain by God or "a human hand."

55. Consult Bowers, p. 746. Bowers sees Rosencrantz and Guildenstern as "traitorous" in their relation to Hamlet, their friend and former schoolmate.

56. Among the wicked cities destroyed by God were Sodom and Gommorah (Gen. 19.24), Shechem (Judg. 9.49, 57), and Nineveh (Book of Nahum and Beard, *Theatre of Gods Judgments* [1597], p. 463). In all of these cities, women, some of whom were innocent, and children were among the victims. Among groups of evildoers destroyed by God were Korah and his coconspirators, as well as "their households" (Num. 16.1-35), the Philistine lords and their attendants (Judg. 16.25-30), and the house of Ba'asha because it worshiped false idols (1 Kings 16.1-4, 10-13).

57. G.W. Knight, *The Wheel of Fire*, enlarged ed. (London, 1949), p. 33.

58. O.J. Campbell, "What's the Matter with Hamlet?" *Yale Review*, 22 (December 1942), p. 313.

59. Bowers speaks of Hamlet, at this late point in the play, as "serene in trust that divine providence will guide him" (p. 748). Richard Helgerson, on a somewhat different tack, arrives at a very similar conclusion. Hamlet, he says, has chosen to leave the resolution of the play's catastrophe "to his own inspired indiscretion," for "the events on the ship [have] revealed to him that divinity that shapes our ends" (Helgerson, "What Hamlet Remembers," *Shakespeare Studies*, 10 [1977], p. 93).

60. No critic, as far as I know, has pointed out the significance of the outcry "Treason! treason!" (V.ii.315), which is the unanimous response, in the closing scene,

to Hamlet's killing of the fratricide Claudius. No one shouts "Hurrah!" So loyal are the courtiers to Claudius, who has purchased their affection with hypocritical smiles, and with Lord knows what else, that Hamlet has had no chance to kill him heretofore without being incarcerated and beheaded. The external obstacles amount to an almost insurmountable barrier.

61. "Sweet Prince," p. 730.

SEVEN: Macbeth, the Devil, and God

1. H.N. Paul, *The Royal Play of Macbeth* (New York, 1950), pp. 292, 294.

2. Ibid., p. 293.

3. Ibid., p. 294.

4. King James, *Daemonologie* (1597), ed. G. B. Harrison, reprint ed. (London and New York, 1924), p. xiv.

5. James, p. 8.

6. Matthew N. Proser, *The Heroic Image* (Princeton, N.J., 1965), p. 62.

7. Cumberland Clark, *Shakespeare and the Supernatural* (London, 1931), p. 94.

8. James, p. 45.

9. Ibid., p. 9.

10. Ibid., p. 75.

11. George Giffard, *A Dialogue Concerning Witches & Witchcrafts* (1603), Percy Society Reprint 24 (London, 1842), p. 62.

12. William Perkins, *A Discourse of the Damned Art of Witchcraft* (Cambridge, 1610), p. 149 (published posthumously). In the introduction to the pamphlet entitled *A Rehearsal . . . of Hainous and Horrible Acts Committed by Elizabeth Stile* (London, 1577), reprint ed. (East Lansing, Mich., 1940), the author writes: "The Witche beareth the name, but the devill dispatcheth the deedes; without him the Witche can contrive no mischief" (p. 3).

13. See Joseph Satin, ed., *Shakespeare and His Sources* (Boston, 1966), p. 564.

14. James, p. 9.

15. Proser, p. 68.

16. Rolf Soellner, *Shakespeare's Patterns of Self-Knowledge* (Columbus, Ohio), pp. 336ff.

17. Timothy Bright, *A Treatise of Melancholie* (1586) (New York, 1940), p. 193.

18. Bright, p. 228.

19. G.R. Elliott, *Dramatic Providence in Macbeth: A Study of Shakespeare's Tragic Theme of Humanity and Grace* (Princeton, N.J., 1958), p. 87.

20. Bright, pp. 189-90.

21. Robert Burton, *Anatomy of Melancholy* (1621), ed. Floyd Dell and Paul Jordan-Smith (New York, 1951), p. 951.

22. Burton, p. 947.

23. Paul A. Jorgensen, *Our Naked Frailties: Sensational Art and Meaning in "Macbeth"* (Berkeley, Calif., 1971), p. 201.

24. Ibid., p. 204.

25. Irving Ribner, *Patterns in Shakespearian Tragedy*, reprint (London, 1962), p. 159.

26. Ibid.

27. Elliott, p. 121.

28. Ibid., p. 93.

29. Jorgensen, p. 201.

30. Ibid., p. 207. Please do not think that I am in total disagreement with Jorgensen's theory that Macbeth's excessive fear of Banquo is an effect of demonic intervention, a type of fear experienced by Cain and Saul because they too had lost God's grace. As a *partial* cause, I accept it; but Macbeth has also logical (and psychological) reasons for his excess of fear.

31. Proser, p. 76.

32. Jorgensen, p. 125.

33. A.C. Bradley, *Shakespearean Tragedy* (1904), reprint ed. (London, 1952), p. 361.

34. Clark, p. 100.

35. Paul, p. 69.

36. Peter De Loier [Pierre Le Loyer], *A Treatise of Specters*, trans. L. Jones (London, 1605), p. 112.

37. Paul, p. 59.

38. Alfred Harbage, ed., *Macbeth* (ca. 1606), in *The Pelican Shakespeare*, reprint ed. (Baltimore, 1960), p. 73n.

39. William Perkins, *A Discourse of Conscience* (1596), 2nd ed. (1608), ed. Thomas F. Merrill (The Hague, 1966), p. 40.

40. Proser, p. 74.

41. Perkins, *Discourse of Conscience*, p. 40.

42. Ibid., pp. 39-40.

43. Ibid., p. 6.

44. I read "ere" in "Ere we will" (1.17) as "rather than."

45. Raphael Holinshed, *Chronicles of England, Scotland, and Ireland*, enlarged ed. (1587), reprint ed., 6 vols. (London, 1808), 5:271.

46. Ibid., pp. 273-74.

47. Ibid., p. 274.

48. James, p. 22.

49. Ibid., p. 76.

50. Ibid., p. 22.

51. Perkins, *Discourse of . . . Witchcraft*, p. 31.

52. James, p. 22.

53. J.C. Bucknill, *The Mad Folk of Shakespeare*, 2nd ed. (London, 1867), p. 29.

54. In Satin, p. 568.

55. Jorgensen, p. 173.

56. Dolora Cunningham, "Macbeth: the Tragedy of the Hardened Heart," *Shakespeare Quarterly*, 14 (1963), p. 44.

57. Ibid.

58. See Thomas Beard, *The Theatre of Gods Judgements* (London, 1597). Under the heading "Of Subject Murderers," Beard argues that kings and princes, "to whom the sword of justice is committed by God to represse wrongs and chastise vices," are to be deemed the most flagrant of evildoers if they slay, rather than protect, their subjects (p.

279). Among rulers who betrayed God by murdering their subjects, and thus inverted the natural order of government, Beard includes accounts of Saul, Jezebel, and Joran of Judah (pp. 279-81). All three were punished, through agents, by God.

59. James, p. xiv.

CONCLUSION

1. Paul A. Jorgensen, *Our Naked Frailties* (Berkeley, Calif., 1971), pp. 196-98.

INDEX